THE SOCIAL IMPACT OF BOMB DESTRUCTION

The Social Impact of BOMB DESTRUCTION

by Fred Charles Iklé

NORMAN : UNIVERSITY OF OKLAHOMA PRESS

The publication of this work has been aided by a grant from
THE FORD FOUNDATION

Library of Congress Catalog Card Number: 58-11611

Copyright 1958 by the University of Oklahoma Press, Publishing Division of the University. Composed and printed at Norman, Oklahoma, U.S.A., by the University of Oklahoma Press. First edition.

PREFACE

ATOMIC AND HYDROGEN BOMBS have now been manufactured by three nations. As long as there remains the risk of a major war, the increasing stock piles of such weapons together with planes and missiles to deliver them against distant targets constitute a permanent threat of nuclear bombing. It is possible that nuclear weapons would not be employed against cities if there should be a new war with full participation of the nations now stock-piling them. Poison gas was available on both sides but was not used in World War II, although it had been employed in World War I. And, after the first two atomic bombs had been used in Japan, the air raids in subsequent armed conflicts—that is, primarily, in Korea—were all confined to conventional incendiary and explosive bombs. Yet, the technical possibility of nuclear attacks against cities is the gravest and most serious peril of the modern world.

In spite of our knowledge of the physical effects of bombing, the social impact remains largely in the field of conjecture. And it is the social, not the physical, effects which are of ultimate importance if cities are bombed. In order to understand what bombing does to the conduct of war, to urban populations and industries, or to nations as a whole, one must look beyond the sheer physical effects and study the social consequences.

The Social Impact of *BOMB DESTRUCTION*

The most precise statements about physical destruction fail to explain how this destruction affects people and society. For example, will people abandon their homes in large cities if the threat of nuclear warfare should become more imminent? How will people live if they abandon their homes, and how will the economy continue to function? Will a nation be able to maintain a war effort if its major cities are bombed? Will nuclear warfare imperil our civilization, destroy the fiber of Western society, and endanger the future of mankind?

Many writers have boldly furnished answers to such questions and have offered horrifying predictions. It is difficult, indeed, not to paint a black and dreadful picture of a future in which nuclear warfare has become a reality. Such predictions are often made with the good intention of arousing world opinion and promoting the forces of peace. However, the global, all-or-none terms into which these prophecies are cast and the almost nonchalant ease with which doom has been predicted make them seem like fantasies that cannot happen, that are too remote and unbelievable to prompt action. Perhaps the present inadequacy of civil defense in the United States and in many other countries can be traced in part to the editorial "off-the-cuff" statements about the alleged social effects of nuclear bombing. These overpowering warnings have obstructed the thinking of many citizens and responsible officials. It is as if people accepted two contradictory realms of facts. The findings of nuclear physics and of tests with nuclear weapons are fully accepted as true facts; but at the same time there is the world in which we live, in itself also more or less rational and factual, yet entirely unreconciled with the world of nuclear bombs.

Although everyone is aware that nuclear bombs exist and can be delivered against cities, most of us are entirely unprepared to face this risk. And practically nothing is being planned to mitigate the potential consequences. It has been said that mankind's choice

Preface

is "one world or none," yet today there are rather "two worlds." City dwellers have been warned that unless nuclear weapons are abolished all cities should be dispersed, yet more and stronger bombs are being produced while cities all over the world continue to grow. It has been claimed that it is irrational to live in cities when nuclear warfare may break out tomorrow, and yet people—including most of the writers who made these statements—remain in the large cities.

The problem is not that these warnings are disbelieved, but rather that rational planning is "switched off" at the point of the real nuclear attack. Up to that point, there is a judicious effort for the production of nuclear weapons, physical research, scientific calculations, and accurate knowledge. After the explosion is assumed to take place, irrational thinking takes over: there is nothing but chaos, doom for all humanity, panic, or suicide—and immediate defeat or immediate victory!

We have deliberately avoided arousing emotions. In this area, which so strongly evokes horror, fear, or hope, a scientist is seriously tempted to relax his standards of objectivity and to give vent to his own subjective feelings. No one can fail to be deeply aroused and disturbed by the facts of nuclear weapons. These sentiments are certainly necessary to motivate actions, but they should not distort an investigation of the truth or factual predictions.

This book deals with the social consequences of actual bombing, starting with different types of destruction as given physical events, tracing step by step the effects upon urban populations—their size, composition, and activities—and finally investigating the repercussions upon national populations and whole countries. Accordingly, problems of international relations in the nuclear age, questions of military strategy, political objectives, and moral implications do not fall within the scope of this study. While we are deeply concerned with the moral and humanitarian implications of bomb destruction, we excluded them from this book,

The Social Impact of BOMB DESTRUCTION

not because we judged them to be of secondary importance but because they are better dealt with separately and in a different context. Moral values and over-all political and strategic objectives are, indeed, the premises which must govern any actions concerning nuclear weapons or bombing and concerning war and peace.

This book is concerned mainly with the adaptive processes of a society which has suffered from bombing and with the rehabilitation of destroyed cities in the months and years following a disaster rather than in the first few hours after an attack. But attention is also given to the effects of partial destruction in cities upon a continued war effort. This problem becomes relevant if one envisages a form of bombing that permits some continuation or rehabilitation of the urban industrial life while the war is still going on. There has recently been an increasing interest in "tactical" nuclear weapons and in other limitations on strategic bombing, which indicates that the question of a continued war effort after partial urban destruction may be of more than historical importance.

The behavior of population groups is of greater interest here than the behavior of individuals, because the main purpose of this study is to encompass the total effect of bombing on cities or on a country as a whole. Accordingly, the approach will be demographic rather than psychological, without neglecting, however, psychological data on individuals in disaster situations. Thus, the problem will be studied largely in statistical terms, abstracted from its value content and devoid of references to personal or national interests. Such an approach is more likely to provide unbiased conclusions.

It is not a pleasant task to deal realistically with such potentially large-scale and gruesome destruction. But since we live in the shadow of nuclear warfare, we must face its consequences intelligently and prepare to cope with them. It is necessary to relate

Preface

the facts of modern technology to man and society if we are to survive as a people and as a nation.

Fred Charles Iklé

Santa Monica, California
August 21, 1958

ACKNOWLEDGMENTS

PROFESSOR KINGSLEY DAVIS of the University of California at Berkeley has given continuous encouragement and advice to the author in preparation of this study. Most of the research and writing was carried out while Professor Davis and the author were at the Bureau of Applied Social Research, Columbia University. Thus, the study has benefited in all stages from the guidance so generously given by Professor Davis and from his critical reading of the manuscript.

The chapter on evacuation was written in coauthorship partly with Eleanor H. Bernert and partly with Harry V. Kincaid. The author is particularly pleased to recall the profitable collaboration with Dr. Kincaid on the study of the Dutch evacuation experience. Among those who have read all or part of the manuscript and to whom the author is indebted are Professor Donald L. Foley, Professor Abram J. Jaffe, and Mr. Paul Berkman. Other colleagues at the Bureau of Applied Social Research frequently offered advice and suggested improvements. Gratitude belongs to the author's assistants, and particularly to Monroe Lerner, Alice Taylor Day, and Bonnie G. Loflin, who helped in various phases of the work with patience and competence.

John C. Hogan and Brownlee W. Haydon of Santa Monica, California, have given valuable editorial advice.

The Social Impact of *BOMB DESTRUCTION*

The study was supported in part by the United States Air Force[1] and in part by the Office of the Surgeon General, Department of the Army.[2] The writing of this book was made possible partly by a grant to the Bureau of Applied Social Research, Columbia University, from the Eda K. Loeb Fund. Appreciation for this support is gratefully acknowledged.

Fred Charles Iklé

[1] Under Contract No. AF 33 (038)-14313, monitored by the Human Resources Research Institute (now Air Force Personnel and Training Research Center), Maxwell Air Force Base, Montgomery, Alabama.

[2] Under Contract No. DA-49-007-MD-454, with the Medical Research and Development Board of the Office of the Surgeon General, Department of the Army, and in co-operation with the Committee on Disaster Studies of the National Research Council, National Academy of Sciences.

CONTENTS

Preface v

Acknowledgments xi

I. Physical Destruction Related to Its Social Effects 3
    The City as a Functional System 5
    The Ratio of Consumers to Resources 7
    Elasticity of Resources 8
    Disproportionality of Effects
    from Increasing Destruction 11
    Deprivations and Perception of Danger
    as Determinants of Behavior 12
    Limited Alternatives and the Problem of Panic 13

II. Casualties and Their Consequences 16
    Disease and Medical Care 23
    Impact of Casualties on Morale 27
    Organizational and Legal Effects of Casualties 34
    Chemical and Biological Warfare 36

III. Destruction of Housing and Its Impact on Population 40
    The Process of Reaccommodation within a City 52
    Additional Factors in the Reaccommodation Process

Evacuation as the Alternative: German vs.
Japanese Cities 59
Billeting and the Post-Attack Period 63
Emergency Housing and Camps 66
The Limits of Housing Elasticity 69
Disproportionality of Population Loss
from Increasing Destruction 71

IV. **Evacuation as a Preventive and Adaptive Process 77**
Preattack Short-Term Evacuation
of the Whole Population 82
Long-Term Evacuation of Nonessential Personnel 85
Bombing Experience and the Problem of Flight 98
Long-Term Evacuation of the Whole Population 106
Evacuee-Host Relationship 115
Summary 120

V. **Transportation, Communications, and Other Utilities 121**
Intra-urban Transportation 121
Communications and Urban Organization 131
Maintenance and Housekeeping Utilities 137

VI. **Food Supply and Other Essentials 141**
Food Supply after Bombing 144
The Supply of Other Consumer Goods after Destruction 152

VII. **The Total Effect on Urban Man Power 156**
Factors Reducing Man Power 157
  Casualties 157
  Homelessness, Evacuation, and Absenteeism 159
  Labor Need for Civil Defense, Repairs, and Dispersal 162
  Time-Loss and Lowered Efficiency
  from Air-Raid Alerts 166
  Inefficiency and Disorganization Due to Destruction 167
  Mobilization for the Armed Forces 168

Factors Increasing Man Power   169
   Employment of Persons Formerly
   Not in the Labor Force   169
   Lengthening of the Work Week   170
Conversion from Nonessential to War Production   171
Summary   174

VIII. **The Cumulative Impact on the National War Effort**   178
   The Economy of the Remainder   180
   National Organization and Decision-Making   183
   Nationwide Transportation   188
   "Broken-backed Warfare"   190

IX. **Postwar Results of Bomb Destruction**   203
   The Heritage of Death and Disease   203
   The Redevelopment of Cities   211
   Survival of Civilization   224

Selected Bibliography   233

Index   243

ILLUSTRATIONS

facing page

Casualties after a Tokyo fire raid of March, 1945   74
A couple leaving their home after the Texas City, Texas,
    explosion in April, 1947   75
Shelter life in London's Picadilly Station during World War II   90
After a night in the air-raid shelters in June, 1942   90
Emergency housing after the World War II raids on Berlin   91
Salvaging personal belongings after a World War II raid on Berlin   154
Mobile soup kitchens in Berlin after World War II bombings   155
Hamburg in August, 1943, after the big fire raids   170
Hiroshima in October, 1945, two months after
    the Atomic bombing   171
Hiroshima, ten years later   171

FIGURES

1.—Destruction and population loss in hypothetical group of cities 42
2.—World War II destruction and population loss in miscellaneous cities 44
3.—Changes in number of rooms and population in 60 German cities, 1939–1948 45
4.—Changes in number of dwelling units and population in 24 Japanese cities, 1941–1948 48
5.—Changes in number of dwellings and population in the districts of Hamburg, July, 1943–October, 1946 50
6.—The relation between "fully compensating increase" and actual increase in housing density among 64 German cities, 1939–1946 54
7.—Reaccommodation within cities versus evacuation 60
8.—The disproportionately larger population loss of a city resulting from increasing housing destruction 72
9.—Evacuation and return compared with housing destruction in Hamburg during World War II 104
10.—Population and man-power loss in Berlin 176
11.—Frankfurt, 1939–1952 214
12.—Nagasaki, 1944–1953 216
13.—Hamburg, 1880–1950 220

TABLES

1. —Destruction and Population Loss in a Hypothetical Group of Cities   43
2. —Comparison of Actual and Calculated Postwar Population for 20 Western German Cities   57
3. —Distribution of Hamburg's Population by Type of Accommodation Two and a Half Months after the Heavy Air Raids   68
4. —Classification of Government-Sponsored Evacuees in Great Britain in 1939 and 1940   86
5. —Changes of the Population's Age Composition in Berlin and Cologne because of Evacuation of Children   87
6. —Percentage Distribution of Cologne's Population by Age Groups Before and After Evacuation   88
7. —Evacuation Arrangements for School Children in Berlin and Frankfurt   94
8. —Destruction of Transit Facilities Compared with Housing Destruction   123
9. —Percentage Distribution of Commuters to Central Areas of Hamburg by Distance Traveled for 1939 and 1946   127
10. —Elasticity of the Consumer-Resources Ratio of Hamburg's Streetcar System   128

The Social Impact of BOMB DESTRUCTION

11.—Effect of Destruction on Communications in Wuppertal: Per Capita Number of Telephone Calls and Letters   134
12.—The Effect of the Atomic Bomb upon Electric Utilities in Hiroshima   138
13.—Wartime Decline in the Supply of Civilian Goods in Great Britain   142
14.—Restaurants and Meals Served in Great Britain   144
15.—Increase in the Percentage of the Total Population Supplied by Community Feeding in Selected German Cities, 1943–45   148
16.—Average Number of Days Lost Per Worker during the First 17 Days after a Raid   159
17.—Drives to Increase the Labor Force for War Industries in Berlin   174
18.—Age-Sex Differentials of the Incidence of Air-Raid Injuries in England during World War II   206
19.—Percentage Distribution of Population in Japan and Western Germany by Size of Community   213
20.—Number of Persons by Place of Residence in Different Zones of Hamburg   218

THE SOCIAL IMPACT OF BOMB DESTRUCTION

Chapter I

PHYSICAL DESTRUCTION
RELATED TO ITS SOCIAL EFFECTS

NUCLEAR PHYSICISTS can obtain much information about the physical effects of atomic and thermonuclear bombs from experimental explosions. Such tests have been conducted in uninhabited areas—the New Mexico and Nevada deserts, the Marshall Islands in the Pacific, western Australia, and Siberia, for example. Social scientists, however, cannot collect new data from these experimental tests. The only empirical evidence of the effect of nuclear weapons on society must come from mankind's only actual experience with nuclear bombings of cities—at Hiroshima and Nagasaki.

Firsthand knowledge of man's reaction to nuclear bombs is therefore—and most fortunately—very limited. Furthermore, the explosions at Hiroshima and Nagasaki were from single atomic bombs which were much less destructive than more modern weapons. In addition, since the bombings occurred near the end of the war, they provided little information concerning their effect upon a continued war effort. These facts help to explain the difficulty of estimating future social and psychological effects of nuclear warfare.

In spite of the lack of direct evidence, it is possible to develop indirectly certain estimates and theoretical principles that will enable us to understand better what can happen in case of nuclear

The Social Impact of BOMB DESTRUCTION

bombing in a future war. First, the effects of physical damage of other wartime and peacetime disasters on social and economic phenomena can be studied. Second, data from natural disasters and World War II bombings can be used to discover how social effects change with varying degrees of destruction. The results of minor physical damage can be compared with those of increasingly greater destruction up to the maximum experienced during World War II. This will provide a trend that can be extended beyond the range of actual experience. However, we must keep in mind that some entirely new social or psychological factors may arise when destruction becomes very great. As a matter of fact, it will be shown later in this book that such new factors do operate, that with significant increase in destruction certain social effects appear that are not present when the physical damage is small.

Since our method here is to relate destruction—any degree of destruction—to its social effects, data on disasters other than wartime bombings will be examined. These include the epidemic plagues of the Middle Ages (destruction of human lives alone), recent natural disasters in the United States, and the 1953 flood in Holland. The most significant data, however come from the World War II bombings in Germany, England, and Japan.

It is necessary to use statistical as well as descriptive material in studying these disasters. An important source on World War II bombings of German and Japanese cities is the *U.S. Strategic Bombing Survey,* including the unpublished documents in the federal archives in Washington.[1] Other information on German and Japanese cities comes from yearbooks, statistical bulletins, and unpublished material received from municipal offices. For England, many published studies,[2] as well as national statistics cover-

[1] *U.S. Strategic Bombing Survey* (cited below as *USSBS,* with the number of the report given instead of its title).

[2] Of particular importance is the series of books *History of the Second World War: United Kingdom Civil Series,* edited by W. K. Hancock (London, H. M. Stationery Office, 1949 ff.).

ing the wartime period, are useful, but English municipal statistics are scanty except for London. In 1949 and 1953, the writer conducted field studies in England and Western Germany and interviewed officials or former officials concerning their World War II experiences. A similar study was made in Holland after the 1953 flood disaster.

The chapters of this book are organized to present an integrated picture of the impact of bombing on urban man power. Casualties, housing destruction, and evacuation (Chapters II to IV) reduce the number of workers available in a metropolitan area. Commuting difficulties and disrupted communications, food shortages, and a general scarcity of consumer goods (Chapters V and VI) are additional factors diminishing man-hours and working efficiency. Aftereffects on urban man power are assessed (Chapter VII), the impact of bombing upon a nation as a whole is appraised (Chapter VIII), a nation being considered as an economic and organizational entity of which the destroyed and damaged cities form a functional part. The final chapter examines the possible long-range consequences after the war is over.

This book is not concerned with destruction in itself. It does not deal with fires, blast, or radioactivity as such. Instead, the emphasis is on the relation between physical cause and social effect.

The City as a Functional System

A city can be understood as a complex of interrelated physical and social functions. It is comprised of a network of many relationships between individuals, groups, and material parts. Thus, urban households depend on markets, housing, and transportation; transportation requires transit workers, and transit workers need food; restaurants or food dealers need utilities; most city dwellers want recreational and educational facilities for their children; and city dwellers form clubs and associations and compete with each other in the labor market.

The Social Impact of *BOMB DESTRUCTION*

This view of the city as a functional composite of material and social factors is well known to urban sociologists and urban planners. It is a convenient approach for a careful assessment of the effects of bombing on cities. It also aids in synthesizing the consequences of physical destruction into a form applicable to the nation as a whole.

A disaster in a city upsets the network of ecological relations. One component may be completely destroyed while another, related one remains undamaged or even increases in importance. Since the primary effects of bombing are physical in nature, the physical components must be considered first, to determine how impairment of physical facilities affects social components. This can best be done by separating the city's maze of interlocking elements into functionally homogeneous relationships. A relationship is functionally homogeneous if it serves basically only one function in the city. For example, housing as the link between dwellings and dwellers is functionally homogeneous because it chiefly serves the one function of accommodating the city's inhabitants. Similarly, the relationships between a city's transit system and its commuters or between the communication facilities and a city's administration are largely functionally homogeneous.

In contrast, if we chose to study the socioeconomic effects of bombing by means of such physical concepts as "fire damage," "blast," "radioactivity," or "radius of total destruction," functionally heterogeneous relationships would become involved. Fire damage, for example, can leave people homeless, destroy transit facilities and thereby impair commuting, or cause fear leading to flight. But by studying functionally homogeneous relationships, one obtains a clearer picture of the over-all effects. A certain amount of housing destruction causes the same population loss in a city whether it is due to fire or to blast. And a given impairment of the transit system, whether from physical destruction, lack of fuel,

The Ratio of Consumers to Resources

or casualties among the transportation workers, leads to the same loss in man-hours among the commuters.

Under normal conditions, the complex mechanism of functionally related components in a city is difficult to trace and defies quantitative measurement. However, an urban disaster reveals many relationships because destruction affects the connected components quite differently, leaving tangible effects in the form of readjustments and measurable discrepancies. In this sense, a study of the "pathological" case helps the urban sociologist to understand the normal situation better, somewhat as physiology profits from medical pathology.[3]

The Ratio of Consumers to Resources

A functionally homogeneous relationship can be studied as a combination of two basic components. One constitutes a supply of goods or services; we call this "resources." The other uses and depends on this supply; these are the "consumers." Resources can be material in form—such as houses, transport vehicles, or water supply—or they can be services—such as medical care, education, or the preparation of food.

There is no clear-cut division of the whole urban system into consumers and resources. Consumers in one relationship may be resources in another. Transportation workers, for example, are part of the resources of the transit system because their services are used or "consumed" by the passengers of the transit system, but at the same time they are also consumers of many other resources such as housing, food, recreational facilities, and the like.

Given quantitative data on consumers and resources, it is possible to establish a ratio between the two for each functionally

[3] The concept of "functionally homogeneous relationships" fits into the theoretical framework of urban sociology (or human ecology), particularly in connection with the concepts of "commensalism" and "competition." Cf. Amos H. Hawley, *Human Ecology* (New York, The Ronald Press Co., 1950), especially pages 39 and 210.

homogeneous relationship. Under normal economic conditions this consumer-resources ratio corresponds to the ratio of supply and demand, and under conditions of free competition it is related to the price of resources or of services. A disaster, such as an air raid, causes changes in these ratios which are greater and more rapid than the normal fluctuations between the amount of resources available and the number of consumers among whom the resources are to be distributed. If a shortage of resources develops and if the resources are vital to many consumers, the government will usually try to abolish price as a regulator of distribution and to substitute rationing instead.[4] Where rationing is inadequate or inapplicable, queueing will result.

An example of a relationship between consumers and resources can be seen in housing. The consumers are the dwellers, families, or households; the resources are the dwellings or houses. Bombing may destroy a great many housing units while most of the inhabitants survive. Thus many people will be homeless unless the ratio between consumers and resources increases, with a larger number of persons accommodated in each dwelling unit.

Elasticity of Resources

A decline in resources on account of destruction is not necessarily accompanied by an equivalent decline in the number of consumers who can be served by those resources. The ratio of consumers to resources is remarkably flexible, permitting a more intensive utilization of the remaining resources to cushion the effects from partial destruction. A city readjusts to destruction somewhat as a living organism responds to injury. Intact sectors of a city can compensate to a degree for the functions previously

---

[4] Statistically speaking, rationing reduces or eliminates the variance of the consumer-resources ratio. When this ratio is mentioned later, the reference is to its arithmetical mean within the specified consumer population (e.g., a city), unless otherwise stated. Rationing, of course, cannot change the mean.

Elasticity of Resources

carried on in a destroyed area. This absorption of destruction takes place not only within a city but also among the different cities of a nation, especially if destruction becomes very great.

If the ratio between consumers and resources were rigid, a certain loss in physical or human resources would necessarily lead to an equivalent decline in the function which depends on them. But this ratio is elastic, and its elasticity is of the greatest importance in estimating the social effects resulting from a given amount of physical destruction. After an air raid, the bombed-out inhabitants who want to stay in the city, for example, can crowd into the undestroyed dwellings. A city which accommodated 60,000 people in 15,000 dwellings at a density of 4 persons per dwelling before destruction can still accommodate 40,000 people, or two-thirds of its inhabitants, with only 5,000, or one-third, of its dwellings left after attack, provided the number of persons per dwelling increases from 4 to 8. Similarly, in case of damage to a city's transit system, the commuters who require transportation to work will crowd into the undestroyed vehicles, increasing the number of consumers for each unit or facility in the transport system. Likewise, as a consequence of queueing and crowding at food stores and restaurants which are still intact, there will be a rise in the ratio of consumers to the city's food-distributing facilities. The same is true for most of the basic services provided by a city.

The greater the elasticity of the consumer-resources ratio, the better destruction losses can be cushioned. But the length to which this ratio can be stretched is not identical for all cities or for all services in a single city. The degree of elasticity is determined by the following factors:

(1) *Pre-destruction consumer density (or resources scarcity).* If housing, transit facilities, eating establishments, etc., have been crowded before attack, or if the supply of water, consumer goods, medical services, etc., was already limited, it is extremely difficult

The Social Impact of *BOMB DESTRUCTION*

to compensate for their destruction by more intensive use of what remains. In other words, more compensation will occur when a greater abundance of resources existed prior to attack.

(2) *Divisibility of resources or consumption.* Some resources cannot be easily distributed among a greater number of consumers than they were originally designed to serve. One of the greatest obstacles to the reaccommodation of homeless survivors, for example, is the difficulty of subdividing dwelling units or of breaking up homeless families. Similarly, there is a serious problem involved in the distribution of transit facilities among all those requiring transportation, because consumption is concentrated at rush hours and cannot be distributed evenly throughout the day to reduce crowding in vehicles.

(3) *Organizational problems.* Redistributing intact resources to compensate for those destroyed often requires a high degree of organization. In some cases, not all of the undestroyed resources can be used to the maximum. Dwellers who could take in homeless families, for example, may conceal the fact that they have available space. Or transportation facilities which are abundant in one part of the city may not be readily shifted to a damaged area where a shortage exists.

In addition to making more intensive use of intact facilities, a city can convert certain resources to the service of its most immediately essential consumers. School buildings can be transformed into dormitories for war-production workers. Sight-seeing buses can be diverted to the regular transit system. Restaurants can be turned into cafeterias to serve a greater number of people. All of a city's resources, however, are not equally susceptible to conversion. The less specialized a function, the greater the possibilities in this direction. Moreover, the organizational problems are considerable, and in most cases there must be provision for financial compensation to the owners of private resources involved.

Disproportionality of Effects from Increasing Destruction

Disproportionality of Effects from Increasing Destruction

It has already been pointed out that while test explosions give nuclear physicists an opportunity to measure physical effects directly and thus to confirm or revise their theoretical calculations, such experiments are not available for studying social effects. Social predictions must, therefore, be based exclusively on an analysis of the fundamental relationship of physical destruction to social phenomena. The intricacies of this relationship must be derived largely from the study of actual disasters; they cannot be deduced solely from general principles of sociology, economics, or other social sciences. Further, it is necessary to find out how nuclear disasters would differ from other disasters in this respect. The relationship between physical destruction and social effects in larger disasters differs from that in smaller ones primarily because of the diminishing "elasticity of resources." Increasing destruction leaves an ever smaller amount of resources to cushion the impact by increasing the consumer-resources ratio. The elasticity of resources is limited. In other words, after physical destruction exceeds a certain percentage of the city's total resources, further increase in destruction will result in a disproportionately greater increase in social effects.

The basic principle of disproportionality is simple and will be illustrated in another chapter in connection with housing destruction. The idea of a maximum number of consumers per unit of a resource, however, is a simplification which will be qualified later. Usually there is no discernible, fixed maximum, but a more complicated limitation results from the interplay of the various forces affecting it.

The phenomena of elasticity and disproportionality apply not only to cities but also to regions or to a country as a whole. In certain functionally homogeneous relationships, consumers and resources are exchangeable within units larger than a city. The housing loss for defense workers, for example, can be cushioned by the housing resources within the whole commuting area of a defense installation; a still wider area contributes to the elasticity of hospital facilities; and losses of raw material in one region can be compensated for by importing supplies from other regions. Thus, the level of destruction at which disproportionality becomes important depends on the type of consumer-resources relationship under consideration.

Deprivations and Perception of Danger as Determinants of Behavior

With the four related concepts of "functionally homogeneous relationships," "consumer-resources ratio," "elasticity," and "disproportionality" in mind, we may now consider two ways in which people confronted by disaster are motivated or forced to follow a particular pattern of behavior.

Civilians who have been bombed are suddenly faced with acute dangers and severe deprivations. They must make momentous decisions in unaccustomed situations and endure prolonged hardships previously unknown. Unlike soldiers, they are not trained to follow orders which may imperil their lives or jeopardize their families, property, and homes. In such a situation, governmental orders and legislation may provide guidance, but they alone cannot force millions of people either to leave their homes and accept the trying life of evacuation for a prolonged period of time or to remain in a target city and brave a nuclear holocaust.

World War II statistics on successive evacuations and return movements disclose that a population reacts more strongly to dangers and deprivations they have experienced or can perceive than to those they have only heard about or have been warned officially to expect, even though the latter may be more disastrous. As a result, people behave in totally different ways before and after they have experienced bombing destruction, or before and after they have experienced an evacuation.

Limited Alternatives and the Problem of Panic

Individuals do not evaluate deprivations by any absolute scale. They judge them within the framework of their own experience or the experience of their friends, neighbors, and colleagues.[5] Therefore, it is not so much the severity of deprivations which determines their reactions, but whether or not these deprivations lie within their personal experience or the experience of a reference group. Thus, deprivations fail to cause substantial changes in the customary behavior of people so long as they lie outside the realm of their personal experience. Likewise, until actually perceived, dangers do not disrupt normal habits of life. The dangers involved in nuclear bombing are particularly difficult to conceive in the absence of precedents. After seeing the charred and mangled bodies of air-raid victims, for example, a city dweller will be more anxious to evacuate, much as someone speeding on a highway will drive more carefully after witnessing an accident.

Limited Alternatives and the Problem of Panic

It is misleading to consider the kind of life which bombing survivors would face as if it were an alternative to the normal, daily life familiar to us. In this book, many reactions to bombing will be described as seemingly voluntary patterns of behavior, i.e., behavior without strong governmental coercion. However, if this behavior is mistakenly compared to life in normal times, it will seem unacceptable to the public. To avoid this misinterpretation, it is useful to map out carefully all possible courses of action that are open to survivors of bombing attacks with the resources that remain after destruction. Thus, the question of whether the public

---

[5] The importance of reference groups for an individual's evaluation of his own personal situation is known in sociology as the concept of "relative deprivation." It has been systematically substantiated through the collected data on attitudes and behavior in the American army during World War II. See Robert K. Merton and Alice S. Kitt, "Contributions to the Theory of Reference Group Behavior" in *Continuities in Social Research: Studies in the Scope and Method of The American Soldier* (Glencoe, Illinois, The Free Press, 1950), 42 ff.

will "accept" a certain situation cannot be answered before examining the alternatives—if any—that are left for the survivors.

In addition to the mistake of rejecting certain courses of action as "unacceptable" to the population, there is another error, of expecting a completely disorganized pathological behavior, which would fail to take advantage even of the limited alternatives remaining. It has occasionally been postulated that large-scale destruction would lead to mass panic, and the attention given to the problem of panic has frequently overshadowed consideration of all other possible social effects from bombing.[6]

"Panic" is defined as individual or collective behavior that is contrary to the interests and safety of the individuals or society. It is characterized by fear and a lack of rational thinking and is prompted by sudden danger or disaster—real or imaginary. Within this definition of panic, a mass flight from the site of explosion is not in itself a panic. A hurried exit from the scene of a nuclear holocaust is perhaps the most rational action a person could take. One could argue, on the contrary, that only those paralyzed by panic would passively await death or certain injury in their dwellings in the face of a nuclear attack.[7]

[6] Cf., for example, Philip Wylie, "Panic, Psychology, and the Bomb," *Bulletin of the Atomic Scientists,* Vol. X, No. 2 (February, 1954), 37ff. Also, much of the literature distributed by state and local civil defense agencies seems to overemphasize the importance of panic.

[7] Contradictory forms of overt behavior have been labeled "panic." For an excellent discussion of panic and the misunderstandings about it, see E. L. Quarantelli, "The Nature and Conditions of Panic," *The American Journal of Sociology,* Vol. LX, No. 3 (November, 1954), 267–75. According to this study, the most striking overt behavior of panic is flight. However, other studies have pointed out that apathy and stunned immobility occur in a context which some observers would characterize as "panic"; namely, as emotional response patterns to a disaster (see Irving L. Janis, "Problems of Theory in the Analysis of Stress Behavior," *The Journal of Social Issues,* Vol. X, No. 3 [1954], 18; and Charles E. Fritz and Eli S. Marks, "The NORC Studies of Human Behavior in Disaster," *ibid.,* 29–34). The view that mass panic occurs rarely is also expressed in the federal Civil Defense Administration's, "The Problem of Panic," *Technical Bulletin TB-19-2* (June, 1955) (Washington, Government Printing Office).

Limited Alternatives and the Problem of Panic

Reports from very large disasters of the past fail to show any significant mass panic among the afflicted population. Findings from Hiroshima, Nagasaki, Hamburg, and other areas of large bombings in World War II do not indicate that serious mass panic occurred at any time.[8]

The idea of "limited alternatives" just set forth may seem obvious when stated plainly. However, it prevents our judging the post-disaster behavior of people within the context of pre-disaster alternatives and avoids the hasty rejection of their behavior as unbearable or unacceptable. Furthermore, consideration of the "limited alternatives" demonstrates the need for an explanation of the unsubstantiated assumption that panic will result instead of an intelligent use of the limited alternatives left.

[8] *USSBS, passim;* John Hersey, *Hiroshima;* Takashi Nagai, *We of Nagasaki;* Hamburg Police President, "[Secret] Report by the Police President of Hamburg on the Heavy Raids on Hamburg in July/August, 1943," translated by Great Britain, Home Office, Civil Defense Department, 1946 (mimeographed); Irving L. Janis, *Air War and Emotional Stress,* 38, 41.

Chapter II

CASUALTIES AND THEIR CONSEQUENCES

THE MOST SERIOUS and certainly the most tragic result of nuclear warfare is the large number of dead and injured. In conventional bombing during World War II, casualties were few and less important in comparison with the other losses suffered by the attacked cities. On the other hand, nuclear bombing not only affects a larger area but creates new, additional hazards to human life. This fact must be borne in mind whenever data from World War II are applied to the effects of nuclear destruction.

During World War II, the number of persons left homeless after a raid using conventional weapons was always greater than the number of casualties. This discrepancy played a decisive role in the rehabilitation and reconstruction of damaged cities. Hamburg, for instance, lost only 3.3 per cent of its population, but 48 per cent of its dwellings in the air raids. In Frankfurt, less than 1 per cent of the population was killed in air raids, but over one-third of the dwellings were destroyed. Air-raid deaths in Kobe amounted to barely 1 per cent of the population, but over one-half of the housing was lost.

Death tolls from conventional bombing were not as high as normal peacetime mortality rates. In London, for example, the total number of civilians killed during the six years of the war was

Casualties and Their Consequences

smaller than the average number of deaths from all causes during a single prewar year.[1] The same is true for those German and Japanese cities where destruction was great.

The estimates of air-raid casualties made before World War II were far too high and resulted in anticipations and preparations out of proportion to what actually happened. In 1924, the British Air Staff estimated fifty casualties per ton of bombs on the basis of losses in the few raids on London during the last year of World War I. Casualty reports from the Spanish Civil War were assimilated, and in 1938 the British Air Raid Precautions Department raised the estimate to seventy-two casualties per ton. As a result, the projected number of hospital beds required for air-raid injuries was staggering.[2]

Actually, the data from World War II show that one metric ton of high-explosive bombs dropped in night raids by piloted aircraft killed about four or five persons in large cities in Great Britain and injured between ten and fifteen. Thus, the total casualty rate per ton lay between fifteen and twenty.[3]

Casualty rates from atomic bombs contrast sharply with those from bombs used during most of World War II. Hiroshima and Nagasaki show that the number of persons killed and injured by atomic bombs is many times greater than from conventional bombing causing the same amount of destruction. In Tokyo, the mortality rate per square mile destroyed by high-explosive bombing was 5,200 persons, while in Nagasaki and Hiroshima the rates rose to 20,000 and 15,000 respectively.[4] The increase is partially due to the added hazards of atomic explosions, such as heat flash and

[1] The number of civilians killed by air raids in the London civil defense region between 1939 and 1945 was 29,890 (see Richard M. Titmuss, *Problems of Social Policy*, 560). The annual average number of deaths from 1936 to 1938 was 37,930.

[2] *Ibid.*, 12–14, 63.

[3] *Ibid.*, 327.

[4] Los Alamos Scientific Laboratory, *The Effects of Atomic Weapons* (Washington, Government Printing Office, 1950), 336.

radiation. The sudden, extreme destruction also contributed to the high casualty rates.

A ratio of dead and injured per square mile destroyed gives only a rough measure of the potential deadliness of an explosion, as it does not take into account the density of the exposed population. A more exact measure for a comparison of physical destructiveness with personnel loss is the ratio of casualties to the number of persons who were not evacuated prior to the explosion and who were left homeless. With data for the city of Hamburg, it was possible to compute this ratio of casualties to the number of homeless fairly accurately and thus to demonstrate that more complete destruction leads to a higher mortality per dwelling destroyed.

Hamburg statistics give the number of air-raid fatalities during the last war by census tracts.[5] These were allotted to tracts according to the deceased's place of residence, not the place where the person was actually killed. Since most of the raids on Hamburg were night raids, the place of death (or fatal injury) and place of residence generally coincided. Such a fatality list could be compared with the percentage of destruction of residences within the tract and thus would enable us to determine whether the ratio of fatalities per dwelling destroyed is relatively constant or whether it depends on the amount of destruction. Investigation proved that this ratio fluctuates between 0 and 0.24 if the census tract suffered less than 90 per cent destruction, but with a destruction above 95 per cent, it rose as high as one fatality per dwelling destroyed.

Data from Hamburg indicates that the ratio of fatalities per dwelling destroyed increased as physical destruction in an area became more nearly total. Several factors contribute to such a rise: the routes of escape become obstructed; small fires develop into large conflagrations; and in the case of a blast, the greater destruction demolishes shelters which could have withstood partial de-

[5] Heinsohn, "Die Menschenverluste der Hansestadt Hamburg im 2. Weltkrieg," *Hamburg in Zahlen*, No. 26 (September, 1951).

Casualties and Their Consequences

struction. Thus, mortality is not constantly proportional to physical destruction—even without the additional hazards of nuclear weapons.

This disproportionality of the personnel effects from destruction is one reason why the ratio of casualties to homeless people is so much higher in nuclear bombing than in conventional bombing. However, the principal reasons for the high casualties from nuclear weapons are the suddenness of the explosive effects over a wide area, the greater danger of fire storms, and radioactivity.[6] Each of these factors will be considered separately.

(1) *Suddenness of widespread explosion effects.* In the case of conventional bombing, people can adopt a wait-and-see attitude before taking refuge in shelters; it is even possible to ignore minor air raids and continue productive activities in cities without exposure to any great risk of death. During the V-1 and V-2 rocket bombings on London, where advance warning was impossible, the population could take this risk since the destructive radius of these missiles was minute in comparison to nuclear weapons. The destruction in Hamburg, which was about equal to that in Nagasaki, took place largely during three midnight raids, lasting about two hours each. A "nominal" atomic bomb could have caused the same destruction within a few seconds, thus depriving the population of an opportunity to take refuge in shelters or to flee after the attack had begun. In the case of nuclear bombing, therefore, protection and evacuation are effective only with advance warning. This means that the population must act before it has perceived the danger, which is difficult according to the principle of "Perception of Danger."

(2) *Danger of fire storms.* Fire storms and conflagrations con-

---

[6] For a discussion of the personnel effects of nuclear weapons, see U. S. Department of Defense and U. S. Atomic Energy Commission, *The Effects of Nuclear Weapons*, Chap. XI.

stitute serious threats to human life because they persist after the initial explosion and cause death by heat or asphyxiation to occupants of shelters who would otherwise survive the short-lived blast or heat flash. Furthermore, avenues of escape are obstructed by the coalescence of fires and the hurricane-like winds peculiar to fire storms. The majority of the air-raid casualties in Hamburg and Tokyo were due to fire storms.

Nuclear weapons are more likely to cause fire storms in densely built-up areas, where many small initial fires are ignited by the heat flash and are fanned by winds rushing toward the center of the explosion.[7]

(3) *Nuclear radiation.* It is estimated that from 5 to 15 per cent of all fatalities in Hiroshima and Nagasaki resulted solely from nuclear radiation.[8] Of course, the number of victims who received a lethal dose of nuclear radiation but who were actually killed by the blast, heat flash, or secondary fires was much larger. However, assuming an attack similar to the early A-bomb, protective measures could further reduce the proportion of casualties from radiation alone, since protection from the initial nuclear radiation is generally less difficult than protection from blast and secondary fires. Therefore, it was justified at that time to assure the public that nuclear radiation was not as important as its mysterious qualities made it seem to many people.[9]

In contrast to the early A-bomb, thermonuclear explosions produce radioactive fall-out that could cause far more casualties than blast, heat flash, and secondary fires. Even without this fall-out, the

[7] For a discussion of the technical aspects of fires from atomic and incendiary bombing see Horatio Bond, *Fire and the Air War* (Boston, National Fire Protection Association, 1946), and "Defense against Fire Effects of Atomic Bombs," *Bulletin of Atomic Scientists,* Vol. VII, No. 11 (November, 1951), 337–40, 352.

[8] U. S. Department of Defense and U. S. Atomic Energy Commission, *op. cit.,* 457.

[9] Cf., for example, Los Alamos Scientific Laboratory, *op. cit.,* 289–90, 334, and 340.

Casualties and Their Consequences

lethal effects of nuclear weapons are beyond the scope of our imagination. Since fall-out leads to the added hazard of widespread radioactive contamination, thermonuclear weapons may ultimately threaten the survival of large parts of national populations. Such a threat overshadows any industrial, military, or property damage.

Fall-out occurs when particles retain residual radioactivity.[10] It may cover an area much larger than that affected by blast and heat and remain a threat to human life for a longer period of time. For example, following the firing of a very large thermonuclear device at Bikini Atoll on March 1, 1954, "over 7,000 square miles was contaminated to such an extent that survival might have depended upon evacuation of the area or taking protective measures."[11] The technical aspects of fall-out radiation need not be discussed here, since we are concerned solely with its social effects, i.e., the fatalities and illness which it causes.[12]

Fatal exposures to fall-out radiation lead to acute radiation sickness, which has a fairly well-established sequence of symptoms. Only in instances of the most severe exposure does death occur within a few hours. In cases involving lethal but not extreme exposures at Hiroshima and Nagasaki, the victims exhibited varying degrees of shock, followed by vomiting and later by severe diarrhea. Afterwards, a few days usually passed without serious symptoms, except perhaps bodily fatigue and malaise. Between the fifth and seventh days, a fever developed which continued until the time of death. However, this experience applies to injuries from the initial radiation, and the sickness due to residual (fall-out)

---

[10] The term "residual" is used here as opposed to the immediate radiation which consists of neutrons and gamma rays released instantaneously with the explosion.

[11] U. S. Department of Defense and U. S. Atomic Energy Commission, *op. cit.*, 423.

[12] Further technical information can be found in *ibid.*, Chaps. IX and X, and 466–502. See also U. S. Congress, Summary Analysis of Hearings before the Joint Committee on Atomic Energy, *The Nature of Radioactive Fallout and Its Effects on Man.*

radiation may lead to a more protracted time sequence of symptoms since the irradiation would be more gradual.

Death from fatal radiation exposures will ordinarily occur in ten days to two weeks. This slowly mounting death toll will have a profound effect upon the survivors. Within the same family or within a small group of evacuees, there are likely to be both victims with fatal exposure and persons who suffered only minor radiation damage, because a great many contingencies affect the dose which people receive in a fall-out area. For example, differences in local shielding or accidental bodily contact with contaminated material may cause substantial variations at essentially the same location. But persons with only minor radiation injuries will exhibit the same symptoms as those with fatal injuries, and hence they will exist in a state of anxiety, believing that their own fate is mirrored in the deaths of others who succumb to this strange disease. Such a situation is likely to discourage active participation in the rehabilitation of a stricken area.

A civilian population can avoid irradiation from fall-out by evacuating from the contaminated area, by seeking protection in a shelter, or by conducting decontamination procedures. The most promising approach is probably a combination of these measures, but all involve serious social and psychological difficulties, particularly if the country has suffered several sudden nuclear bombings. Thus, if protection in a shelter is to be effective, people may have to remain there for a long time, perhaps many days or weeks, spending only very brief periods outdoors. Many may not have the perseverance to remain in uncomfortable quarters with inadequate facilities, since the danger will be absolutely indiscernible except with special measuring equipment and since homes and workplaces may be completely intact. Unless there has been effective instruction before the attack and there is continuous guidance afterwards, many people may disregard the proper precautions because the danger of radiation is not directly evident.

Disease and Medical Care

Evacuation from contaminated areas may present even greater difficulties than prolonged stays in shelters. The greatest problem is to find safe areas. These may be too far away, inaccessible because of disrupted transportation, or without facilities to receive evacuees. Furthermore, because the safe areas and the contaminated areas can be distinguished only with measuring instruments, useful evacuation depends on a swift, extensive monitoring and communication system. And this complex guidance will have to operate immediately, at a time when the normal channels of communication and transportation may all be disrupted. Finally, areas which are safe after the initial attack, and hence become crowded with evacuees, may soon be subject to fall-out from a later attack.

Decontamination can begin only when the radiation level is sufficiently low that exposed personnel will not suffer serious irradiation. Like evacuation, it is contingent on measuring instruments. While decontamination methods are quite simple, their effectiveness is another matter, because most of the work would probably be carried out by inexperienced civilians. A certain hazard in the general environment will always remain because decontamination must necessarily be limited to readily accessible parts of buildings, factories, and perhaps the main streets.

In this connection it should also be remembered that civilian casualties from fall-out could occur even in areas which were not the principal targets of attack. Nuclear weapons delivered against military targets could, under certain conditions, lead to serious fall-out hazards in densely populated areas.

Disease and Medical Care

During World War II the number of persons injured and requiring hospitalization was usually larger than the number of persons killed. In England, the ratio of injured to killed was between 3 to 1 and 4 to 1. Counting only the injured who were admitted to hospitals, the ratio of persons seriously injured to persons killed was 5 to 3 in the London civil defense region from 1939 to 1945.[13] But in the big raids on Hamburg the number of injuries and deaths was about equal.[14]

With two exceptions, the injuries from nuclear bombing are the same as those from conventional bombing. Both forms of bombing cause heat injuries from burning buildings and fire storms, and mechanical injuries from blast and collapsing buildings. (Conventional incendiary bombs occasionally also cause direct heat injuries.) The two additional causes of injuries peculiar to nuclear bombs are the heat flash and nuclear radiation.[15] Protection against the direct effects of the heat flash is easily possible with only short advance warning. Heat-flash injuries were the main cause of the grossly altered physical appearance of victims in Hiroshima and Nagasaki, which had a most disturbing emotional impact upon the other survivors.

On the basis of estimates, the ratio of injured persons to those killed in Hiroshima and Nagasaki was roughly 1 to 1.[16] This compares with the 3 to 1 or 4 to 1 ratio for England's air-raid victims and with Hamburg's 1 to 1 ratio mentioned above. In the case of nuclear explosions, where mortality is very high near the center of the blast, most nonfatal injuries occur at the fringe of the devastated area or in regions contaminated by fall-out. Since the number of injured people depends primarily on the width and population density of this vulnerable, nonfatal fringe and on the extent of the fall-out area, it is also possible that the number of injured

---

[13] Titmuss, *op. cit.*, 558, 560–61.

[14] Hamburg Police President, *op. cit.* According to this source, there were 37,214 injured persons and 31,647 persons known by December 1, 1943, to have been killed during the raids. Those killed but unknown to the police at that time were estimated at another 4,000 to 8,000.

[15] For a summary of the relative incidence of mechanical, burn, and radiation injuries in Hiroshima, see Mardelle L. Reynolds and Francis X. Lynch, "Atomic Bomb Injuries among Survivors in Hiroshima," *Public Health Reports*, Vol. LXX, No. 3 (March, 1955), 261–70.

[16] U. S. Department of Defense and U. S. Atomic Energy Commission, *op. cit.*, 455.

Disease and Medical Care

persons would be much larger than the number of fatalities, especially if the protective measures in outer areas are insufficient.

Even if there were no cases of radiation sickness, the medical resources remaining after a nuclear attack would not permit adequate treatment of all nonfatal casualties. Medical facilities and personnel, which are largely concentrated in central areas of cities, are themselves subject to attack. In Nagasaki, over 80 per cent of the hospital beds were completely destroyed, and the mortality of the patients and medical staff who were in the hospitals at the time of the explosion was about 75 to 80 per cent.[17] Hamburg lost 14,000, or 66 per cent, of its 21,105 hospital beds during the big raids.[18] In comparison, only 45 per cent of Hamburg's dwellings were destroyed in these raids.

The elasticity of a city's medical resources is very important for the care of casualties. Where there is no shortage of doctors, nurses, and hospital beds before destruction, the increased load of patients can be more easily absorbed. In London, for example, hospital space was cleared at the beginning of World War II by evacuating patients to country hospitals or nursing homes outside of the city and by discharging patients sooner than in normal times.

Sickness resulting from residual radiation overshadows the medical problem created by all other injuries. The initial symptoms of the radiation syndrome from a non-lethal dose are about the same as those from a lethal dose, but they generally develop somewhat later and are less severe. After two weeks there will be continued illness with marked tendencies to bleeding, diarrhea, loss of hair, and—more serious—a strong susceptibility to secondary infections.[19] Furthermore, people who come in direct contact with

---

[17] *USSBS*, Pacific report No. 13, p. 10.
[18] Karl Vincent Krogmann, in a lecture given as mayor of Hamburg, at a meeting of German mayors in Posen on February 12, 1944.
[19] See, for example, C. P. Miller, C. W. Hammond, and M. Tompkins, "The Role of Infection in Radiation Injury," *Journal of Laboratory and Clinical Medicine*, Vol. XXXVIII, No. 3 (September, 1951), 331–43.

fall-out material may contract skin injuries which can become infected or ulcerated.[20] Thus, not only will the victims of non-lethal radiation sickness be incapacitated for several weeks because of the radiation syndrome itself, but many will also develop secondary infectious diseases. The lack of proper medical care and the weakened condition of these patients will impede their recovery or lead to death, in many cases on account of secondary infections that normally could have been cured.

The many seriously ill people will be scattered widely over the country since the fall-out pattern itself will be widespread, and subsequent evacuations will distribute the afflicted populations still further. With the undestroyed hospitals filled to capacity, relatives or hosts will undertake to nurse people through radiation sickness in homes and temporary billets. Many patients may require care for months. This burden of disease may constitute an excessive drain on the nation's man power. The slow recoveries or disappointing deteriorations of the sick people who are scattered among many families will tax large population groups more severely than the material devastation and initial fatalities, thus diverting much time and energy from rehabilitation or from the war effort itself.

In addition to the irradiation from external sources of residual radioactivity, there is the hazard of internal radiation from ingested bomb residues, although in areas of intense radioactive fall-out, external radiation is considered overwhelmingly more important.[21] The danger of ingested radioactive substances arises because plants and subsequently animals may absorb certain long-lived radioactive materials. The actual or presumed hazard from consuming these products may limit the food supply of the surviving populations. However, if the choice lies between starvation and accepting the vague risk of ingested radioactive substances—which scien-

[20] U. S. Department of Defense and U. S. Atomic Energy Commission, *op. cit.*, 483–88.
[21] *Ibid.*, 493.

Impact of Casualties on Morale

tists as yet can scarcely evaluate—most people will not refuse available, normal-tasting foodstuffs. The effects from ingested radioactive substances upon the health of human beings would generally not be noticeable for a considerable time, perhaps even for two to twenty years; hence, these may be regarded as postwar effects.

Impact of Casualties on Morale

The effect of casualties upon the functioning of the labor force and upon the socioeconomic life of a nation is not a homogeneous one. It is one of four principal types:

(1) *The direct man-power loss.* The number of workers killed or seriously injured will reduce the size of the labor force.

(2) *The indirect man-power loss.* The number of man-hours worked by the survivors will be reduced because casualties require care. This indirect loss becomes particularly serious in the case of widespread disability.

(3) *Disorganization.* Casualties among business leaders or important government officials can cause disorganization of the economy.

(4) *The effect upon "morale."* The fact that there are casualties among a population, as well as the risk of future casualties, will affect the emotions and motivations of the survivors and might consequently influence their behavior.

The energy and determination with which people meet an adverse situation depends on morale, although the concept of "morale" is not synonymous with the reaction of people toward difficult situations. It is not easy to formulate a brief definition of "morale." For the present we prefer to define it by a process of elimination. We are concerned here with the possible effects of casualties upon the economic and social functioning of a nation

The Social Impact of *BOMB DESTRUCTION*

which are not due to a decline in man power, to the time and effort necessary for the care of casualties, or to the loss of administrators. With these three factors eliminated, it appears that the remaining factors largely coincide with phenomena that are commonly thought of as relating to morale.[22]

The impact of casualties upon morale stems mainly from actually seeing dead or injured persons and from the emotional shock resulting from the death of family and friends. When casualties have occurred among a group of persons, they are forced to realize that they face the risk of death now or in the future. No other aspect of an air raid causes as severe an emotional disturbance as the actual witnessing of death and agony. Interviews with persons who have experienced an atomic explosion reveal that one-third of them were emotionally upset because of the casualties they saw, while only 5 per cent or fewer experienced fear or some other form of emotional disturbance on account of the flash of the explosion, the noise, the blast, the devastation, and the fires.[23]

An atomic bombing raid causes more severe emotional reactions than a conventional raid. Janis declares:

> Apparently it was not simply the large number of casualties but also the specific character of the injuries, particularly the grossly altered physical appearance of persons who suffered severe burns, that had a powerful effect upon those who witnessed them.

---

[22] Our usage of the term "morale" does not include all the differentiated meanings which this concept has acquired in some sociological or psychological studies; it comes closer to military parlance, such as in the expression "morale of troops," for example, which means simply the will to win a battle. There has been a considerable amount of research on morale with all its many meanings, sometimes introducing an ethical aspect, sometimes building up elaborate hypostatizations and indices of "high" and "low" morale. Cf., for example, Robert C. Angell, "The Moral Integration of American Cities," *American Journal of Sociology*, Vol. LVII, No. 1 (July, 1951), Part II; also, Samuel A. Stouffer *et al.*, *The American Soldier*, I, II. (Princeton, Princeton University Press, 1950.) (Studies in Social Psychology in World War II.)

[23] Janis, *Air War and Emotional Stress*, 16–17.

Impact of Casualties on Morale

Hence, it appears to be highly probable that, as a correlate of the exceptional casualty-inflicting properties of the atomic weapon, there was an unusually intense emotional impact among the uninjured evoked by the perception of those who were casualties.[24]

The strong emotional disturbance that results from the sight of mangled bodies has also been reported from lesser peacetime disasters, such as a plant explosion.[25]

We are interested here in this emotional agitation only as it affects the overt behavior of city dwellers. Two contradictory reactions could be suggested as short-range effects. It can be argued that apathy and disorganization will prevail. On the other hand, it is conceivable that the emotional disturbance from casualties will intensify rescue or defense activities. While there is evidence of both forms of reactions after a disaster, the latter is encouraged by effective leadership which directs survivors toward useful activities.

These two short-range effects will diminish and decline in importance, if they occur at all. But there is another effect from the sight of casualties which has a much greater influence on the behavior of a population after an air-raid. This is the "Perception of Danger" principle. Nothing can make people more fully aware of the risk of death and injury from bombing than seeing air-raid casualties around them. Therefore, if there is a threat of further attacks, city dwellers are impelled to action to avoid the risk of death or injury. In the event of very large disasters, such as nuclear explosions, where shelters and ordinary precautions may not offer sufficient protection, many urbanites will leave the city. This exodus—probably one of the most important morale effects from

---
[24] Ibid., 20-21.
[25] Unpublished study by the National Opinion Research Center's disaster research team, at the University of Chicago, March, 1951.

nuclear bombing—will be dealt with in the discussion of evacuation in Chapter IV below.

Daylight raids with conventional bombs against defense plants create a localized danger which leads to absenteeism in the factories rather than flight from the city. Such absenteeism occurred during World War II and probably also in North Korean defense plants which were attacked in daylight raids by the United Nations forces.

The second factor determining the impact of casualties upon morale is the emotional distress caused by the loss of friends or family and results in increased anxiety about future dangers and protection of surviving family members. Such anxiety may enhance the attraction of evacuation much as the sight of casualties does. It is conceivable, also, that widespread casualties would make surviving relatives apathetic toward the war effort and that they would work less efficiently or become reluctant to fight. Such a reaction could be particularly significant among troops in the field who learn of the loss of family members in bombed cities, although studies made of troop morale after news had reached them of casualties and other air-raid losses during World War II disclosed no evidence that the efficiency of troops had been substantially reduced or that desertions had increased.[26] In the event of nuclear bombings, however, entire military units rather than single soldiers, as in World War II, might suffer bereavements which would have serious repercussions on troop morale.

Some information is available regarding the effect of family deaths upon the civilian population, too. In the big raids of 1943, 3.3 per cent of the total population of Hamburg was killed in addition to heavy battle casualties among Hamburg soldiers at the front (in the Russian counteroffensive after Stalingrad). Shortly

[26] *USSBS*, European report No. 64b, Vol. II. In the German army, furlough was granted to soldiers who suffered losses of family members or total destruction of their homes as a result of city bombing (*USSBS*, European report No. 65, p. 350).

Impact of Casualties on Morale

after these air raids the local newspapers carried notices of the deaths of soldiers whose families lived in Hamburg as well as lists of the city's air-raid victims. It is significant that, whatever the "morale" effect of this double impact, there was no noticeable decline in industrial production nor were there important political repercussions.

Finally, the question arises whether very heavy casualties might not lead to political agitation for surrender or have a direct influence on government leaders to negotiate a surrender. It is impossible, of course, to make general predictions on this subject because it depends on the political structure of each country. There are historical examples where heavy casualties did not discourage the surviving population from continuing the fight, just as there are examples to the contrary. A general sociological analysis cannot provide a satisfactory answer to this problem, but political science or history might suggest somewhat more definite predictions in terms of individual countries and specific situations.

It is necessary to restate this open question precisely in order to distinguish it from the sweeping, all-inclusive question of whether or not bombing will cause a "breakdown of morale." Thus, the unanswered question is whether the "personal or ethical" loss from casualties—and, particularly, anticipated future casualties—could prompt citizens to force their government to surrender or could directly influence government leaders to capitulate. By "personal or ethical" loss is meant the feeling of bereavement or a humanitarian sympathy for the general loss of human life, in contrast to the impersonal loss of industrial and military man power or of administrators. The effects of the latter, more tangible losses are more easily analyzed and will be considered in a later chapter.

Special attention must be given here to the impact on morale of repeated casualties. The experiences of Hiroshima and Nagasaki give no indication of how a continued threat of death or

The Social Impact of *BOMB DESTRUCTION*

bodily injury might affect a population. The plague epidemics of the Middle Ages provide more pertinent historical examples, for at that time city dwellers were continually exposed to a great risk of death, which was emphasized by the daily sight of plague victims.

London lost about one-sixth of its population in the plague epidemic of 1603.[27] This was a proportionately higher death toll than that suffered by Hiroshima from the atomic bomb. And yet London was able to recover quickly and resume its functions as the leading city in England. Its population increased sharply during the next sixty years. Then, in 1665, a new epidemic caused an equally high mortality rate. It has been said that "Never did so many parents carry their children with them to the grave, and go together into the same house under the earth, who had lived together in the same house upon it. Now the nights are too short to bury the dead."[28]

The result of this continued threat to human life was a mass flight from London. Thus:

> The flight was so fast that for most of July the houses left empty and forsaken by their owners were far more numerous than those marked by the red cross, where the Plague had entered. There were yet many intending to fly, both in the out-parishes and the City, who lingered too long and fell victims to the Plague before they could get away. For weeks the tide of emigration flowed by every outlet from London towards the country, the smaller traders who were fortunately circumstanced following in the steps of the rich merchants. It was checked at last by the refusal of the Lord Mayor to grant further certificates of health, and by the effective opposition of the neighboring townships, which in self-defense set armed guards upon their roads and formed a barrier around the stricken capital.[29]

[27] F. P. Wilson, *The Plague in Shakespeare's London* (Oxford, Clarendon Press, 1927), 114–15.
[28] Thomas Vincent, *God's Terrible Voice in the City* (1667), 30–31.

Impact of Casualties on Morale

The efforts of the authorities to stem the flight from London by refusing to grant certificates of health provides a curious parallel to the situation three hundred years later in cities subjected to severe air raids when German and Japanese authorities curbed indiscriminate evacuation by refusing departure certificates.

The plague epidemics, however, throw little light on the consequences of casualties in a modern city because the style of living and social organization were so different at that time. It is reported that the wealthy were the first to flee from London, having the means to travel and somewhere to go. As a result, the poor, who depended largely on private relief, were abandoned without means of support. Some narratives complain of the callousness that was shown toward the dead, especially by those charged with the disposal of bodies, but this was partly a mark of the time and the people involved rather than a consequence of the plague. On the other hand, no acts of mass violence or political disturbances are reported from the two epidemics in London. "The spirit for violence was broken, and all isolated instances were of rare occurrence."[30] But in other cities, such as Milan, the plague led to mob actions and persecutions. It must be remembered that all these reactions can be properly evaluated only within the context of the time. More interesting for our purposes are the long-range demographic, economic, and cultural effects of plague epidemics, which will be discussed later.

In general, repeated occurrences of casualties will intensify the perception of danger and hence induce more people to avoid exposure than would a single attack. The possible political reaction from the impact of the "personal and ethical loss" of casualties arises presumably because many citizens or the government wishes to prevent future casualties. Now, if not only is there a risk of

---

[29] George Bell, *The Great Plague in London, 1665* (London, John Lane, the Bodley Head, Limited, and New York, Dodd, Mead, and Company, 1924), 94.
[30] *Ibid.*, 173.

future casualties, but the death toll actually increases with repeated attacks, this particular political reaction becomes more likely. (Again the reader should be cautioned against presuming a vague "breakdown of morale," and urged to refer to the above, more precise formulation of this problem.)

While the long-range morale effects of casualties are likely to be intensified by repeated disasters, the short-range emotional shock from the sight of casualties will become weaker after the first occurrence. The following report from Nagasaki suggests that survivors become accustomed to casualties even after a single attack:

> In an atom-bomb war, I realized, there were just too many dead people; there weren't enough living ones to take care of the dead. They had to leave the bodies where they were. People got used to seeing corpses lying around; they came to take it as perfectly natural; they came to joke about it.[81]

Organizational and Legal Effects of Casualties

In all modern nations the government, in order to function properly, needs trained personnel and officials invested with formal authority. In normal times continuity of government operations is assured by the existence of an experienced core of officials, among whom replacements take place gradually. A war fought with nuclear weapons would suddenly swell the tasks of governments enormously, and at the same time, heavy casualties would deprive national and local administrations of essential personnel.

In the event of nuclear attacks, the normal mechanisms provided for the replacement of important government functionaries will break down in many instances. A replacement procedure based on popular elections will be out of the question in such an extreme emergency; and if it is based on predesignated substi-

---

[81] Nagai, *op. cit.*, 124.

Organizational and Legal Effects of Casualties

tutes (vice-president, undersecretary, deputy chief, etc.), the large area of mortality from nuclear bombs may frequently bring death or injury to all the replacements at the same time, for substitutes usually work in the same buildings as the officials they are to replace or live in the same general neighborhood. In cases of conventional bombing, this was not serious because the area of mortality from a single explosion was small, usually encompassing only a few rooms in a building.

Let us call the area affected by the same bomb the "area of identical vulnerability." Under conventional bombing, important officials and their substitutes are generally not in an area of identical vulnerability, but they frequently would be in nuclear bombing. If a government official or a business leader and his substitute are located in an area of identical vulnerability, the risk that this important position will become vacant after a bombing attack is exactly the same as if no substitute were provided at all. The legal replacement mechanism for the office of President of the United States, for example, would thus be entirely inadequate in case of a surprise nuclear attack. At a time when Congress is in session, the President, the Vice-President, the Speaker of the House, and all cabinet members are often simultaneously in downtown Washington, which is an area of identical vulnerability from a thermonuclear bomb.[32]

While it is relatively easy to suggest replacement mechanisms for top officials of a national government, the problem becomes more difficult in the case of local officials. In order to avoid with certainty the areas of identical vulnerability, it would be necessary to provide that residents of another community could become sub-

[32] Legislation has been suggested which would invest state governors with the power to appoint a replacement for the office of the President in such an emergency. Since most American state capitals are not large target cities, the state executives would be particularly suited for appointing replacements of important federal officials in case of a nuclear war, provided the necessary legislation has been enacted in advance.

35

stitutes—a condition contrary to the principles of local administration. Incidentally, it should be remembered that judges will also be highly important officials immediately after an emergency with heavy casualties, because they are frequently invested with the authority to appoint successors, administrators of estates, and the like.[33] An organizational chaos arising from inadequate replacement provisions and the resulting vacuums in legal authority could be prevented only by very general reserve emergency legislation co-ordinated on national and local levels. The existing civil defense treaties among adjacent states in the United States are a step in this direction.

Some of the organizational effects of casualties will be cushioned by the elasticity of "human resources." Surviving administrators or business leaders will be able to take over part of the most important duties of colleagues who are air-raid victims. Furthermore, an emergency always gives rise to spontaneous leadership on the part of persons previously in lower positions.

Chemical and Biological Warfare

We cannot adequately treat the possible social effects of chemical warfare (poison gas) and bacteriological or virological forms of attack, because too little is known to the public about these weapons. However, we can sketch the framework into which more detailed knowledge could be placed.

The principal technical impediment to the use of poison gas or biological poisons against civilian populations has been—and probably still is—the difficulty of delivering and spreading the toxic substances over large targets.[34] Poison gases with devastating

---

[33] For a discussion of the legal difficulties which would result from nuclear casualties, the reader should consult David F. Cavers, "Legal Measures to Mitigate the Economic Impact of Atomic Attack," *Bulletin of the Atomic Scientists*, Vol. IX, No. 7 (September, 1953), 269–72.

[34] The British White Paper on defense confirms this view: "Having regard to difficulties of mounting a successful gas attack, it appears improbable that even the most deadly nerve gases would be used against urban areas by an enemy who

Chemical and Biological Warfare

effects upon human lives had been developed during World War I. Mustard gas, for example, which was first used some forty years ago, affects the skin as well as the respiratory organs, so that gas masks do not offer adequate protection. Thus, aside from improving the ease of delivering or spreading the gas, it is hard to see what technical developments could add to the effectiveness of such long-known toxics as mustard gas. However, the techniques of chemical warfare have progressed since 1918, and governments of all the large nations have been concerned with new developments in this field.[35]

The use of biological or chemical weapons against livestock or crops seems remote, since the only purpose would be to reduce the food resources of a nation. It is scarcely conceivable that a belligerent would choose such a circuitous and—compared with nuclear weapons—such an ineffective method of attacking a population. There are several reasons why this indirect form of attack would be ineffective as compared with direct attacks against the war potential of a country:

(1) Since livestock or crops are more widely and evenly distributed than population, the delivery and spread of toxic agents would be immensely more costly in terms of planes or missiles than attacks against cities.

had nuclear weapons and the means to deliver them available to him." (Great Britain, *Statement on Defence: 1956,* Cmd. 9691 [London, H. M. Stationery Office, 1956], 28.) Humanitarian restrictions, international conventions, and historical traditions are certainly also of great importance as checks against the use of chemical and biological weapons. They are not dealt with here, because like physical, chemical, or medical aspects of an air war, they lie outside of the scope of this book.

[35] The fact that research is taking place in the United States for protection against new types of poison gas which could be used by an enemy was brought to public attention by an accident in which seventy employees at a research station had received mild doses of a deadly gas, the so-called "G-gas," which affects the nervous system. (The *New York Times,* May 7, 1954, p. 25). Regarding this nerve gas, see John R. Wood, *et al.,* "Treatment of Nerve-Gas Casualties," *U. S. Armed Forces Medical Journal,* Vol. II, No. 11 (November, 1951), pp. 1609–17.

The Social Impact of *BOMB DESTRUCTION*

(2) The great diversity of the food supply of a nation means that only a small part would be destroyed by a single agent (certain blights, for example, affect only grain, or certain bacteria or viruses only cattle or poultry).

(3) The great time lag between an attack on the food supply and its ultimate effect would be the most important deficiency in nuclear warfare, in which speed is so decisive. It would take months or years to affect a population seriously by such attacks, because a nation's food supply is quite "elastic" (especially at the beginning of a war), and considerable time normally elapses between production and consumption of a great many important types of food, such as grain and meat.

Diseases caused by bacteriological or virological attacks upon a population can spread indirectly through contagion. Biological warfare is a serious problem only because of the danger of epidemics, since the direct infection of large targets is technically difficult. This threat of epidemics in a modern war, however, should not be overrated. After the air raids of World War II, no increase of epidemic diseases was noted, in spite of widespread housing destruction.[36] Furthermore, modern antibiotics make the spread of most epidemic diseases still less likely than during World War II.

The possibility of disease and death from chemical and bio-

---

[36] *USSBS*, European report No. 65, pp. 82ff. This section, entitled "Why There Were No Epidemics," is an instructive example of the possible discrepancy between the real effects of bombing and the effects that would be expected on the basis of "common sense" or erroneous extrapolations. Much of the literature on biological warfare seems to overrate the risk of epidemics, especially in the absence of other destructive effects of bombing. Further discussions of biological warfare will be found in Theodor Rosebury, *Peace or Pestilence* (New York, Whittlesey House, 1949); Alexander Langmuir, "The Potentialities of Biological Warfare against Man—An Epidemiological Appraisal," *U. S. Public Health Reports*, Vol. LXVI, No. 13 (March 30, 1951), 387–99; and John J. Phais, "The Threat of Biological Warfare," *Armed Forces Chemical Journal*, Vol. VIII, No. 1 (January–February, 1954), 14–16.

Chemical and Biological Warfare

logical warfare would probably be completely obscured by the effects of radioactivity from nuclear weapons. As mentioned above, radiation sickness leads to reduced resistance to infectious diseases; hence bacteriological weapons might increase the casualty tolls *after* a nuclear attack.

In principle, the social effects of chemical and biological warfare, in contrast to those of nuclear and conventional bombing attacks, consist of all the effects of casualties without the effects of destruction, such as homelessness, disrupted transportation and communication facilities, and shortages of consumer goods. Consequently, the ratio between consumers and physical resources would decrease, not increase as in nuclear and conventional bombing (with the exception of medical supplies). The impact of these types of warfare upon morale would basically correspond to the general impact of casualties upon morale.

Chapter III

DESTRUCTION OF HOUSING
AND ITS IMPACT ON POPULATION

OF ALL the urban services affected by bombing, housing is most susceptible to quantitative statistical study. It represents a functionally homogeneous consumer-resources relationship which is clear-cut and readily identified; consumers are the city's total population, resources the dwelling units. The effect of destruction upon resources is immediate, obvious, and easily recorded. The effect upon consumers can be determined in a large part from analysis of changes in the consumer-resources ratio.

The typical World War II bombing attack, as we have seen, destroyed a much larger proportion of a city's housing than of its population. The homeless survivors were faced with two major alternatives. On the one hand, they could evacuate, leaving the ratio of consumers to resources the same as it was before the bombing. Or they could double up with others whose dwellings were still serviceable, thereby raising the consumer-resources ratio. Actually they did both. Consequently, the consumer-resources ratio rose, but not as much as it would have done had all the homeless sought accommodation within the city.

Hamburg's wartime population after the big raids was about 64 per cent of its prewar size, whereas only 51 per cent of its prewar dwellings remained intact. Within a year after the atomic

Destruction of Housing and Its Impact on Population

bombing, Hiroshima's population reached 50 per cent of its former size, but only 31.5 per cent of its prewar buildings still stood. Plymouth's population in 1945 stood at 79 per cent of its prewar size, but only 47 per cent of its prewar buildings were still habitable.

These cases suggest the degree to which housing elasticity can cushion the impact of air attacks. They also provide a commentary on a now obsolete concept of strategic air power, whose advocates in World War II "expected . . . great results from a systematic destruction of housing."[1] But this expectation was based on the assumption that a city's man-power loss would be roughly equivalent to its housing destruction. As it was, instead of fleeing the city, a substantial number of homeless survivors found habitation within its undestroyed structures. In short, an increase in housing density took place.

A series of hypothetical cases covering various degrees of destruction will illustrate systematically the theoretical effect of an increase in housing density on population size. In order to isolate the influence of the housing factor alone, casualties will be disregarded at first. Assume that a group of seven cities all had a housing density of four persons per dwelling before destruction, rising to five persons per dwelling after destruction. In each instance, therefore, the remaining dwellings will be occupied by five-fourths as many people as before. Assume further that the extent of housing destruction ranged progressively from none (0 per cent) to 90 per cent. It is then possible to calculate the percentage of population loss for each level of destruction and in effect produce a theoretical trend of population loss based on the extent of housing destruction as the independent variable. This trend, derived from Table 1, is plotted in Fig. 1.

---

[1] Stefen T. Possony, *Strategic Air Power*, 159. On page 54, Possony correctly points out the fallacy of this strategic concept: "Destruction of houses does not mean total destruction. The German example showed that even widespread demolition of dwellings and factory buildings does not make it impossible to carry on."

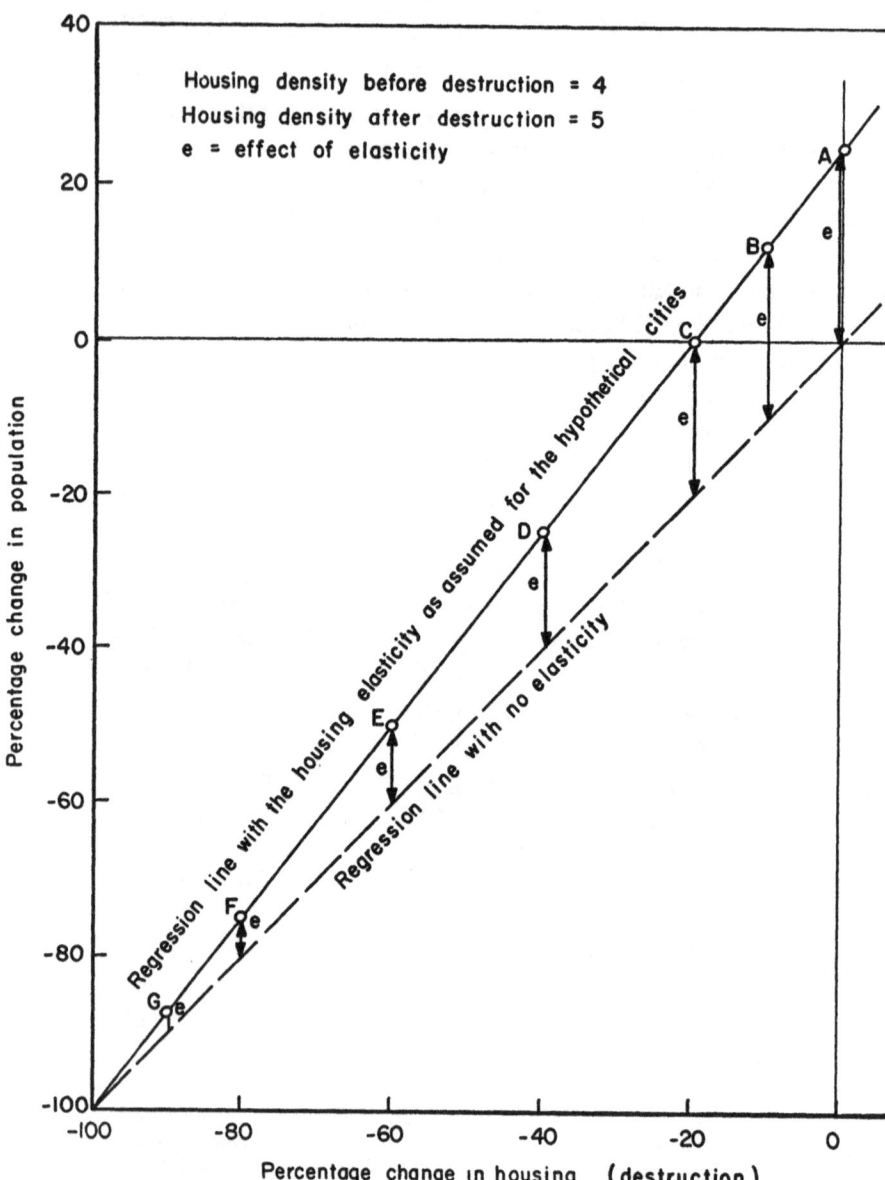

Fig. 1. — Destruction and population loss in a hypothetical group of cities.

Destruction of Housing and Its Impact on Population

TABLE 1

DESTRUCTION AND POPULATION LOSS IN A
HYPOTHETICAL GROUP OF CITIES*

(1)	(2)	(3)	(4)	(5)
City	Percentage Destruction	Per Cent of Housing Remaining	Per Cent of Population That Can Be Accommodated	Percentage Population Loss†
		100% − (2)	5/4 × (3)	100% − (4)
A	0.0	100.0	125.0	−25.0
B	10.0	90.0	112.5	−25.5
C	20.0	80.0	100.0	0.0
D	40.0	60.0	75.0	25.0
E	60.0	40.0	50.0	50.0
F	80.0	20.0	25.0	75.0
G	90.0	10.0	12.5	87.5

*In per cent of pre-destruction figures.

†The population gain in cities A and B could, for example, represent in-migration of inhabitants from cities D to G.

Figure 1 also includes the comparable trend (designated by the broken line) that would apply if there were no post-destruction increase in housing density—in other words, if the relationship between consumers and housing resources remained inelastic. The vertical distance between the two trend lines represents for any given level of destruction the theoretical effect of housing elasticity on the size of a city's population. Stated as a general rule, a post-destruction increase in housing density produces a percentage of population loss that is smaller than the percentage of housing units destroyed.

It will be noted, however, that the trend lines converge as housing destruction approaches totality. That is, with an increasing extent of destruction, housing elasticity declines in relative significance as far as the total population of a city is concerned. In practical terms, this means that as destruction mounts, a city will

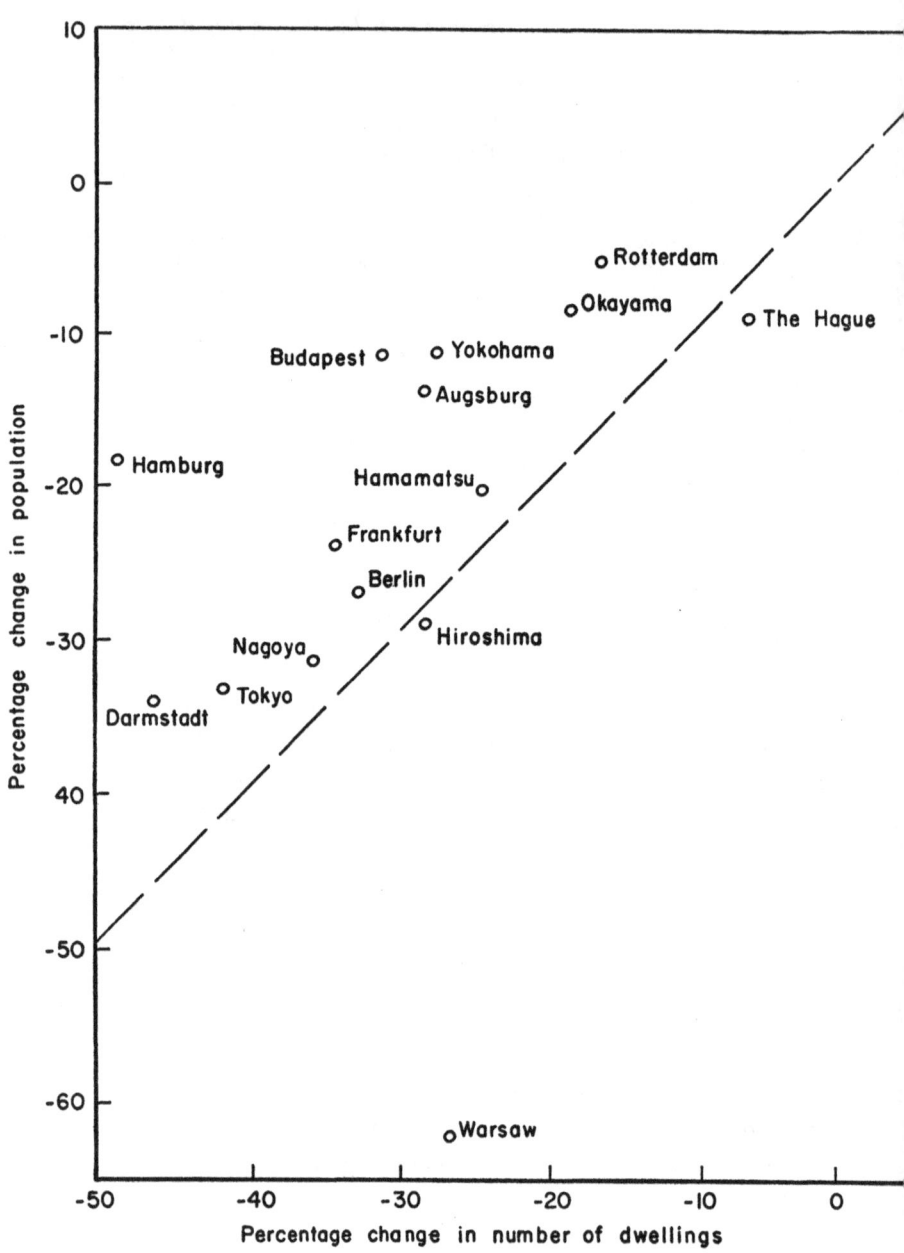

Fig. 2. — World War II destruction and population loss in miscellaneous cities.

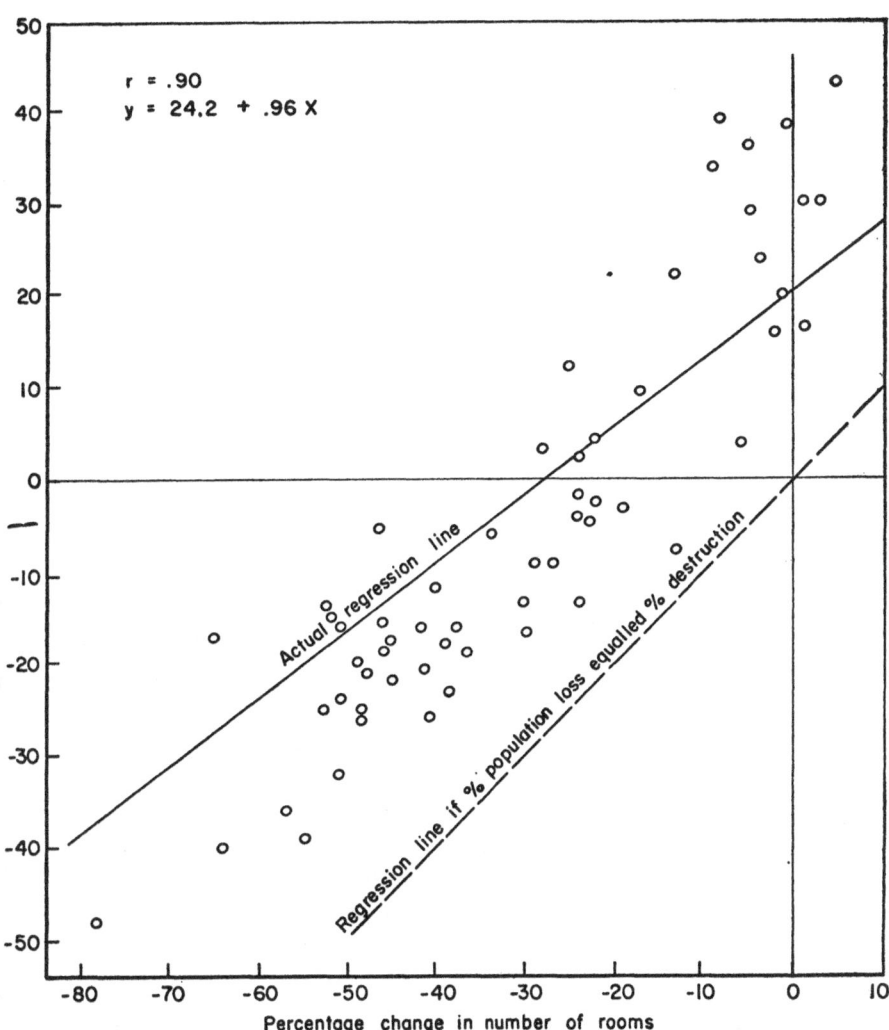

Fig. 3. — Changes in number of rooms and population in 60 German cities, 1939—1948.

The Social Impact of BOMB DESTRUCTION

experience disproportionately greater difficulties in absorbing the impact of further demolition.

Application of the reasoning used in the construction of our hypothetical model to the empirical evidence of World War II (Figs. 2, 3, and 4) demonstrates that the great majority of cities studied actually did experience a post-destruction rise in housing density. This is reflected in the observed differences between population loss and extent of destruction. Like the model, the percentage of population loss in most of the cities was smaller than the percentage of dwelling units destroyed.

In Fig. 2, the percentage of population loss is plotted against the percentage of destruction for a heterogeneous group of fifteen cities in several countries bombed in World War II.[2] The diagonal broken line passes through every point on which the cities would have fallen had their housing densities in 1946 been identical to those in 1939; that is, had a given percentage of housing destruction been accompanied by an equal percentage of population loss. As it is, all of the cities but three lie above the points on the diagonal which mark the extent of their destruction. In each case, the vertical distance above the diagonal represents the percentage by which the population loss was less than the extent of destruction and, inferentially, the relative amount by which housing densities increased after destruction.

Figures 3 and 4—in which population change is plotted against housing change for sixty German cities[3] and twenty-four Japanese cities,[4] respectively—are comparable to Fig. 1, with the following

[2] The 1939–46 decline in population is expressed as a percentage of the 1939 population, and the 1939–46 decline in number of dwellings is expressed as a percentage of the number of dwellings in 1939. (The terminal dates 1939 and 1946 apply to all the European cities; the corresponding dates for the Japanese cities are 1940 and 1948 for the population, and 1941 and 1948 for the number of dwellings.) The recorded change in the number of dwellings between the two terminal dates is usually somewhat smaller than the total amount of housing destruction suffered by these cities because of emergency construction, repairs, and subdivision of dwellings.

Destruction of Housing and Its Impact on Population

additions: (1) each includes several cities which suffered little or no war damage and which actually possessed more housing facilities in 1946 (or 1948) than immediately before the war; (2) the trend (correlation) of actual population change associated with concurrent changes in housing resources is represented graphically by the "actual regression line," and the trend that would exist had the housing density of each city remained constant is called the "regression line if percentage of population loss equaled percentage of destruction"; (3) the coefficient of correlation, "r," and the equation for the actual regression line are indicated here for analytical use later; and (4) Fig. 3 uses the percentage change in number of rooms instead of dwellings, as the measure of housing change, because it is somewhat more precise and because German data on rooms are available.[5]

From the scatter of cities in the portion of Figs. 3 and 4 marked by a loss in housing resources, one readily sees that, as with the miscellaneous cities in Fig. 2, most of the German and Japanese cities suffered a percentage of population loss that was smaller than the percentage of housing destruction. The differences between the two for Japan, however, are not as great as the differences for

[3] All but one (Berlin) are West Germany cities. All but eight of the West Germany cities with a population of over 100,000 and all but twelve of the cities between 50,000 and 100,000 in 1946 are included. The population data are from the 1939 and 1946 censuses.

[4] Those for which prewar housing data are available, including all cities with a prewar population of over 200,000, plus a number of others. The base population data come from the 1940 population census, and the base housing data come from the 1941 housing census; but it is safe to assume that there was little change in Japanese urban housing resources between 1940 and 1941. The source of the 1940 population data and the 1941 housing data is the *Statistical Yearbook* (Nihon Statistical Association, Tokyo, 1949), 43, 374; of the 1948 population data, the *Report on the Resident Population Census, 1948,* (Tokyo, Prime Minister's Office, Statistics Bureau), II, 18–160; and of the 1948 housing data, the *Report on the Housing Census of 1948* (Tokyo, Prime Minister's Office, Statistics Bureau, 1950), 136–41.

[5] The source of the data on rooms is an unpublished study of the Statistical Office of Düsseldorf: H. W. von Guérard, "Bevölkerungsdefizit und Zerstörungsgrad" (March, 1950). (A kitchen is counted here as a room.)

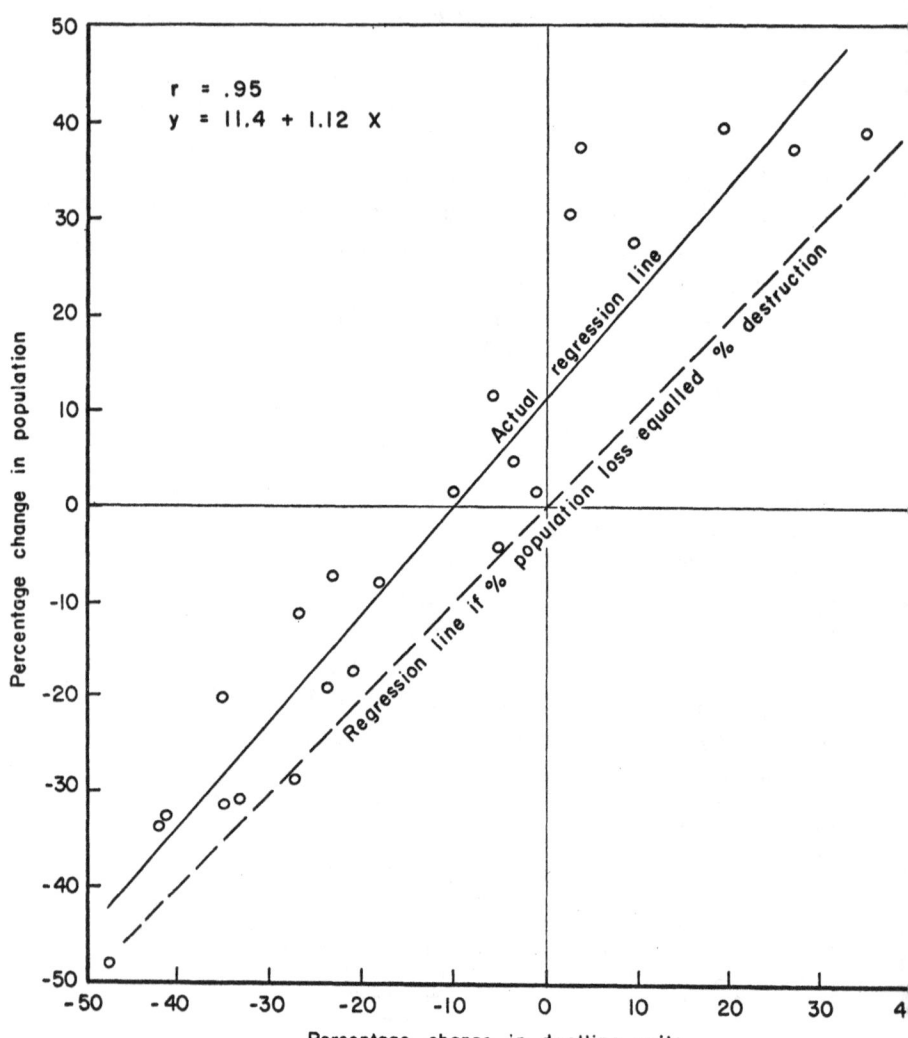

Fig. 4. — Changes in number of dwelling units and population in 24 Japanese cities, 1941—1948.

Destruction of Housing and Its Impact on Population

Germany. In other words, the post-destruction housing densities of the Japanese cities rose somewhat less. Thus, the Japanese urban housing resources proved less elastic than the German resources.

Figures 3 and 4 also show the extent to which cities with relatively little or no destruction serve to compensate for the housing losses of the more severely bombed cities. In the great majority of the cities with the least damage (less than 25 per cent destruction in Germany, Fig. 3, and less than 10 per cent in Japan, Fig. 4), absolute population as well as the housing density was greater after destruction than before. Moreover, most of these increases are larger than can be accounted for by a natural increase in population. It may then be inferred that these gains are largely attributable to an influx of homeless survivors from more damaged cities. In a sense, these are rough, quantitative measures of the extent to which urban survivors of air strikes migrate from their damaged cities to others that are still intact.

The results of the preceding analysis based on city totals are confirmed on a smaller scale by corresponding population and housing data from districts within a bombed city. The study of urban districts is of methodological value because it reveals the internal mechanism of a city's housing elasticity. Moreover, some districts experienced a proportionately greater housing destruction than cities as a whole during World War II. Such areas provide empirical data on the effects of nearly total destruction, such as might be caused by nuclear bombs.

For several European and Japanese cities information was available which permitted such an analysis by urban districts. The findings can be illustrated with the data from Hamburg.[6] In Fig. 5, percentage of population change is plotted against percentage of change in number of dwellings for the districts of Greater Ham-

[6] The other cities studied internally are Berlin, Düsseldorf, Warsaw, Budapest, Tokyo, Osaka, Yokohama, Nagoya, and Nagasaki.

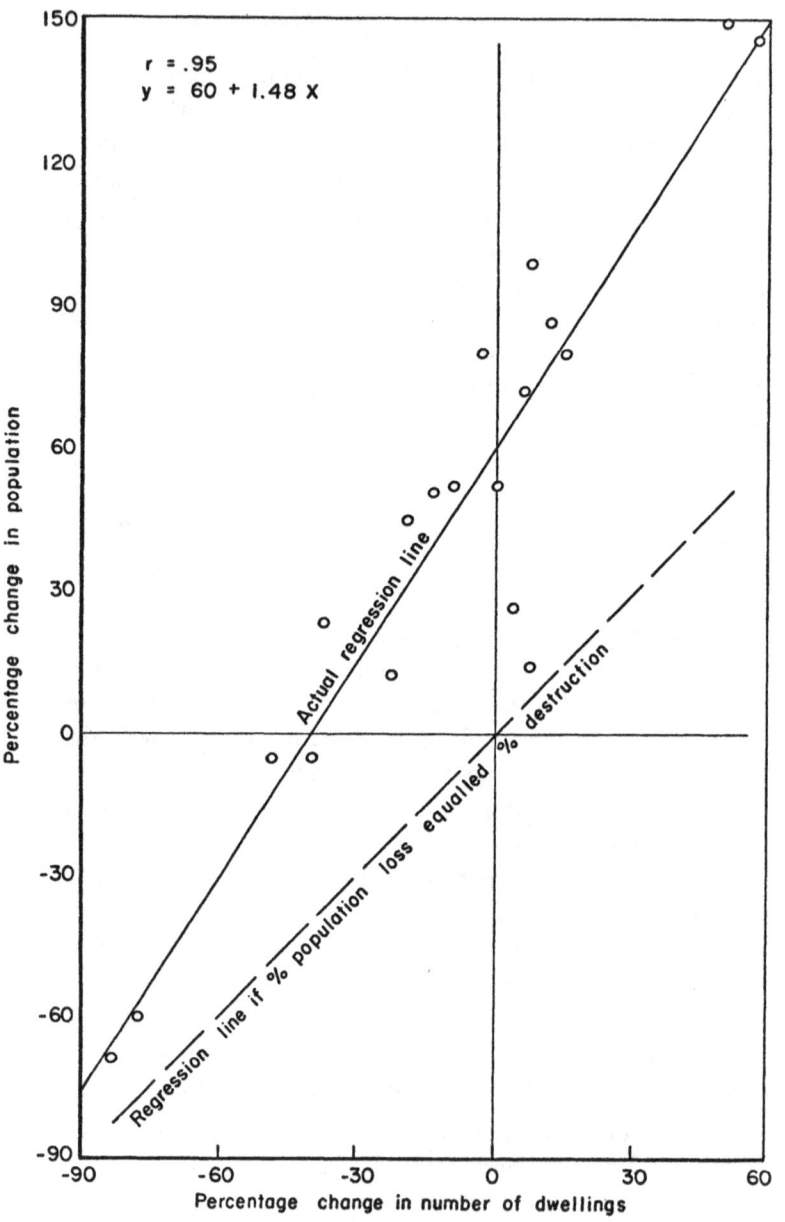

Fig. 5.—— Changes in number of dwellings and population in the districts of Hamburg, July, 1943–October, 1946.

Destruction of Housing and Its Impact on Population

burg, as was done in Figs. 1 to 4.[7] Evidently, the actual regression line in Fig. 5 converges with the trend (broken line) that would have occurred had housing density in each district remained constant. Thus, our hypothetical Fig. 1 is confirmed by these data from districts with nearly total destruction.

The population gain of the districts on the right side of Fig. 5 clearly demonstrates how an elastic consumer-resources relationship works: undestroyed resources partly absorb the loss from destroyed resources by accommodating more consumers. In terms of this concrete example, Hamburg's undestroyed districts partly absorbed the homeless survivors from destroyed sectors.

Supplementary statistical analysis—not shown in Fig. 5—reveals that the districts which were least crowded originally experienced the greatest increase in housing density regardless of percentage of destruction. As a result, the densities of all districts were more nearly uniform after destruction than before. It is as if the remaining serviceable dwellings had all been filled to the same high level of crowding. This is analogous to the effect of rationing of food or clothing, which also equalizes the consumer-resources ratio.[8]

[7] The period studied was from July, 1943, after which most of Hamburg's destruction occurred, to October, 1946. Between these dates Hamburg's total population declined by 6.8 per cent, and its number of dwellings by 48.3 per cent; consequently, there was an increase in the city's average housing density from 2.72 to 4.87 persons per dwelling. As can be seen from Fig. 5, fifteen districts increased in population (one remained stable), while only five decreased; but since the latter are large, the city's total population declined. The sources for the population and housing data are Kinder and Pause, *Soziographische Untersuchungen im Raume Hamburg* (Hansestadt Hamburg, Baubehörde, 1949); *Aus Hamburgs Verwaltung und Wirtschaft*, Sondernummer 7 (June 20, 1944); and information supplied by the Hamburg statistical office.

[8] An allocation of scarce housing resources by the government, similar to rationing, actually did take place. The equalization of housing density can be expressed statistically with the coefficient of variation (i.e., the standard deviation in percentage of the mean) among the housing densities of a city's districts. This coefficient decreased in Hamburg from 22.1 in July, 1943 (before destruction) to 8.2 in October, 1946. Similarly, in Düsseldorf, it dropped from 20.0 in 1939 to 7.6 in 1946, and in Warsaw from 13 in 1939 to 11 in 1945.

The Social Impact of *BOMB DESTRUCTION*

The Process of Reaccommodation within a City

To an extent, housing destruction reduces the size of a city's population. It has been shown that the percentage of destruction and the percentage of population loss are not equivalent because of housing elasticity. Nonetheless, Figs. 3 and 4 suggest a relatively high linear correlation between the two; in other words, although the two magnitudes are not the same, they are roughly proportional to each other.

Thus, the percentage of population loss in cities bombed in World War II can be statistically related to the percentage of destruction through a linear regression. The regression equation for Germany is quite different from that for Japan, but within each country the effect of housing destruction upon population size is described fairly accurately by these equations.[9] It is a simple problem of arithmetic to determine with these equations how great the destruction in a city must have been, on the average, to produce any population loss at all. In Germany this minimum level of destruction was 25 per cent; in Japan, 10 per cent.[10]

The above equations generalize the relations actually prevailing between urban population change and housing change in Germany and Japan during World War II. They are purely descriptive and cannot be used to predict the possible effects of housing destruction by nuclear bombing, because this type of bombing leads to a greater number of casualties and higher percentages of destruction than conventional bombing.[11] In order to arrive at

[9] For the sixty German cities of Fig. 3 the regression between percentage population change, Y, and percentage change in number of rooms, X, is $Y = 24.18 + 0.96 X$, with a Pearsonian correlation coefficient $r = 0.896$, and a standard error of estimate of 9.64. For the twenty-four Japanese cities of Fig. 4 the regression is $Y = 11.39 + 1.12 X$ (X here is percentage change in number of dwellings), with an $r = 0.947$, and a standard error of estimate of 8.38.

[10] These are the values the variable X takes in the equations if $Y = 0$. It must be remembered that the equations apply to the postwar population; the post-destruction population before the end of the war is generally smaller because of other factors besides housing destruction.

[11] It becomes apparent that the above equations cannot be applied to very

The Process of Reaccommodation within a City

more general relationships applicable to nuclear bombing, the reaccommodation within a city must be analyzed as a dynamic readjustment process in which the billeting of homeless survivors leads to an increase in housing density.

The immediate effect of bombing on housing is a decline in the number of dwellings through destruction and a loss in the number of inhabitants because of fatalities. Theoretically, a new potential consumer-resources ratio, consisting of all the surviving inhabitants divided by the city's undestroyed dwellings, would follow. In the conventional and atomic attacks of World War II, there were always homeless survivors; that is, the percentage of housing destruction was always larger than the percentage of fatalities. Barring very high fatalities from radioactive fall-out, this result might also be expected from nuclear bombing. Now, owing to housing elasticity, the actual post-destruction housing density will be higher than the density before destruction, making the reaccommodation of homeless survivors possible. In order to reaccommodate all homeless survivors within the city, housing density would have to increase to the above potential ratio (the city's surviving population divided by its remaining dwellings). This increase from the pre-destruction ratio to the potential ratio will hereafter be called the "fully compensating increase," since it would compensate fully for the loss in resources.

This fully compensating increase can be formulated in terms of the following symbols:

P_1 = Population of a city before destruction.
P_2 = Population of a city after destruction.
H_1 = Number of housing units before destruction.
H_2 = Number of housing units after destruction.
F = Number of fatalities.

high levels of destruction. If one lets $X = 100$ (i.e., total destruction) then the percentage population still housed according to the German equation would turn out $100 + Y = 28.18$, instead of O.

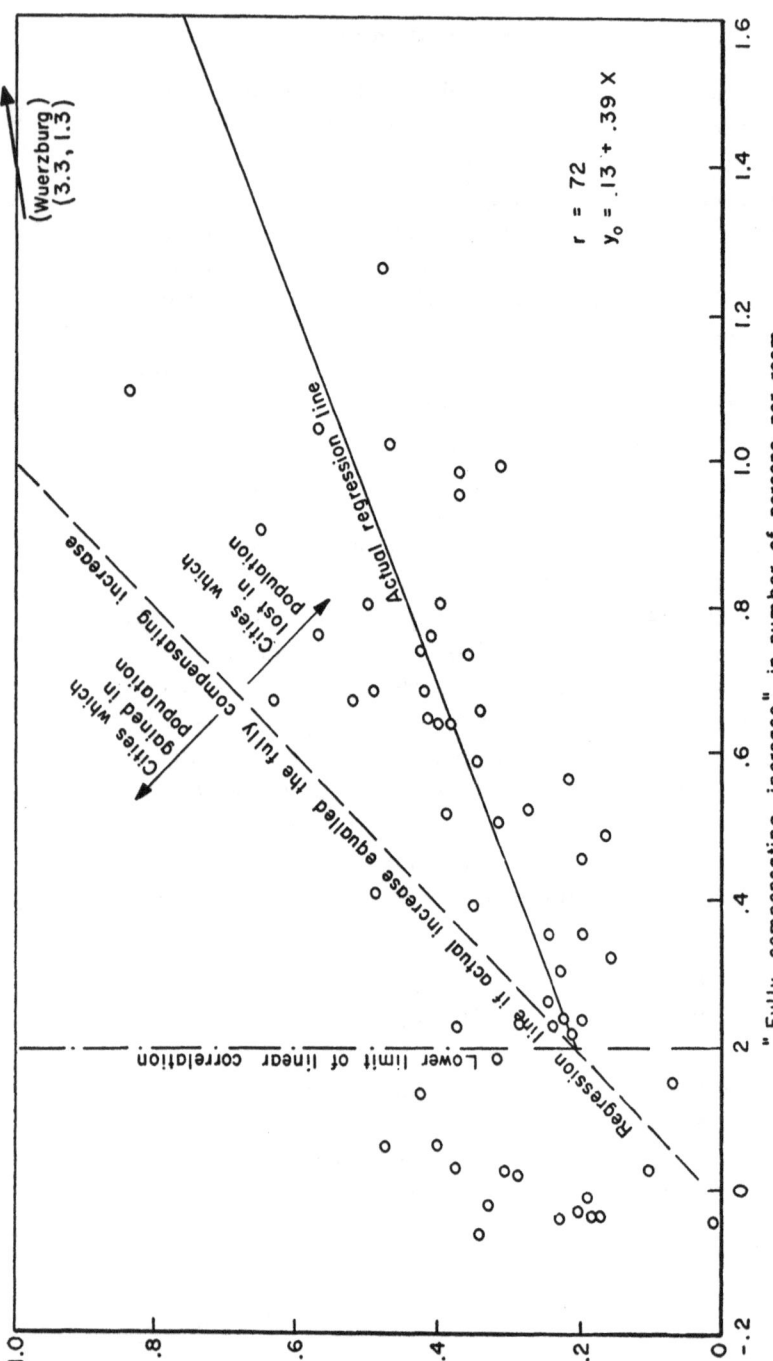

Fig. 6. — The relation between "fully compensating increase" and actual

The Process of Reaccommodation within a City

Thus, a city's potential housing density after destruction becomes

$$\frac{P_1 - F}{H_2} ; \qquad (1)$$

that is, pre-destruction population minus fatalities, divided by the number of dwellings that remain undestroyed after attack. Since the pre-destruction housing density is $\frac{P_1}{H_1}$, the fully compensating increase in housing density becomes

$$\frac{P_1 - F}{H_2} - \frac{P_1}{H_1}, \qquad (2)$$

whereas the actual increase in housing density is

$$\frac{P_2}{H_2} - \frac{P_1}{H_1}. \qquad (3)$$

With these formulas, it is now possible to clarify the relationship between the actual post-destruction population (P_2) and the housing remaining after attack (H_2). Given the necessary data, the fully compensating increase (2) can be calculated and plotted against the actual increase in housing density (3) for any group of war-damaged cities. This was done in Fig. 6 for sixty-four cities in Western Germany.[12] In this case, it can be readily seen that the relationship is not linear for the whole range of the independent variable, or the fully compensating increase. As the latter becomes very low or negative, the regression line curves.

To the left in Fig. 6 fall the cities which suffered very little or

[12] All but four of these cities are the same as in Fig. 3, and the same sources were used for population and housing data, along with municipal statistics for the added cities. Fatality figures could sometimes be found in the *USSBS*, but for the majority of cities they had to be estimated. This was done by assuming that fatalities amounted to 5 per cent of the number of bombed-out people.

The Social Impact of BOMB DESTRUCTION

no destruction and hence accommodated an influx of homeless evacuees from more heavily bombed cities, much as undestroyed districts within a city absorbed bombed-out survivors from destroyed districts (cf. Fig. 5). The broken line shows the trend that would apply if the actual increase in housing density equaled the fully compensating increase. In cities which fall on this trend line, housing destruction was fully compensated for by the increase in housing density, hence no population loss occurred except as fatalities. Most cities on the left side of the chart (those with little or no destruction) fall above this broken line, so that the actual density increase overcompensated for the loss of dwellings, permitting immigrants from other cities to be accommodated.

The roughly linear trend in the scatter of cities on the right side of Fig. 6 suggests a linear regression equation to describe the relationship between actual increase and a certain minimum level of the fully compensating increase in housing density.[13] This equation can then be used to calculate the actual density increase for each city on the basis of the figures of pre-destruction population (P_1), pre- and post-attack housing (H_1 and H_2), and number of fatalities (F). This calculated density increase plus the known pre-destruction density (P_1/H_1) yields the calculated post-destruction housing density; the calculated post-destruction population equals the product of this calculated density times the number of post-destruction housing units (H_2). Computation of calculated percentage of population loss then becomes a matter of simple arithmetic.

The post-destruction population thus calculated can now be

[13] This lower limit of the linear range has been estimated by inspection, at a fully compensating increase of 0.20. Forty-six cities fall within the linear regression, whose equation becomes:

$$\frac{P_2}{H_2} - \frac{P_1}{H_1} = 0.130 + 0.392 \left(\frac{P_1 - F}{H_2} - \frac{P_1}{H_1} \right)$$

with a Pearsonian correlation coefficient $r = .718$. The upper limit of the linear range will be discussed later; all cities in this group, except perhaps Würzburg, appear to fall below it.

TABLE 2

COMPARISON OF ACTUAL AND CALCULATED POSTWAR POPULATION FOR 20 WESTERN GERMAN CITIES

Cities	Prewar Population (1939 Census)	Actual Postwar Population (1946 Census)	Calculated Postwar Population	Percentage Difference Between Calculated and Actual Postwar Population*
Above 100,000				
Aachen	162,164	110,462	120,809	+ 9.4
Augsburg	185,374	160,055	169,750	+ 6.1
Bielefeld	129,466	132,276	125,664	− 5.0
Bochum	305,485	246,477	235,490	− 4.5
Bremen	450,084	385,266	344,799	−10.5
Bremerhaven	112,831	99,208	95,039	− 4.2
Düsseldorf	541,410	420,909	426,551	+ 1.3
Duisburg	434,646	356,408	358,804	+ 0.7
Essen	666,743	524,728	542,229	+ 3.3
Frankfurt a. M.	553,464	424,065	468,718	+10.5
Below 100,000				
Bottrop	83,385	80,724	81,249	+ 0.7
Giessen	46,560	39,709	36,696	− 7.6
Hamm	59,035	49,751	50,113	+ 0.7
Herne	94,649	97,389	85,285	−12.4
Hildesheim	72,101	58,973	57,975	− 1.7
Lünen	46,310	51,989	44,620	−14.2
Offenbach	87,063	75,479	83,564	+10.7
Pforzheim	79,011	46,752	52,030	+11.3
Recklinghausen	86,313	89,787	84,167	− 6.3
Schweinfurt	49,321	37,331	36,634	− 1.9

*Calculated minus actual postwar population in per cent of the latter.

compared with the actual post-destruction population from the census. The differences between calculated and actual values indicate the accuracy of this method in establishing the relationship between population loss and housing destruction for these German cities.[14] The last column of Table 2 lists these differences for twenty cities (selected at random within each of two size groups from the forty-six cities which fell within the linear range).

A basic process of reaccommodation within a city can now be generalized. In principle, the number of homeless survivors leads to an increase in housing density, and the larger this number, the greater the increase (up to a certain maximum to be discussed later.) Thus, the concept of "elasticity" seems fully justified, for the resources yield increasingly to growing pressure. However, since actual increase in housing density is lower than the fully compensating increase in most cases, elasticity does not completely absorb the loss from destruction, much as an elastic body does not fully absorb a mechanical impact. In other words, only a certain percentage of the homeless survivors find accommodations within the city, and this percentage declines gradually as the number of homeless survivors becomes larger in relation to the undestroyed housing resources.[15] Although housing density apparently increases as the number of homeless persons becomes larger, it does so at a slower rate.

This framework and, particularly, the concept of the fully compensating increase in housing density permit us to extend the World War II experience to situations in which the number of casualties would be greater and the level of destruction higher. But

---

[14] The standard error of estimate of the percentage of population loss in this group of forty-six cities proves to be 7.02.

[15] According to the linear regression equation of the forty-six German cities, all of the homeless survivors find reaccommodation if the fully compensating increase amounts to only 0.21 persons per room; if it amounts to 1 person per room, 52.2 per cent find reaccommodation; and for a fully compensating increase of 2 persons per room, the percentage reaccommodated is only 45.7.

Evacuation: German vs. Japanese Cities

the problem of estimating the effect of nuclear or conventional bombing of housing upon the size of a city's population cannot be solved with this basic framework alone. Additional factors which play an important role in the reaccommodation process must also be considered.

Additional Factors in the Reaccommodation Process
Evacuation as the Alternative: German vs. Japanese Cities

For homeless survivors, the alternative to reaccommodation within the city is evacuation to villages, towns, or other cities. Figure 7 illustrates these two alternatives schematically. The greater the percentage of people who evacuate, the lower the degree of reaccommodation.[16]

Loss of homes is not the only reason that city dwellers evacuate after attack. But at this point it is important to note that evacuation of survivors reduces the actual increase in post-destruction housing density regardless of whether these survivors had living quarters or not. Hence, a given percentage of housing loss and a given number of fatalities can lead to different percentages of population loss, depending on the extent of evacuation among the survivors.

Instances where the actual post-destruction increase in housing density was much smaller than in the German cities are found in World War II data from Japan. Of the twenty-four Japanese cities shown in Fig. 4, it was found that six did not produce a positive fully compensating increase in housing density. Therefore, like the German cities with little or no such increase, they fall below

---

[16] In reality, not only homeless people evacuate after attack but also some of those who are still housed. The latter thereby make room for homeless persons who stay in the city (as do those who evacuate before attack). The total numerical effect is the same whether a certain number of homeless people fail to find reaccommodations and hence evacuate or whether an equal number of persons with housing evacuate; however, there are qualitative differences between persons evacuating because of homelessness and other evacuees (see Chapter IV).

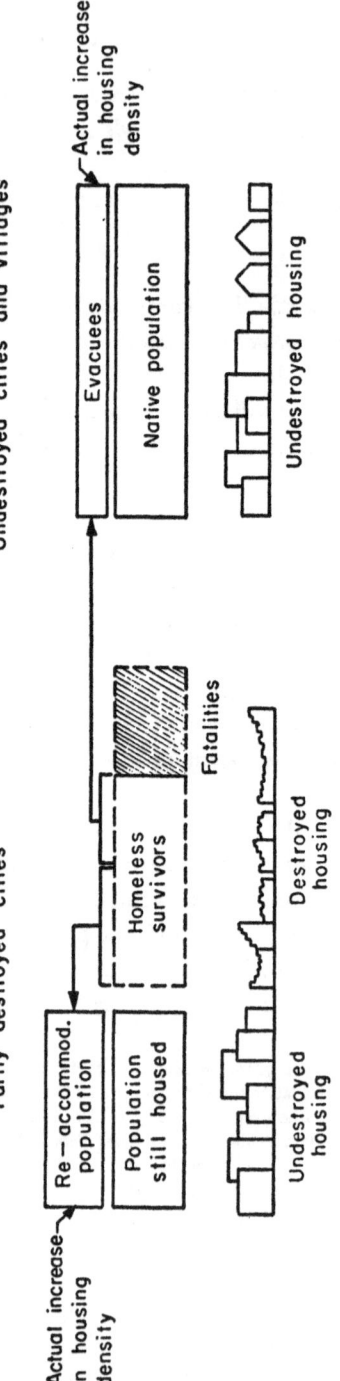

Fig. 7. — Re-accommodation within cities versus evacuation.

the range of linear regression. Among the remaining eighteen cities, however, Osaka deviates so markedly that no satisfactory regression line can be established between actual increase and fully compensating increase in housing density. By omitting Osaka, the trend becomes more pronounced, and the regression line then shows that the percentage of reaccommodated homeless survivors is only about half as large as that for the German cities.[17]

The housing densities of war-damaged cities showed considerably greater increases in Germany than in Japan. Thus, the German cities successfully survived partial housing destruction without losing any of their population. It has already been pointed out, for example, that among the German cities plotted in Fig. 3, little or no population loss occurred as long as housing destruction was below the 25 per cent level. Among the Japanese cities (Fig. 4), on the other hand, the population began to decline in size as soon as housing destruction exceeded 10 per cent.

There is no ready explanation for the greater degree of evacuation in Japanese cities, or for the accordingly smaller degree of reaccommodation than in German cities. Several general reasons, however, can be plausibly advanced. Urbanization is a more recent phenomenon in Japan than in Germany.[18] Accordingly, the urban

[17] Comparing here, of course, cities with the same degree of destruction and fatalities (i.e., the same fully compensating increase). For the eighteen cities, including Osaka, the Pearsonian correlation coefficient is $r = 0.05$. Without Osaka it becomes $r = 0.30$, and the regression equation for these seventeen cities is:

$$\frac{P_2}{H_2} - \frac{P_1}{H_1} = .022 + .225 \left(\frac{P_1 - F}{H_2} - \frac{P_1}{H_1} \right)$$

where H_1 and H_2 represent the pre- and post-destruction number of dwellings. With this equation, the actual increase in housing density can be calculated and used to compute the percentage population loss (as was done for the German cities above). The standard error of estimate of this calculated percentage population loss becomes 6.70 (slightly lower than the 7.02 of the forty-six German cities). Incidentally, if Osaka is included in the regression equation and subsequent computations, the standard error of estimate of percentage population loss increases only to 7.02.

[18] The recent rural-urban migration in Japan and the rural ties of the city dwellers are discussed by Irene B. Taeuber, "Family, Migration, and Industrialization in Japan," *American Sociological Review*, Vol. XVI, No. 2 (April, 1951), 149–57.

way of life may be less of a social and economic necessity for many Japanese city dwellers than for their German counterparts. Many may still retain close ties with the countryside through relatives and ownership of rural property. If so, when bombed out of their urban dwellings, they would be more inclined than the German urbanites to move into the country. Once there and readjusted to familiar rural life, they would then be less anxious to return to the bomb-scarred city.

A further reason for a smaller degree of reaccommodation—and consequently more evacuation—may be the somewhat higher pre-destruction housing density which prevailed in Japanese cities. Therefore, if it is assumed that a high initial density limits the housing elasticity of a city,[19] the Japanese cities had a smaller capacity for additional crowding. Furthermore, Japanese housing does not lend itself as readily as German housing to subdividing and doubling up.[20]

Finally, two additional reasons can be given for the different degrees of reaccommodation in Japan and Western Germany which are not pertinent to the social effects of bombing as such, but rather reflect imperfections in data. First, Western Germany experienced a considerable postwar influx of refugees from the eastern part of the country, who swelled the potential number of city dwellers. In Japan, on the other hand, the refugee movement from former territories of Nippon's Co-Prosperity Sphere was not as large.[21]

[19] An assumption partially validated by the data on variations in housing density among several districts in Hamburg (see Fig. 5).

[20] "There is no privacy in a Japanese house. There are several rooms but they are like a large Western-style room subdivided or partitioned by curtains. Therefore, unless it is a large house or a Western-style house, no one likes to live together with other families under the same roof." Goroh Itoh, *Postwar Housing Situation and Policy of Japan* (Tokyo, Ministry of Construction, 1950), 6.

[21] West Germany's population increased by 13.4 per cent from 1939 to 1946, mainly because of immigration from the east. In contrast, Japan's population increase (due to repatriations and excess of births over deaths) between 1940 and 1948 amounted to 8.7 per cent.

Billeting and the Post-Attack Period

Second, much of the difference may be simply an artifact of the varying definitions used for the indices of housing density. For Germany, it was possible to use the number of rooms before and after destruction as the measure of housing. The resulting index of density was therefore based on a relatively invariant type of housing unit. But Japanese data on rooms were not available. Instead, the index of housing density had to be based on the number of "dwelling units," as defined by the Japanese census. This definition obscured the effect of subdividing, tending to underrepresent increases in density. To be specific, the Japanese housing census of 1948 defines a structure "arranged to accommodate two or more households ... as two or more dwelling units" and instructs that it be tabulated accordingly.[22] Thus, a structure occupied by one household and counted as one dwelling unit before destruction would be counted as two dwelling units after destruction if it had then been subdivided to accommodate two households. Actually, the density of the structure as such would have doubled. In short, it is likely that increases in the housing-structure densities of Japanese cities were greater than the data indicate, and consequently that the real situations in Japan and Germany were more nearly alike than would at first appear.

The difference between the German and the Japanese findings reveals the complex interplay of factors involved in the final population effect of a given amount of housing destruction. To estimate properly the social effects of housing destruction, however, additional factors must be considered.

Billeting and the Post-Attack Period

As long as destruction is relatively limited, the reaccommodation of bombed-out persons can proceed in an informal fashion through private arrangements with friends or relatives. Govern-

[22] *Report on Housing Census of 1948* (Tokyo, Prime Minister's Office, Statistics Bureau, 1950), 8.

ment assistance, if necessary at all, can be confined to providing mass shelters and financial aid. In Great Britain, swift accommodation after attack was facilitated by advance private arrangements with friends. According to a World War II report from the city of Hull, "Citizens have been continually reminded that they should make mutual arrangements with friends for accommodation in the event of their house being damaged or destroyed by enemy action. This propaganda has yielded a rich harvest, for up to the present time, although thousands of families have been billeted, on no occasion has compulsory billeting been necessary."[23]

Thus, in a disaster with only minor housing destruction, reaccommodation with friends generally prevails. That this is so is also confirmed by reports from smaller air raids in Germany as well as from recent natural disasters in the United States.

However, if a sudden attack should bring widespread destruction to a city, the government will have to provide housing for the homeless by means of compulsory billeting in undestroyed private dwellings. Germany had two different laws to accomplish this end. The less stringent one gave the hosts or involuntary landlords some time to select the homeless they would prefer to accommodate and offered them the choice of letting or removing their furniture. The other law (*Reichsleistungsgesetz*), for a more immediate emergency, authorized billeting officers to place the homeless directly into available dwellings or rooms and provided that the hosts must leave the necessary furniture in the billets. After the big raids in Hamburg, only the second, more stringent law was found to be sufficient.[24] To expedite billeting in case of emergency, the local administrations of Hamburg's districts prepared card files in advance which indicated the capacities of each dwelling.[25]

Essentially, compulsory billeting of the homeless amounts to

[23] Great Britain, Ministry of Health, "Air Raid Welfare in Hull" (mimeographed) (December 1, 1941), 11.
[24] Krogmann, *loc. cit.*
[25] *Ibid.*

Billeting and the Post-Attack Period

a forced subletting. Gradually, the billeting arrangements can be improved for both the hosts and the homeless through structural changes which facilitate the subdivision of dwellings and give greater privacy, such as the partitioning of rooms, addition of kitchenettes, remodeling of attics, and the like. So far as these changes require skilled labor or construction materials, they are severely limited by the shortages prevailing after bombing attacks. The most satisfactory answer to the housing shortage is the repair of partly destroyed dwellings. These repairs are, however, a drain on man power and materials. Vacant buildings provide relatively few accommodations since they ordinarily account for only a small percentage of a city's housing resources.

As more time elapses without further attack, billets tend to improve and become more plentiful because of repairs and subdivision of dwellings and because of administrative allocation of every underoccupied structure and every vacant room. Consequently, the degree of reaccommodation will increase, or, in other words, the increase in housing density will gradually become greater. But progressive increase in housing density does not arise solely from these improvements in billeting. In addition, evacuation becomes less desirable after the raids stop and life in bombed cities becomes more normal. Furthermore, the longer evacuees remain in reception areas, the more anxious they become to return to their city.

For this reason, the data from German and Japanese cities analyzed above represent the minimum population loss on account of housing destruction under given social conditions, inasmuch as the post-destruction figures on population and housing date from after the war (1946 and 1948, respectively). The above statistical analysis was deliberately designed to estimate the percentage of urban population loss associated primarily with a progressive decrease in housing facilities, although other factors which influence the population of bombed cities, such as fear of future

The Social Impact of *BOMB DESTRUCTION*

attacks, disrupted utilities, and lack of food, were not considered. In this way, the postwar data could serve better than wartime figures on post-destruction population and housing.

For Hamburg, statistics are available which illustrate how housing density increases progressively following destruction, both during the war and after. Hamburg's housing density in early July, 1943, was 0.73 persons per room. This was just before the big air raids at the end of that month. Two months later the density had risen to 0.97 persons per room. From then on, despite some small further attacks which served to emphasize the danger of bombing but scarcely raised the number of homeless, housing density increased gradually to 1.03 in February, 1944, and to 1.26 in October, 1946. Thus, during the first two post-raid months, enough homeless survivors remained to boost the city's density from 0.73 to 0.97. But at the same time, many persons deserted the city for reasons other than, or in addition to, the loss of their homes and the difficulties of reaccommodation. Then, as time passed without additional bombing, the population gravitated back, continuously pushing up the city's housing density.

Emergency Housing and Camps

So far it has been tacitly assumed that all the inhabitants who remain in a city after bombing destruction are housed in dwellings which existed before the attack. These dwellings might either be undestroyed, only slightly damaged, or repaired. So far the possibilities that new housing structures would be erected or that people would remain in a city without housing have been neglected.

The acute man-power shortage and the scarcity of all raw materials which prevail in a country after bombing attacks, particularly after nuclear bombing, preclude the possibility of any significant new housing construction until some time after the war is over. All available building materials and construction workers will be marshaled for repairs or the construction of defense in-

Emergency Housing and Camps

stallations, such as airports, factories, and docks. Whatever can be spared for civilian housing needs will not be used for new construction but for the repair of slightly damaged dwellings which would provide the greatest amount of living space for the labor and materials employed.

The case of Hamburg, which lost almost half of its housing within a few days in 1943, can again serve as an illustration. At first, after the raids, the administration and the public expected that a program for the construction of emergency homes would provide shelter for the homeless. People were even urged to assist the building workers by laboring on their prospective homes on Sundays. Regulations were issued prescribing the number of hours defense plant workers could be absent for this purpose and where they could obtain building tools. However, five months later no more than 1,625 emergency homes (each for one family) had been erected, accommodating less than 2 per cent of Hamburg's homeless.[26] The other 98 per cent were required to find accommodations in existing dwellings if they wanted to remain in the city. It must be remembered that Hamburg's recuperation was the most remarkable of all the heavily bombed cities in World War II and that the resources of the whole German *Reich* could still be rallied at that time to aid in the recovery. How much less can then be expected from emergency construction after nuclear attacks upon several cities of a nation!

While construction of new dwellings can be expected to accommodate only an insignificant percentage of the homeless, the possibility of camps or bivouacs is of somewhat greater significance. Where the climate is temperate, or during the summer, a substantial number of people could conceivably live in a city with no housing at all. There are cities where many inhabitants bivouac even in peacetime, as in India.

[26] Data from the records of Hamburg's Chamber of Commerce (Industrie- und Handelskammer, May 16, 1944).

The Social Impact of BOMB DESTRUCTION

In the relatively intemperate climates of Germany and Japan, however, the proportion of a city's population living in camps, makeshift shacks, or bivouacs was not very large during World War II. Table 3, for example, shows that two and one-half months after the big raids only 7.8 per cent of Hamburg's population were living in structures which were not regular dwelling units. Immediately after the raids, in the summer months, this percentage was probably larger: 12 per cent is the estimate given by local authorities. In April, 1946, only 3.6 per cent of Berlin's population were

TABLE 3

DISTRIBUTION OF HAMBURG'S POPULATION
BY TYPE OF ACCOMMODATION TWO AND A HALF MONTHS
AFTER THE HEAVY AIR RAIDS

	Percentage	
Ordinary dwellings	90.2	
Institutions and hotels	2.0	
Rooms converted into dormitories	0.6	
Camps and barracks	2.9	
Cottages or shacks in allotment gardens		7.8
("victory gardens")	3.8	
Bunkers, offices, stables, etc.	0.5	
	100.0	

Source: *Aus Hamburgs Verwaltung und Wirtschaft*, Sondernummer 7 (June, 1944), 6. These data are from a housing census taken on October 10, 1943.

living in cottages or emergency shacks.[27] And in most war-damaged cities of Japan, when the 1948 housing census was taken, less than 4 per cent were living in makeshift shelters, such as sheds constructed of metal sheets or scrap lumber, huts built within burned buildings, office buildings, or barns. The comparable figures

[27] "Wohnungen und Wohnräume in den Gross-Berliner Verwaltungsbezirken am 13. April, 1946." *Berliner Statistik*, Vol. I (1947), 52.

The Limits of Housing Elasticity

were 4.2 per cent in Hiroshima, 4.7 per cent in Kobe, and 5.9 per cent in Yokohama.

For the purpose of keeping the workers in a city, factory dormitories are probably more effective than individual shacks and barracks. In Kobe's steel company, 17 per cent of the adult shop force was made homeless during the raids of March, 1945, but about one-third of these bombed-out workers were reaccommodated in factory dormitories.[28]

Accommodations in barracks or dormitories near the plants make it possible to keep the working force together, but usually imply that the workers are subject to strong governmental or military controls. Part of Germany's forced foreign workers and prisoners of war were housed in this manner, so that they could make a substantial contribution to the labor force in bombed cities.

The Limits of Housing Elasticity

In the preceding statistical analysis of the relationship between housing destruction and population loss, little attention has been given to the absolute level of housing density. Instead, the increase in density has been related to the physical destruction of a city. Thus, it has been found that an increase in housing density permits a certain percentage of the homeless survivors to be reaccommodated and that the percentage of reaccommodation tends to become smaller as the number of homeless survivors rises (relative to existing housing resources). However, housing density cannot increase indefinitely, and a point will be reached where no more reaccommodation can take place despite a further increase in the number of homeless. At this point the elasticity of a city's housing resources will be exhausted.

The elasticity of resources can easily be determined if it is limited by physical factors alone. For example, urban transit facilities have a certain maximum capacity; thus, a bus or a subway

[28] *USSBS*, Pacific report No. 58, p. 213.

The Social Impact of *BOMB DESTRUCTION*

car can be filled to the last standing room and no more. In the case of housing, however, this limit is determined by an exceedingly complex combination of influences, including the possibilities of evacuation, strength of government controls, standards of living, climate, and season. The limit of housing elasticity can never be considered alone, but only in the context of the alternatives which are open to homeless survivors. Housing elasticity is largely limited to the accessibility and desirability of the accommodations in areas to which homeless survivors can evacuate.

It is probably more realistic to visualize the limit in housing elasticity as asymptotic; it approaches a fixed limit but never actually reaches it. As the housing density approaches this theoretical limit with increasing destruction in a city, the percentage of reaccommodated survivors will rapidly become smaller, and the trend line will curve, as it is no longer proportional. In other words, the actual increase in housing density will become very small for each additional increment in the fully compensating increase.

In Fig. 6, Würzburg is the city with the highest fully compensating increase in housing density, and consequently with the highest actual increase. However, its actual increase falls somewhat short of what it should be according to the relationship between these two increases which applies, on the average, for the other forty-five cities.[29] Hence, this city is perhaps a case where housing density became so high that the asymptotic limit of elasticity caused the increase in density to be smaller than what it would have been if the absolute level of density had been lower.

The case of Würzburg, however, cannot be generalized. The

[29] Würzburg's fully compensating increase is 3.31 persons per room, and its calculated actual increase (on the basis of the linear regression equation) becomes 1.43, whereas its observed actual increase amounts to only 1.34 persons per room. Würzburg's pre-destruction density is 0.96 persons per room, and the post-destruction density in 1946 is 2.30, the highest of all German cities for which data were available.

Disparity of Population Loss and Increasing Destruction

numerical value for the limit of housing elasticity is likely to be different in a new situation because of the great many factors which determine it. For instance, in countries of a different culture there are cities which normally have a much higher housing density than has ever been observed in a European city after destruction.[30] Or, to give another example, at the time South Korean civilians followed the United Nations forces in their temporary southward retreat to Pusan, housing resources were so limited and alternative accommodation areas so inaccessible that densities of fifteen to twenty people per room could be observed.[31] Finally, it must be remembered that a city's housing density is always an average. There are usually a great many dwelling units far above this average density, eliminating the possibility of a generally applicable, rigid upper limit.

Disproportionality of Population Loss from Increasing Destruction

The principle of disproportionality is based on the fact that there is a limit to the elasticity of resources. Applied to housing, it means that after destruction exceeds a certain percentage of the city's total number of dwelling units, a further loss in housing will result in a disproportionately greater population loss.

A hypothetical example will demonstrate how this principle works. Three assumptions will be made for the computations:

(1) For the basic regression equation between actual increase

---

[30] In Bombay, the average number of persons per room in 1931 was 3.50 and in Karachi 3.02 (Kingsley Davis, *The Population of India and Pakistan* [Princeton, Princeton University Press, 1951], 147). Similarly, in the Soviet Union housing density is much higher than in Western countries. It has been reported that the typical pattern in Moscow is one family per room, and that the per capita housing space was only about thirty-eight square feet in 1950 and forty-five square feet in 1955 (*New York Times*, October 24, 1950, and November 28, 1955).

[31] J. Donald Kingsley, United Nations agent general for Korean reconstruction, in the *New York Times*, March 1, 1951.

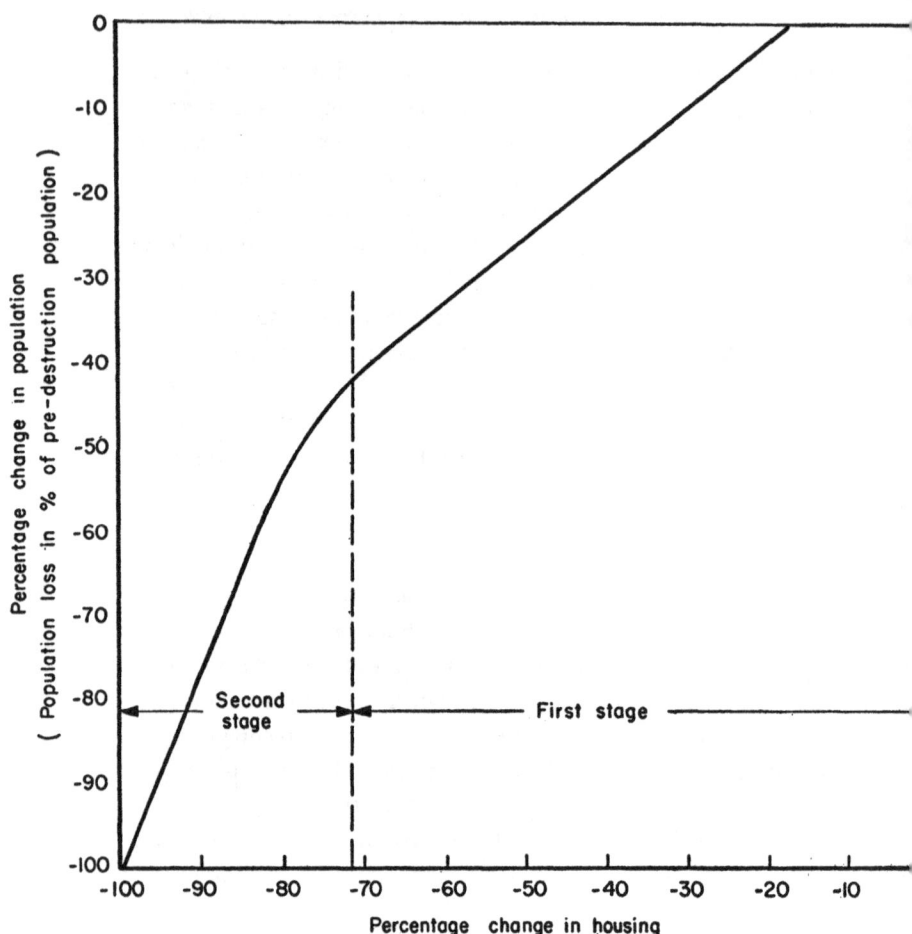

Fig. 8. —— The disproportionately larger population loss of a city resulting from increasing housing destruction.

Disparity of Population Loss and Increasing Destruction

and fully compensating increase in housing density, it is assumed that the parameters of the above equation for the forty-six German cities apply.

(2) This linear relationship is not applicable with total destruction, because it presumes a continuously increasing housing density to absorb those who become homeless. For the purpose of this illustration, therefore, it is assumed that the actual increase in density associated with the fully compensating increase will begin to taper off after housing density has doubled and will reach zero at complete destruction, as it obviously must.

(3) In order that percentage destruction may be the only independent variable, it is assumed that the number of fatalities amounts always to 15 per cent of the number of bombed-out persons.[32]

With these assumptions we can now estimate for any given degree of destruction the population loss of a city which occurs because of destruction of housing and fatalities. Figure 8 gives the results of these estimates. The curve shows how the percentage of population loss changes with increasing destruction, illustrating that population loss grows disproportionately after destruction has reached a certain level. In the first stage, population loss increases more slowly than housing destruction; in the second, it increases faster. Whether the first or the second stage will result from a certain explosion does not depend on the absolute size of the destruction, but on the percentage of destruction relative to the whole city (or metropolitan area) within which reaccommodation can take place. Therefore, the larger the city, the greater must be

---

[32] This percentage is assumed to be at least three times higher than that which prevailed in World War II because nuclear bombing tends to produce a higher number of casualties than conventional bombing with the same amount of housing destruction. Actually, as has been shown in Chapter II, the number of fatalities per bombed-out persons increases somewhat as destruction becomes more nearly total, hence this constant percentage is merely an approximation.

the destruction in order to produce the second stage. Thus the prevailing notion that the largest cities are the most vulnerable ones needs to be qualified.[33]

In summary, we can now delineate clearly the process by which destruction of housing affects the population of a city. To begin with, because housing resources are elastic, the bombed-out survivors who elect to stay in the city can find reaccommodation in the remaining dwellings. In addition, some survivors may be billeted in camps, emergency shacks, or even bivouacs. Newly constructed houses, however, no matter how hastily prepared, can contribute only a negligible number of accommodations in time of war. For this reason, the actual percentage of survivors who stay in the city depends greatly on the proportion of housing that remains habitable after bombing. Conversely, the percentage is also affected by the alternative opportunities for housing outside the city. The pull which these outside accommodations exert on the homeless survivors depends on many factors, such as the threat of future bombing, governmental controls, and the availability of food and employment. Finally, the absolute level of housing density in the city becomes an important factor if it is very high in relation to the customary level or in relation to the physical capacity (floor space) of the dwellings. Theoretically, there is, of course, a maximum housing density determined by this physical capacity, but the practical limit of housing elasticity becomes effective before the physical limit is reached. It has an asymptotic effect, leading to a rapidly decreasing and eventually vanishing degree of reaccommodation in existing dwellings, as crowding becomes greater.

While the dynamic relationship between housing destruction and population loss can thus be analyzed in principle, it is impossible to determine it quantitatively without further knowledge of

---

[33] Larger cities have a greater potential to cushion a given amount of destruction of all types of resources. For example, London had a greater capacity to absorb bomb damage than smaller English cities (Titmuss, *op. cit.*, 305–306).

Casualties laid out in a park for identification after a Tokyo fire raid of March, 1945.

COURTESY USSBS, NATIONAL ARCHIVES

A couple prepares to leave their home after the explosion in Texas City, Texas, in April, 1947.

COURTESY AMERICAN RED CROSS

Disparity of Population Loss and Increasing Destruction

a concrete situation, because it depends on such an exceedingly intricate combination of many factors.

Reflecting on the bombing attacks of World War II, it can be noted that "area raids"—which caused housing destruction primarily—hit what was physically the most vulnerable but socially the least effective component of a city. Of all the urban consumer-resources relationships, housing is probably the most elastic one; hence partial destruction is here least disruptive. Thus strategic bombing in World War II did not become decisive until technical developments made it possible to hit less elastic resources, such as transportation facilities and factories (mainly in daylight raids).[34] Housing destruction can cause more decisive consequences to a

[34] Sir Arthur Harris makes it plain that the area attacks of his bomber command (the bomber force of the R.A.F.) were aimed at the densely built-up centers of German cities and not specifically at any one factory. "The objective of the campaign was to reduce production in the industries of the Ruhr at least as much by the indirect effect of damage to services, housing, and amenities, as by any direct damage to the factories or railways themselves." Referring to the technical obstacles to precision attacks, Harris explains: "At this stage of the war there was no alternative method or means of attacking German industry, but at the same time I had good reason to believe that the indirect effects of this general damage would be extremely important in the long run." (Sir Arthur Harris, *Bomber Offensive* [New York, The Macmillan Company, 1947], 147.)

Here we are explaining why the "indirect effects of this general damage" were much smaller than had been expected from the number of acres destroyed. In retrospect, the fact that the elasticity of resources can cushion partial destruction looks obvious. But at the beginning of World War II the social effects of bombing (or what Sir Arthur Harris calls the "indirect effects") were not well understood; and they were least understood by those who at the time professed special knowledge in this area and confidently predicted "morale effects," without a clear notion about either "morale" or the relation between physical destruction and social phenomena. Therefore, the errors in bombing strategy that were committed in World War II should perhaps be blamed not on the military commanders but rather on their scientific advisers who dealt with social problems. However, it must also be granted that another kind of indirect bombing effect was of great importance, even though the effects on population and man power did not materialize. This was the diversion of a great portion of the German and Japanese air force, military personnel, and war production to the defense of cities, thus substantially weakening other military efforts. (Cf. Harris, *op. cit.*, 193.)

The Social Impact of BOMB DESTRUCTION

nation's war effort only if it reaches higher percentages within a city (or metropolitan area) than it did in World War II. In case of more nearly total destruction, the elasticity of housing will be exhausted and the consequences will rapidly become more severe.

Chapter IV

EVACUATION AS A
PREVENTIVE AND ADAPTIVE PROCESS

EVACUATION HAS a decisive influence upon the population of a bombed city. It separates the surviving urbanites into two groups: those who stay in the city and those who move into safer areas. Thus the impact is felt not only in the city but also far into the hinterland. On the one hand, it breaks up and diminishes the community of city dwellers; on the other, it carries into the remoter areas a surge of urbanites, who for some period of time must live away from their homes. Casualties and loss of homes are the most important direct or primary social effects of bombing. Evacuation is a secondary effect of equal significance. It represents the predominant reaction of people to bombing, either as a precaution before attack, or as an escape from the disaster area with its shortages, its possible fall-out, and perhaps its risk of future attacks. Moreover, it is one of the principal civil defense measures in the era of nuclear warfare.

Evacuation is usually thought of as the temporary removal of people from areas of potential danger or areas where life has actually become too difficult or too hazardous. In contrast to industrial dispersal or migration, it is always intended to be temporary, although it may later lead to lasting changes in the distribution of population. Industrial dispersal—sometimes suggested as

The Social Impact of BOMB DESTRUCTION

an alternative to evacuation—attempts a permanent relocation of plants and offices, with the workers and their families, from the large urban areas to smaller cities or new industrial sites. Because it requires construction of new factories or the transplanting of old ones, industrial dispersal can be accomplished rapidly only on a small scale.

Thus the term "evacuation" is easily distinguishable from "industrial dispersal." However, apart from this distinction, it includes several different types of population movements. Failure to recognize this fact will result in confusion and contradictions, especially in connection with civil defense planning. In order to assure clarification and a systematic treatment, three types of evacuation will be discussed:

(1) *Pre-attack short-range evacuation of the whole population* from a prospective target city (leaving only a core of maintenance personnel behind). This type is sometimes called "tactical evacuation." Its purpose is to reduce casualties by removing the city dwellers from the expected bombing target. This type of evacuation requires preliminary warning to allow sufficient time to put the plan in effect. With only a few hours' warning before an attack, people would have to leave the city quickly and efficiently. Until recently, most civil defense plans in the United States included only this measure.

(2) *Long-term evacuation of nonessential personnel,* such as children, unemployed women, and the aged, from potential or actual target cities. Its purpose is to reduce casualties and alleviate the emotional stress from threatened attack. In the case of a partially damaged city, it would reduce the number of inhabitants to be housed and fed ("remedial evacuation"). To function properly, this type of evacuation must last as long as enemy attacks are likely to occur, that is, for weeks, months, or possibly longer. This kind

Evacuation as a Preventive and Adaptive Process

of evacuation was used widely in World War II and is the predominant form in recent British civil defense plans.

(3) *Long-term evacuation of the whole population,* both nonessential people and workers, leaving only a core of maintenance personnel and other nonevacuable workers in the target city. This type might become a necessary civil defense measure to reduce casualties in case of nuclear bombing, but it would generally require advance (strategic) warning. It might also develop as a spontaneous reaction of a bombed population, regardless of planning; to some extent this happened in Japan toward the end of World War II. In such a case evacuated workers would be lost to the war effort or industrial rehabilitation unless they could be profitably re-employed in the reception areas.

Types (2) and (3) are sometimes called "strategic evacuation."

In actual fact, these kinds of evacuation seldom occur singly, but are usually found in various combinations and sequences. Moreover, evacuation is usually only partial; that is, only a fraction of all the persons who are theoretically included in a given category actually leave the target area.[1] Thus the typical pattern is a combination of two or all three types of evacuation, involving varying fractions of the total number of potential evacuees. The social consequences and defense implications, however, are distinctly different for each type, so that separate treatment is warranted. The effects and implications vary for the evacuated area (the target city) and the area into which evacuees move or resettle (the reception area).[2]

[1] The fact that only a portion of all persons included in a given evacuation scheme actually do evacuate is of great importance for civil defense planning. By way of illustration, the proportion of the total evacuable number of mothers and children who actually left English cities at the outbreak of World War II varied between 57 per cent in Newcastle, 44 per cent in Manchester, 37 per cent in London, 21 per cent in Birmingham, and 13 per cent in Sheffield. Titmuss, *op. cit.*

[2] The term "reception area" will be used here to mean the area (village, town, or city) in which the evacuees are reaccommodated or billeted. This term is used

The Social Impact of BOMB DESTRUCTION

Sometimes the term "evacuation" is used to mean only population removals which are organized by the government, and not the voluntary, individual exodus of civilians. But, as will be shown below, private evacuation and government-organized evacuation are supplementary. Civil defense plans must take the voluntary, private movement into account, because it dictates the number of people who may have to be removed later under government-organized schemes, and it also influences the number of available accommodations in the reception areas.

Dispersion of industries has been frequently advocated as the principal defense measure against nuclear attack.[3] The most important limitation is that it cannot be effected both quickly and on a large scale. Particularly after widespread destruction has occurred, the ensuing shortage of labor, building materials, and transportation facilities will thwart construction of new factories at scattered sites. The difficulties are analogous to those of emergency housing construction after attack. However, if workers are evacuated, some makeshift removals of undestroyed machinery into provisional structures farther from target areas will probably occur. This hardly qualifies as industrial dispersal, nor is it advocated as a civil defense measure.

Hence, if industrial dispersal is to reduce the vulnerability of cities significantly, it must be a long-range undertaking before bombing occurs. Next to underground facilities it is perhaps the best passive defense measure against nuclear attack, but to be wholly effective, it probably would have to be combined with

---

with this meaning also in British literature. The term "evacuation area" is avoided because it can mean the area either from which or into which the evacuees move. "Support area," sometimes used synonymously for "reception area," might better be reserved for a region adjacent to a target city from which support (such as fire-fighting equipment, food, medical aid, etc.) may be sent to the bombed area.

[3] Cf. Project East River, "Reduction of Urban Vulnerability," Part V (New York, Associated Universities, Incorporated, 1952); and *Bulletin of the Atomic Scientists*, Vol. VII, No. 9 (September, 1951). (This is a special issue on dispersal, with a useful bibliography.)

Evacuation as a Preventive and Adaptive Process

shelters, especially in view of the fall-out hazard.[4] Industrial dispersal is cheap as long as it entails simply the building of new factories away from large target cities, leaving existing plants where they are. Through the decades, such a policy might effect a valuable reduction in industrial vulnerability. However, large metropolitan population centers will remain or even grow larger in spite of this piecemeal dispersal movement.[5]

A radical breaking-up of large cities into smaller industrial communities, including the transfer of many existing firms and factories, would be very expensive in direct costs as well as in indirect losses in efficiency and economy. In the free world, it would lead to excessive political controls and curtail our individual liberties and economic freedom.[6] The economic and social forces which influence the growth and permanence of urban concentrations cannot, apparently, be offset by a potential danger, however serious it may be. Indeed, these forces operate even after houses and plants have been destroyed.[7] The integration of the firm

---

[4] The Swedish civil defense program demonstrates that extensive underground shelters and plants are economically and technically feasible. Cf. G. Alison Raymond, "Sweden Digs In," *United States Naval Institute Proceedings*, Vol. LXXX, No. 11 (November, 1954), 1223-25.

[5] In the United States, dispersed plant construction of military value has been encouraged in the past by means of tax incentives which permit more rapid amortization of plant investments.

[6] Even in the Soviet Union, where the political and economic obstacles to the breaking up of large cities could conceivably be ignored (the attendant costs and losses would, of course, accrue just the same), the large cities continue to grow larger. Thus, Moscow's population grew from 4,137,000 in 1939 to about 4,500,000 in 1946-48, and Leningrad's population grew from 3,196,000 in 1939 to about 4,000,000 in 1956. (Theodore Shabad, *Geography of the USSR* [New York, Columbia University Press, 1951], 506; and the *New York Times*, April 4, 1956, 7.) It has been reported, however, that many plants and industries of military value have been dispersed or placed underground. It is likely that significant piecemeal dispersal is taking place, enhanced by the makeshift World War II dispersals which had been carried out to escape the advancing German armies.

[7] Cf. Chapter IX below and Fred C. Iklé, "Reconstruction and Population Density in War-damaged Cities," *Journal of the American Institute of Planners*, Vol. XVI (Summer, 1950), 131-39. On the costs of dispersal, see also Amos H. Hawley, "Urban Dispersal and Defense," *Bulletin of the Atomic Scientists*, Vol.

The Social Impact of *BOMB DESTRUCTION*

and its labor supply, its fixed investment in plant and facilities, and the attachment of urbanites to their traditional homes present formidable obstacles to prewar dispersal.

Preattack Short-Term Evacuation of the Whole Population

This type of evacuation consists of the temporary removal of all the inhabitants from the urban areas which are considered to be likely targets. The removal will take place only upon warning that an enemy air raid is imminent and will last until the attack or threat of attack is over. The purpose of this quick, short-term evacuation is to remove people from the target area in order to reduce fatalities and injuries. Thinning out the population will lessen the probability of a large number of casualties, even though the bombs may not hit the city centers and may explode in suburban areas, along evacuation routes.

This type of evacuation is designed primarily for a surprise nuclear attack, but World War II experience provides some information on it. At that time, it was frequently called "nighttime evacuation" because in the first years of the war conventional bombing raids occurred almost exclusively at night and people who wanted to escape attacks without leaving their city jobs moved to the outskirts in the evening and returned to the city center in the morning. In England, this nightly exodus was referred to as "trekking." During the first heavy raids on London a great many people drove out of the city and slept in their automobiles. When the subways were later opened for shelter, trekking declined in London, but it continued in smaller cities such as Southampton, Plymouth, and Hull. Since the areas surrounding these smaller cities were not equipped to receive the nightly influx of evacuees, serious

---

VII, No. 10 (October, 1951), 307–12. The importance of comparing the possible gain from dispersal and its high cost with alternative defense measures is stressed by Gershon Cooper and Roland N. McKean in "Is Dispersal Good Defense?" *Fortune*, Vol. L, No. 5 (November, 1954), 126ff.

Preattack Short-Term Evacuation of the Whole Population

billeting problems arose. Rural rest centers were already crowded with permanent evacuees, and many trekkers had to find shelter "in barns, churches, quarry tunnels and every conceivable kind of building. Many, too, lay down in ditches, under hedges and in the open country."[8]

In Germany, this type of evacuation was less important, except at one time in Hamburg. There, a mass exodus occurred after the second large raid in the summer of 1943.[9] Then, when the third attack caused widespread damage, many casualties were averted by this evacuation.

There is one crucial difference between the short-term preattack evacuation of World War II and its counterpart envisaged for defense against nuclear attack. Trekking began only after air raids had occurred. To be effective in a nuclear attack, evacuation must take place before the first bomb has exploded. People would have to react toward a danger they have not yet perceived or experienced. Since strong motivation is lacking in this instance, this plan of evacuation is likely to be abandoned in face of obstacles or deprivations. The "trekkers" who moved out of English cities did so because they saw the havoc wrought by the night raids when they returned to work. Under the threat of nuclear bombing, city dwellers might rush out of the city once, twice, or even three times. But without visible evidence of nuclear destruction, the deprivations and troubles of evacuation would soon appear worse than the potential danger. Fewer and fewer persons would cooperate, and many would cease to evacuate at the warning.

This is one reason that more permanent evacuation will be necessary in the event of a war in which nuclear bombs may eventually be used. Another reason, even more cogent, follows after nuclear destruction has become a reality. Then the devastation

[8] Titmuss, *op. cit.*, 307–308.
[9] The *Reich's* defense commissioner appealed to all women and children to evacuate voluntarily because of the danger of further attacks. (Hamburg Police President, *op. cit.*)

will be so great that many temporary evacuees will be unable or unwilling to return to the demolished city, possibly through fear of another attack. Loss of housing alone, as shown in the preceding chapter, will force part of the city's population to find accommodations in other localities. Therefore, other types of evacuation will follow in case of nuclear bombing.

In America, short-term evacuation has been considered in most civil defense plans and public discussions. The sociological problems are of secondary importance, except for the difficulty of motivating people to participate without having perceived the danger. The crucial problems are more of a logistical nature. There must be: sufficient advance warning that will reach the whole population; organization of the enormous traffic for quick outward migration; a second type of warning for imminent danger of a sudden nuclear explosion, so that evacuees en route can take cover to avoid the direct blast and heat wave;[10] emergency shelters against fallout and weather, to be provided in the areas into which people move, and perhaps arrangements for mass feeding; and, after the danger is over, instructions and directions for the return of evacuees to the city, provided more permanent evacuation is not necessary. In the United States, the goal of temporarily thinning out the population has received so much attention that a more permanent, long-term evacuation has hardly been considered. This is probably because the quick, temporary removal of a whole city population (excluding maintenance personnel) would be the first move if an attack should come with only a few hours' warning. However, the war will not end miraculously after the people have been moved into the nearest fields, and further problems of evacuation will then arise.

[10] In the United States the final warning is a "Red Alert," while the earlier warning, in time for evacuation, is the "Yellow Alert." For a presentation of recent official views on evacuation, see Val Peterson, "Mass Evacuation," *Bulletin of the Atomic Scientists*, Vol. X, No. 7 (September, 1954), 294–95.

Long-Term Evacuation of Nonessential Personnel

Two situations call for long-term evacuation of nonessential persons: when bombing attacks are very likely to occur at an unspecified time and when bombing raids take place repeatedly without causing enough devastation to stop industrial production. The first case occurred in England one week before the beginning of World War II. A similar situation might well develop again if the tension between the world powers which possess nuclear weapons should become seriously aggravated.

The second situation obtained throughout World War II, except when greater disasters caused even workers to leave the stricken areas. These exceptions included Hamburg and Cologne, where everyone had to evacuate for a few days, and some Japanese cities toward the end of the war.

In both these situations calling for long-term evacuation, governments have favored evacuation of children, mothers, and other people not essential for urban production, in order to avoid unnecessary casualties and to reduce the number of persons who have to be housed, fed, and cared for in partially destroyed cities. The public tends to accept such plans at first, but the willingness soon wears off as the hardships of evacuation become apparent.

The extensive evidence from World War II on long-term evacuation of nonessential personnel is indeed instructive. The British experience has been carefully studied. In 1939, the British government organized and financed a substantial evacuation movement. Table 4 shows that over one-half of the official evacuees in September, 1939, were school children escorted to the reception areas by their teachers and other school personnel. Their removal was organized around the school structure, and classes were evacuated intact. Mothers with children of preschool age formed an additional third of the official evacuees. The data for January, 1940, in Table 4 reveals the rapid decline in the number of evacuees.

TABLE 4

CLASSIFICATION OF GOVERNMENT-SPONSORED EVACUEES IN
GREAT BRITAIN IN 1939 AND 1940

	September, 1939		January, 1940	
	Number	Percentage Distribution	Number	Percentage of 1939 Evacuees
1. Unaccompanied school children	826,959	56.1	457,600	55.0
2. Mothers and accompanied children	523,670	35.5	64,900	12.0
3. Expectant mothers	12,705	0.9	1,140	9.0
4. Blind persons, cripples, and other special classes	7,057	0.5	2,440	35.0
5. Teachers and helpers	103,000	7.0	46,500	45.0
Total:	1,473,391	100.0	572,580	39.0

Source: Titmuss, *op. cit.*, 103, 172. The original tables have been rearranged here, for greater clarity.

In addition to the official movement of almost 1,500,000 evacuees, there was an unofficial exodus. Under private arrangements of one sort or another, an estimated 2,000,000 persons moved into safer areas in England and Wales between the end of June and the first of September, 1939. So great was this movement into the western half of England that in many areas private evacuees greatly outnumbered those moved under government auspices. As a result, the number of billets available for government-sponsored evacuees was substantially reduced. A survey made as early as February, 1939, half a year before the war started, revealed that 1,100,000 billets—one-sixth of the potential accommodations in reception areas—had been reserved privately.

For Germany, direct data on the total number of evacuees are not available. From changes in the age composition of city populations, however, it is possible to infer that a great many children

Long-Term Evacuation of Nonessential Personnel

were evacuated. As can be seen from Table 5, the number of children under three years of age in Berlin declined by 61 per cent between December, 1942, and December, 1944, while persons aged three to eighteen decreased by 53 per cent, and adults by only 18 per cent. The pattern of evacuation in Cologne was similar, though more precipitate, during the winter of 1944–45, when the Allied troops were approaching the city. The extent of the evacuation of children is further reflected in Table 6, which shows that persons under eighteen years of age comprised 26 per cent of Cologne's population in 1942, but only 14 per cent in the winter of 1944–45.

TABLE 5

CHANGES OF THE POPULATION'S AGE COMPOSITION IN BERLIN
AND COLOGNE BECAUSE OF EVACUATION OF CHILDREN

(Number of persons in each age group expressed as a percentage of the number present in December, 1942.)

	All Ages	Under 3 Years	3 to 18 Years	Over 18 Years
Berlin				
December, 1942	100.0	100.0	100.0	100.0
August–September, 1943	86.0	65.0	73.0	90.0
January–February, 1944	76.0	50.0	54.0	82.0
May–June, 1944	66.0	29.0	37.0	75.0
August–September, 1944	65.0	31.0	39.0	73.0
December, 1944–January, 1945	66.0	39.0	47.0	72.0
Cologne				
December, 1942	100.0	100.0	100.0	100.0
July–August, 1943	76.0	50.0	63.0	79.0
March–April, 1944	78.0	52.0	69.0	80.0
July–August, 1944	71.0	42.0	57.0	75.0
November–December, 1944	41.0	13.0	22.0	44.0
December, 1944–January, 1945	29.0	6.0	12.0	31.0

Source: ration card statistics from *USSBS*, European reports No. 39, 41, and unpublished records.

The Social Impact of BOMB DESTRUCTION

TABLE 6

PERCENTAGE DISTRIBUTION OF COLOGNE'S POPULATION
BY AGE GROUPS BEFORE AND AFTER EVACUATION

	Under 3 Years	3 to 18 Years	Over 18 Years	All Ages
December, 1942	5.0	21.0	74.0	100.0
December, 1944	2.0	12.0	86.0	100.0

Source: ration card statistics from *USSBS*, European report No. 41, and unpublished records. The data exclude foreign workers and the population supplied by community kitchens.

In Tokyo, the proportion of children also declined during the war years because of evacuation. Before the war, children under fourteen years of age constituted 32 per cent of the total population, but in the summer of 1945, they comprised only 29 per cent of the total, even though part of the evacuees had already returned.[11] (By 1950, the percentage of children in Tokyo had again reached the prewar level.) The evacuation of school children in Tokyo was accelerated after the heavy attacks. Between August 4 and September 24, 1944, 203,400 pupils were removed in classes or other groups, primarily to the prefectures in the northwestern part of the island.[12]

The present evacuation plans in Great Britain are again focused on the pre-attack long-term removal of nonessential personnel. The following population groups constitute priority classes which are to be evacuated: school children over five years of age, handicapped children, children under five years of age and their mothers, and expectant mothers. The evacuation would be put into effect when there is imminent danger of war. Train schedules for this mass migration have already been prepared. The policy makers hope that the political situation prior to an attack would indicate in advance when the exodus should begin.

[11] *Tokyo-to-Tokei-sho* (statistical yearbook of Tokyo), *1950*, 20.
[12] *USSBS*, unpublished records to Pacific report No. 10.

Long-Term Evacuation of Nonessential Personnel

Long-term evacuation of nonessential persons can begin even while the danger of attack is still doubtful, because it does not disrupt the urban economy. For example, it has been estimated that all children could be transported from New York City in private automobiles and buses in from one to three days without disrupting normal traffic and commuting of workers.[13] (Less time would be required on week ends, because during the week commuter traffic absorbs a large share of the highway facilities.) This estimate ignores railroad facilities which could further reduce the evacuation time. However, evacuation by automobiles has the advantage that the children could be transported directly to their final destinations in distant reception areas.

An exodus from the cities is only the beginning of long-term evacuation, and the difficulties are by no means over after the nonessential persons have been transported to reception areas. In fact, the more permanent difficulties might provoke a premature return to the target cities and thus defeat the very purpose of evacuation. This happened in World War II in both England and Germany. Over 60 per cent of the British government-sponsored evacuees had returned to their cities four months after the war began. Table 4, above, indicates that unaccompanied school children were more apt to remain in the reception areas than any of the other groups of evacuees. While more than 50 per cent of these school children stayed, only 12 per cent of the mothers and their young children did so. Apparently, the separation of children of school age from their families was more tolerable than the separation of wives from their husbands. Another reason for the proportionately greater return of mothers with young children lies in the difficulties which evacuated housewives found in sharing kitchens with their hosts.

In Germany, too, an increasing number of children were

[13] Fred C. Iklé and Harry V. Kincaid, *Social Aspects of Wartime Evacuation of American Cities,* Committee on Disaster Studies, National Academy of Sciences, National Research Council *Publication No. 393* (Washington, 1956), 66.

brought home by their parents during periods that were free from attacks. The premature return of German evacuees was so prevalent that city authorities tried to take measures to prevent it. For example, the city government of Dortmund sought to stem the returning tide of evacuated children by refusing to provide schooling for them or by withholding their ration cards. Mothers who returned without their children were permitted to stay in the city only if they worked in war industries.[14] In Munich, parents who refused to evacuate their children without special permission had to sign a statement assuming full responsibility for the hazards to which the children might be exposed. In general, however, the German authorities hesitated to force parents to evacuate their children. Indirect measures, such as the closing of city schools, were not sufficient to overcome public opposition.

In Great Britain, the flow back to the cities was uneven. In some places and among certain groups the return was rapid; in others it was slow and selective. From reception areas close to the cities, the return movement was stronger, and more evacuees came back to the poorer areas of East London than to the more prosperous districts of West London. Shorter distances between home and billet, poverty, and a lower education level may all have contributed to the premature return of evacuees.[15]

This premature return of nonessential evacuees during World War II shows the great strength of the backward pull of the city. The attraction of better social services in the city combined with the hardships of less adequate provisions in the reception areas to impel return. There were also economic factors: the cost of keeping two homes, transportation fares for visiting, extra clothes, dissatisfaction with billeting allowances to foster parents, etc.[16]

[14] *USSBS,* unpublished records to European report No. 64.

[15] Titmuss, *op. cit.,* 177–80.

[16] Economic difficulties seem to have been particularly strong obstacles to private evacuation in the Soviet Union, where the people were fleeing from the

Shelter-life in London's Picadilly Station during World War II.

COURTESY UNITED PRESS PHOTOS

COURTESY WIDE WORLD PHOTOS

Residents of Canterbury, England, return from a night in the air-raid shelters in June, 1942.

Emergency housing after the World War II raids on Berlin.

COURTESY *USSBS*, NATIONAL ARCHIVES

Long-Term Evacuation of Nonessential Personnel

The usual troubles in the reception areas were accentuated by a general misunderstanding of different customs and habits and a hostility to "foreigners." In short, the general interference and inconvenience caused by billeting in private houses was not acceptable in the absence of air attack. "The principal enemy of evacuation was the solidarity of family life among the mass of the people."[17]

Apart from the cohesion of the family there are other social relationships which tie urbanites to their city. Many are attached to their familiar neighborhood. According to the World War II experience, this attachment is especially strong for elderly people in the economically poorer areas. Often such residents were found to be unwilling to evacuate to safer areas even after their homes had been destroyed.[18]

Dissatisfaction with evacuation also prevailed among the reception hosts. The billeting of mothers and small children meant added financial burdens and increased domestic responsibilities for them, as well as a violation of family privacy. As the war went on, it became increasingly harder to persuade householders to give up so much of their freedom and time to care for other people's children. The differences in economic, religious, educational, and rural-urban backgrounds between evacuated children and their hosts led to widespread friction. Evolving along with the cultural and class tensions were psychological difficulties such as homesickness, jealousies between foster and real parents, and divided loyalties on the part of the children. Irreconcilable conflicts arose

---

advancing German armies rather than from bombing attacks. See Herbert Dinerstein and Leon Gouré, *Moscow in Crisis*, 162.

[17] Titmuss, *op. cit.*, 180. The conflict between loyalty to the family and loyalty to the community in an emergency situation has been clearly brought out by Lewis M. Killian in his study of peacetime disasters in America: "The Significance of Multiple-Group Membership in Disaster," *The American Journal of Sociology*, Vol. LVII, No. 4 (January, 1952), 309–14.

[18] "The people of the East End objected to being transferred to distant parts of London with different social standards and habits of life." Titmuss, *op. cit.*, 259.

between the social and moral standards of the children's own families and those of their temporary hosts. But, as one British study explains, "far greater than the difficulties attendant on the billeting of unaccompanied school children were the irremediable problems of billeted mothers. Both the evacuee mother and the hostess inevitably resented the curtailment of privacy in daily living and were unavoidably critical of each other's standard of living, domestic skill and child management."[19] Conflicts also arose because evacuees and country householders suddenly found themselves living in intimate contact with forms of speech, behavior, dress, diet, morality, religious faiths, and habits of worship to which they were not accustomed. Thus, the discomfort of living in reception areas was largely caused by intermingling of different social customs.

Yet, in spite of these difficulties, the system of billeting in private houses remained the keystone of the British, German, and Japanese evacuation systems throughout the war. This policy was much criticized, but no feasible alternative could be suggested. For example, before the beginning of World War II, rural communities in England voiced strong opposition to billeting in private homes. The British government was urged by members of Parliament representing rural districts to build a vast network of camps instead of relying on private households. Obviously this was not feasible, because the standards of temporary accommodations would have been too low, labor and materials would not have been available, and the expense would have been prohibitive. It was argued that rural households would not take "the dregs of London," and it was suggested that evacuees might be accommodated in golf clubhouses or in racecourses.[20]

Billeting in private homes would be even more necessary in

[19] Richard Padley and Margaret Cole (editors), *Evacuation Survey: A Report to the Fabian Society*, 162.
[20] Titmuss, *op. cit.*, 35, 36.

Long-Term Evacuation of Nonessential Personnel

case of nuclear attacks, because the percentage of the urban population evacuating would be much larger than in World War II. This type of billeting is necessary because of lack of alternative accommodations, and, in the case of unaccompanied school children, the experience of living with a family in a private household, no matter how trying, is preferable to the impersonal atmosphere of a hostel.

If children or mothers can be evacuated to the homes of relatives, many social difficulties can be minimized. Many sources of friction, such as differences in social background and religious or racial discrepancies, are thus avoided. According to a sample survey of evacuees in Germany, "two specific reasons were given by those who reported a satisfactory [evacuation] experience: the evacuees were friends or relatives, or they stayed so briefly there was no time for friction to develop."[21]

For civil defense planning it is important to know how many urban evacuees could find accommodations with relatives or friends and how many would have to be billeted with strangers. As noted above, private evacuees outnumbered those who moved under official sponsorship in England during August and September, 1939. But only part of the private evacuees moved in with relatives or friends (exact figures are not available). According to Table 7, some two-thirds of the evacuated German children found accommodations with relatives. Preliminary statistics are available on the percentage of New York's inhabitants who could evacuate to the homes of relatives or friends in the country. In a sample of one thousand interviews, a little less than one-third (31 per cent)

[21] *USSBS*, European report No. 64b, Vol. I, 72. In the case of adult evacuees, however, it is not necessarily advantageous that they be related to their hosts. In the evacuation after the Dutch flood disaster of 1953, kinship relation or previous friendship between hosts and evacuees did not reduce the number of households reporting tension. (C. J. Lammers, *Survey of Evacuation Problems and Disaster Experiences* [Instituut Voor Sociaal Onderzoek Van Het Nederlandse Volk and Committee on Disaster Studies of the National Academy of Sciences–National Research Council, *Studies in Holland Flood Disaster, 1953*, II] 68–70.)

The Social Impact of BOMB DESTRUCTION

TABLE 7

EVACUATION ARRANGEMENTS FOR SCHOOL CHILDREN
IN BERLIN AND FRANKFURT

	Berlin September 15, 1943‡	Frankfurt November 15, 1944§
Evacuated to relatives	51.2%	42.4%
Evacuated to camps*	15.4%	5.5%
Evacuated with mothers by special trains†	3.9%	—
Evacuated with entire schools	—	16.9%
Remaining in the city	29.5%	35.2%
All children of school age	100.0%	100.0%
In absolute figures	266,018	43,187

*Kinderlandverschickung (specially organized camps).
†Aktion Mutter und Kind.
‡Source: USSBS, unpublished records to European report No. 39.
§Source: USSBS, unpublished records to European report No. 64b.

of the respondents had a place to go in the event of a nuclear attack on the city. This figure is so small because less than one-half of those queried had given any thought to what they would do in case of attack. However, those who did know a place to which they could evacuate planned almost exclusively to go to relatives, friends, or a country home of their own.[22] In a nationwide survey in the United States it was found that 31 per cent of the persons in metropolitan areas had some place in mind to go if evacuation became necessary.[23]

Measures designed to make the evacuation program more acceptable in World War II varied from country to country. For example, in England and Germany free transportation was pro-

[22] Iklé and Kincaid, op. cit., 51–52. This survey was conducted in September, 1954.
[23] Stephen B. Withey, *Fourth Survey of Public Knowledge and Attitudes concerning Civil Defense* (Ann Arbor, Michigan, Survey Research Center, University of Michigan, 1954), 127. The survey was conducted in March, 1954.

Long-Term Evacuation of Nonessential Personnel

vided for nonessential evacuees, and eligible persons were strongly urged to take advantage of this service. The breaking up of families for long periods of time naturally leads to a strong desire to visit evacuated children or wives, and thus creates problems of transportation and accommodations. The British government reduced Sunday railway rates to allow family members to visit evacuated relatives. But in Germany the transportation situation had deteriorated so much toward the end of the war that parents were urged to refrain from visiting the reception areas. Nevertheless, the difficulty of communicating with separated relatives was felt to be a severe deprivation, especially when members of the same family had been billeted in different areas. As a result, many German parents and children set out on foot or used any available transportation to find one another.[24]

The British sought to make evacuation more desirable by establishing welfare services in the reception areas. Hostels and residential nurseries were opened to accommodate evacuated children when they or their hosts became ill. Community centers offered opportunities for recreation and made it possible for evacuees to take meals outside the homes of their hosts, thus providing occasional relief from the burden of sharing cooking facilities. Weekend hostels permitted visiting husbands to stay overnight in the reception area. Special homes were established to handle evacuees who were difficult to billet for educational or psychiatric reasons. Naturally, there was a great demand for social workers. This need was filled partly by volunteers and partly by professional social workers who were moved from the cities to the reception areas. The latter were most useful because they understood the problem of city dwellers which were so puzzling to many authorities in rural communities. In Germany, an attempt was made to improve the administrative co-ordination between cities and reception areas by delegating special representatives from both sides.

[24] *USSBS*, European report No. 47, p. 8.

The Social Impact of *BOMB DESTRUCTION*

The most important improvement in the British evacuation system was probably the liberalization of the financial support given to private evacuees. Of the four million persons who were eligible for evacuation, the government expected some 80 per cent to take part in the official scheme, but less than 40 per cent actually did so. The financial support granted to private evacuees consisted of full compensation for the railway fare to the reception area, and, if children's parents were poor, an additional allowance was granted to cover part or all of the cost of board and lodging.[25] Based on this World War II experience, the present British evacuation plans envisage similar aid to private evacuees. According to a recent British evacuation manual, "such private arrangements will be given every encouragement, for not only do they avoid separation of school children from their mothers but they enable families leaving home to know their destination in advance and to have the greater comfort of staying with friends or relatives instead of in a strange household."[26]

Conflicts in government administration also tend to arise from the long-term evacuation of nonessential personnel. The administrative problems which accompany long-term evacuation of the whole population are, of course, even more complex. The principal cause of conflicts in local administration is the fact that when millions of people move across local boundaries to live temporarily in strange communities, many need some sort of aid owing to the distress caused by war destruction, broken families, and transportation and billeting costs. But since the traditional forms of relief are the responsibility of local governments (county or state), the reception communities are reluctant or unable to support needy evacuees, since they already feel the burden of providing

---

[25] Titmuss, *op. cit.*, 368.
[26] Great Britain, Home Office, Civil Defense, *Manual of Basic Training*, I, Welfare Section, Pamphlet No. 2 (London, H. M. Stationery Office, 1951), 16.

Long-Term Evacuation of Nonessential Personnel

housing, utilities, and general communal facilities for the sudden influx of city dwellers.

In addition to the problems of jurisdiction and financial responsibility for government services rendered to nonresident evacuees in reception communities, conflicts occur among the various national governmental agencies charged with different administrative aspects of evacuation. In Great Britain no fewer than ten departments were concerned with the housing of persons away from their homes, with no co-ordinating agency provided to force them to agree.[27] The administrative difficulties in England reflected the conflict between the traditions of local relief responsibilities and the need for aid on a national scale in order to cope adequately with such an unprecedented emergency.[28] It is likely that similar conflicts between local communities and various federal agencies would arise in the United States in the event of long-term evacuation. Yet the problem cannot be solved simply by superimposing an autonomous organization to cope with all the aspects of local and national evacuation, because effective civil defense has to be built upon the existing authorities and administrative personnel.[29] County welfare officials, state relief agencies, and various federal departments must provide the core for the administrative bodies dealing with evacuation and must contribute their experience, their existing legal powers, and their functioning interrelationships with other branches of the government.

[27] The departments were the War Office, the Admiralty, the Air Ministry, the Ministry of Health, the Board of Education, the Ministry of Labour, the Ministry of Supply, the Ministry of Works and Buildings, the Ministry of Aircraft Production, and the Ministry of Home Security. (Margaret Cole, "Wartime Billeting," *Research Series No. 55*, issued by the Fabian Society [London, 1941], 10–13.)

[28] The detrimental effect of these local administrative conflicts upon the whole evacuation program in England is well described in Titmuss, *op. cit.*, 150–71, 203–35. This British experience, so well chronicled, is very instructive for present administrative evacuation planning.

[29] This point is stressed by Marc Peter in "Lessons from the Last War," *Bulletin of the Atomic Scientists*, Vol. VII, No. 9 (September, 1951), 252–55.

The Social Impact of BOMB DESTRUCTION

Bombing Experience and the Problem of Flight

The reaction of people toward evacuation depends largely upon both their experience with actual bombing raids and their acquaintance with life in reception areas. The response to evacuation is distinctly different when a population has experienced the terror of a severe air attack and when it has suffered prolonged family separation and the hardships of billeting in a previous evacuation experience. Awareness of danger and the experience of deprivations condition human behavior in every evacuation program.

In the first stage of a war, city dwellers who have experienced neither bombing nor evacuation may be unwilling to embark upon a pre-attack evacuation program prompted by official or unofficial warnings of impending bombing attacks. Full awareness of the imminence of an attack must exist, and popular inertia must be overcome by dramatic political developments or well-timed government instructions. Otherwise, most city dwellers will probably not move, because they do not realize the danger. The feasibility of initiating pre-attack evacuation merely on the basis of threatening political events and official instructions is demonstrated by the exodus of some three and one-half million women and children from London and other English cities in August, 1939, prior to the outbreak of World War II.

In the second stage, when bombing remains only a potential threat or a minor, sporadic disturbance, evacuees become increasingly dissatisfied with life in reception areas and tend to flock back to the cities. The hardships of billeting, family separation, and abandonment of the home will not be acceptable in the long run if the alternative is only a vague risk of bombing. In such instances, life in the city seems preferable. Indeed, a return movement took place in England and Germany as soon as the intensity of attacks decreased or turned out to be less severe than expected. In London, the government sponsored a drive to re-evacuate returned children and mothers eight months after the first evacuation movement.

Bombing Experience and the Problem of Flight

But the public responded less willingly than it had to the first program, because many had experienced difficulties in reception areas at a time when serious air raids were still unknown.

In the third stage, city dwellers will have lived through actual bombing destruction and will have perceived the danger of air attack and witnessed injury and death among their neighbors. The threat to their lives will then be no longer a vague, potential risk, but a real and present danger. Under these circumstances the deprivations of evacuation will decline in importance. The incentive to evacuate after a heavy attack will be particularly strong for people who have never experienced evacuation and disillusionment from the conditions in reception areas. Therefore, if destruction should occur in a surprise attack prior to any evacuation movement, the exodus from cities will be precipitate. Those who have lost their homes will be more willing to evacuate than will the city dwellers who have merely witnessed an attack but are still housed. During World War II, essential persons who had not been bombed out rarely evacuated their cities. The statistics for German cities indicate that those whose homes had not been destroyed generally remained in the cities. Destruction of the home, on the other hand, forces urban families to move: the homeless must find shelter, either temporary or permanent. After the frightening experience of an attack and in face of the prospect of future attacks, the homeless will seek reaccommodation outside the threatened city rather than remain and double up in undamaged homes.

During World War II, when air raids varied so much in destructiveness and frequency, these three stages in a population's reaction toward evacuation became clearly apparent. As already mentioned, many British evacuees returned when heavy bombing failed to materialize. Similarly, German evacuees trickled back to their partially damaged cities as soon as the vividness of their experience with bombing faded and a recurrence of attacks seemed less likely. By contrast, the increasing blows against Japanese cities late in 1944 and early in 1945 intensified the evacuation of all nonessential persons. Thus, in August, 1944, before the large-scale bombing attacks, only 53 per cent of the school children had left Japanese target cities; but in April, 1945, after the heavy raids, 87 per cent had been evacuated.[30] In summary, it appears that urbanites decide to evacuate, to remain in reception areas, or to return to their cities largely on the basis of their past experiences of bombing and their past life as evacuees rather than on the more rational basis of anticipation of future dangers.

With this evidence on the different stages in evacuation behavior before us, it is now possible to consider the problem of flight. The idea of a mass flight from cities immediately before or after a nuclear attack has received wide attention. Frequently, the concept of "mass flight" has carried with it a sinister connotation of defeatism or even of rebellion against the national war effort. But speedy retreat from cities in times of war is not necessarily a cowardly, unpatriotic, or chaotic reaction of the public. The derogatory connotation of the word "flight" conceals the fact that that there are situations when flight is in the interest both of individuals and of the national war effort. Sometimes it may reduce casualties and preserve man power. Flight can only be properly evaluated in the context of the situation in which it occurs, with due attention to the alternative courses of action that are left for the population. It is helpful to distinguish three situations in which flight from cities may take place: avoidance of a potential danger, which is usually equivalent to pre-attack evacuation (short-term or long-term); escape from actual peril; and withdrawal from a hazardous disaster area, otherwise known as post-attack (remedial) evacuation.

Flight to avoid a potential danger is merely the precipitate, initial phase of pre-attack evacuation. Thus, what has been said

[30] *USSBS*, Pacific report No. 11, p. 167.

Bombing Experience and the Problem of Flight

about the motivation for the latter applies also to this form of flight. The decision to flee depends on the extent to which a population realizes the threat, and the exodus is not likely to be repeated many times if the anticipated danger does not materialize. City dwellers may flee once or twice upon advance warning, but if the bombing attack does not take place, the number of persons fleeing in subsequent alerts will diminish.

In the face of actual and evident peril, flight may occur in a more dramatic fashion, with throngs of people racing to escape, often in disorganized fashion and with little regard for the social inhibitions that normally govern human relations. It is this form of flight which looms like a nightmare in the minds of those who are opposed to pre-attack evacuation. All too frequently, the mental image of such a mass flight is associated with panic. But the prevalence of panic tends to be overestimated, and many forms of extraordinary behavior are mistakenly labeled as "panic," even though they may be quite rational and wise in the light of the disaster situation. Moreover, no alternative course of action may exist that would be better than the alleged "panic flight." Flight and panic are not necessarily related. Undoubtedly, survivors of a nuclear explosion who are endangered by the ensuing fire storms will flee as fast as they can. Mass flight may save many from death by asphyxiation or heat. However, if the fleeing masses fear that they may be entrapped or that escape routes may become blocked, panic is likely to follow. Therefore, it is most important to facilitate immediate post-attack evacuation if adequate shelters are not available.[31]

[31] Considering this, one of the most ill-advised civil defense measures in the United States was the placing of signs on the outgoing highways from the large cities which indicated that those escape routes would be closed in the event of enemy attack. The possible gain of having unobstructed access routes for rescue operations does not offset the psychological danger of making the population feel entrapped. Concerning the relationship between threatening entrapment and panic, see Quarantelli, *loc. cit.*, 273; and Paul B. Foreman, "Panic Theory," *Sociology and Social Research*, Vol. XXXVII, No. 5 (May–June, 1953), 303.

The Social Impact of *BOMB DESTRUCTION*

The psychological problems of panic after a disaster are overshadowed by the sheer logistical difficulties of co-ordinating an orderly escape movement and organizing constructive rehabilitation efforts. Thus, "compared with other reactions panic is a relatively uncommon phenomenon."[32] It occurs only under quite restricted conditions and only to some of the persons involved in the disaster;[33] there is no evidence from any of the World War II bombings that widespread panic occurred anywhere. Irving L. Janis, after a careful review of the available reports on Hiroshima and Nagasaki finds it "probable that overt panic and extreme disorganized behavior occurred in some local circumstances during the two atomic disasters, but it is unlikely that such behavior was widely prevalent among the hundreds of thousands who survived the atomic explosions."[34]

The third form of population exodus from bombed cities that is sometimes referred to as "flight" is withdrawal from a disaster area after the immediate peril has passed. This exodus is motivated by the difficult and hazardous living conditions in the stricken area as well as by a fear of repeated attacks and a general uneasiness about remaining at the scene of devastation and past sufferings. The physical reasons impelling people to evacuate are mainly lack of housing and food and, in the case of nuclear attacks, prolonged radioactivity dangerous to health. Since the physical effects of radioactivity do not become apparent for some time, the public reaction to it will depend on official warnings and instructions or—in the absence of these—on rumors.

The dramatic aspects of flight tend to exaggerate its economic and military importance. Flight is harmful for the urban economy only so far as it reduces the man power available for production or for the maintenance and repair of essential facilities. If flight

---

[32] Quarantelli, *loc. cit.*, 275.
[33] Fritz and Marks, *loc. cit.*, 41.
[34] Janis, *Air War and Emotional Stress*, 41.

Bombing Experience and the Problem of Flight

reduces casualties among workers, it is obviously not harmful but beneficial to the urban economy. It must also be remembered that the total number of workers who flee is not an adequate measure of the loss in man-hours, because absence from the city's productive facilities can be either short or prolonged. The first two forms of flight—avoidance of a potential danger and escape from actual peril—are, as a rule, of very short duration. Workers usually return to the city quickly. Indeed, as was shown above, even nonessential persons flock back to the city from pre-attack evacuation, oftentimes sooner than the government would wish.

Records for the city of Hamburg support this contention and illustrate the fact that flight after a large disaster has only a short-lived effect, whereas long-term pre- and post-attack evacuation and reaccommodation of the homeless are much more important for urban man power. In Fig. 9, Hamburg's population loss is compared to its housing loss. The scales for both have been matched so that they coincide at the time before any destruction or evacuation took place. Hence, if housing density (the number of persons per dwelling) had always remained the same, the two lines would never diverge. But Fig. 9 shows three areas of divergence which illustrate three different and highly important social effects of bombing. The first area, in the early part of 1943, is formed by pre-destruction evacuation. As can be seen from the broken line (number of dwellings), no loss of housing had yet occurred, but a portion of the population had left the city in anticipation of serious air raids. On the basis of other available information it can be inferred that those who left at this stage were primarily nonessential persons. Then, in the middle of 1943, Hamburg was struck by the big fire raids, so that only 282,000 of its 557,000 dwellings remained habitable. In the first days after the raid, practically all homeless people fled from the city, as did probably some of those who were still housed. This gives us the second area of divergence, where the population trend drops temporarily below the housing

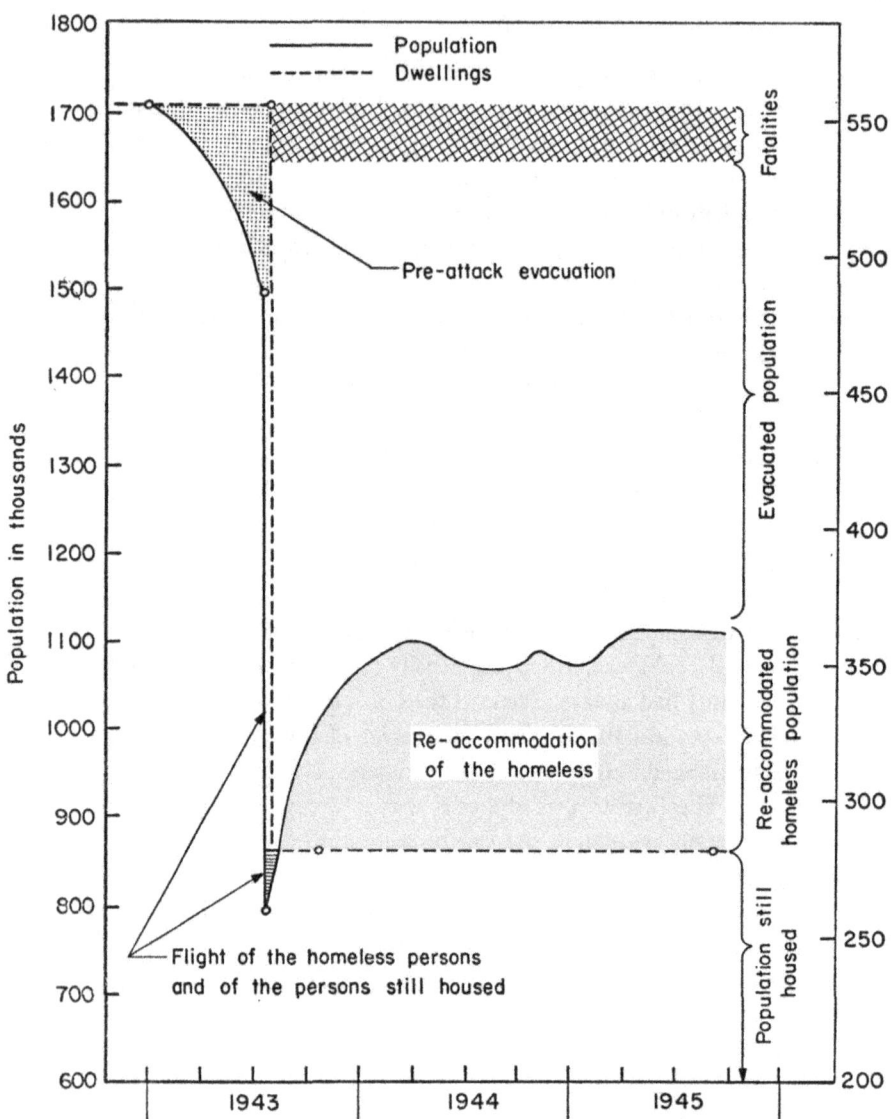

Fig. 9. — Evacuation and return compared with housing destruction in Hamburg during World War II.

trend.³⁵ However, this flight was of little consequence to the size of Hamburg's population in the long run because the return movement set in very rapidly. Not only did people whose dwellings were still serviceable return, but many homeless persons found shelter within the city by doubling up. The reaccommodation of the homeless through an increase in the housing density of the remaining dwellings is illustrated by the third area of divergence in Fig. 9, where the population trend moves above the housing trend. Fatalities, shown in the hatched portion of Fig 9, amount to about 3.3 per cent of the pre-attack population.

Although the return of Hamburg's inhabitants was rapid and the degree of reaccommodation quite substantial, there were complaints that some workers had fled from the city and failed to return. The government introduced various measures to bring male workers back, but female workers were permitted to remain in evacuation. This policy provoked protests from employers in Hamburg who were short of female labor. One month after the raids even more stringent measures were enacted to enforce the return of evacuated workers.³⁶

These findings illustrate the three principles which govern human behavior in disaster situations: the perception of danger, the experience of deprivations, and the limited alternative courses of action. Each individual faces serious dilemmas. Should he

---

[35] After the summer of 1943, the curves of Fig. 9 actually reflect the combined effect of pre-attack evacuation and post-attack evacuation or flight. The separate effect of the two is expressed more clearly by the housing density. In 1939, prior to pre-attack evacuation, the housing density was 3.0 persons per dwelling. In the summer of 1943, after the pre-attack evacuation but before the heavy raids, it had dropped to 2.7. Immediately after the raids, in spite of the mass exodus, it increased a little to 2.8 persons per dwelling, indicating that a few homeless persons found reaccommodation without ever leaving the city. Then, with the progressing reaccommodation, the housing density increased in 1944 up to between 3.8 and 4.2 persons per dwelling, which was substantially above the pre-attack as well as the pre-war figure.

[36] Records from the Industrie- und Handelskammer Hamburg, September 3, 1943.

evacuate or stay in the city? Should he remain in evacuation or return to the city? Should he flee at the last minute or take a chance? Individuals must determine a course of action on the basis of the dangers they perceive, the deprivations they have experienced, or the alternative courses of action which appear to remain.

The conflicts between inertia and danger, vested interests and calculated new risks, and the customary way of life and sheer survival are perhaps the basic dilemmas of our nuclear age. But they have been faced before by city dwellers, as shown by the following passage from a description of the London plague epidemic in 1665, which epitomizes the problems of the modern urbanite in times of nuclear warfare:

> I now began to consider seriously with myself, concerning my own case, and how I should dispose of myself; that is to say, whether I should resolve to stay in London, or shut up my house and flee, as many of my neighbors did. . . . I had two important things before me; the one was the carrying on my business and shop, which was considerable and in which was embarked all my effects in the world; and the other was the preservation of my life in so dismal a calamity, as I saw apparently was coming upon the whole city.[37]

Long-Term Evacuation of the Whole Population

The preceding discussion, based largely on World War II findings, has shown the relationship between past bombing experience and the way people react to evacuation. We are now in a better position to estimate public response to nuclear bombing attacks.

After the first nuclear attacks have occurred, evacuation assumes very different aspects, scarcely encountered in World War

---

[37] Daniel Defoe, *History of the Plague in London in 1665* (London, n.p., 1834), 3.

Long-Term Evacuation of the Whole Population

II. After nuclear explosions, those persons who escaped by pre-attack evacuation will face the serious problem of whether or not to return to their partially damaged cities. Similarly, those who did not evacuate, but escaped death because of shelters or some other protection, may afterwards be impelled to flee (for example, because of fire storms or radioactivity) and then face the question of whether to return to the city or remain permanently in a reception area. After conventional bombing in World War II, essential personnel usually favored a return to the cities, so that they could quickly resume work in industries only partially damaged. After nuclear attacks the population may be less likely to return. And thus a very different situation will exist from that envisaged in most civil defense plans.

It has often been argued that all able-bodied men will march back into the devastated cities to rebuild, repair, and resume industrial production as soon as possible and that the government will not permit a prolonged evacuation of the workers. This contention fails to take into account the very serious possibility of repeated bombings, such as would take place in a "limited" war when tactical nuclear weapons are being employed near cities. If such attacks do occur, or if the government or the public seriously expect them to occur, the question of returning to the endangered cities appears in an entirely different light. The risk of repeated attacks cannot be met by a program of repeated pre-attack movements alone, because when nuclear weapons are being used, evacuation upon advance warning is too precarious an operation to be repeated as easily as were the World War II nighttime evacuations. There is always the danger that any warning will be too late. In such circumstances, the government will be faced with the dilemma of whether to urge or somehow force the working members of the evacuated population to return after the first attacks have occurred in tactical situations or even in some cities and thus repopulate targets of possible future attacks, or to organize a more permanent

The Social Impact of BOMB DESTRUCTION

form of evacuation that would include these workers. The gain in production from a return of workers may be relatively small, because many urban industries may already have been destroyed or disrupted. On the other hand, the risk in human lives may be very great, because each additional pre-attack exodus will be a hazardous operation. It is true that long-term evacuation will displace the urban labor force and interrupt production, but it is preferable to have evacuated workers rather than dead or injured workers.

More important than the government's views about returning civilians to the cities after attack are the individual decisions of the workers themselves, since the enforcement of an official policy without the co-operation of broad population groups will be very difficult in time of nuclear war. Each individual's decision, as we have seen, will be shaped primarily by the way in which his past experiences are projected into the future. After the first nuclear attacks, the thinking and planning of the survivors will be shaped by the sudden terror of the explosion, by the attendant holocaust of fires, by the widespread, utter devastation, and—above all—by the shocking number of casualties. Hence, if further attacks appear likely, the impulse to avoid a repeated experience will be overwhelming. Instead of the expected march back to the cities, there may rather be a further exodus of those survivors who failed to evacuate the first time. With all the attention that has been focused on panic, this deliberate, long-range reaction of the urban population has received very little consideration in civil defense plans.

In other words, not only nonessential persons but most of the workers will remain evacuated as long after the first nuclear attack as further attacks appear likely. The decisive element will be the public evaluation of the likelihood of additional attacks. This evaluation may be based on sound advice from the government, or the incidence of further alerts, on raids in other cities, or on sheer speculation and rumor. Of course, if repeated attacks actually

Long-Term Evacuation of the Whole Population

do occur, the evacuees will have a most convincing argument for not returning.

It is likely that the government will adapt its policy to this situation and will try to organize the long-term evacuation of workers in such a way as to minimize the loss in industrial man power. Under conditions of repeated attacks, evacuation of workers will not only reduce casualties substantially but will also provide better conditions for a minimum level of industrial production than a policy which attempted to enforce the return of workers to target cities.

The reintegration of the evacuated workers into the labor force has to be accomplished in the reception areas. There exist three basic possibilities for the re-employment of evacuees away from their cities:

(1) *Employment at new, dispersed industrial or business facilities constructed after evacuation.* New plants in reception areas can make only a minor contribution toward the immediate employment of evacuees, since construction takes considerable time. Under a situation of extreme emergency and shortages, new plant construction, as well as the dispersal of old plants from target cities, will be particularly difficult. By combining the new facilities with existing establishments, industrial expansion in reception areas can probably be accomplished more quickly.

(2) *Employment at industrial and business establishments, such as plants, offices, and shops, which were already in the reception area prior to evacuation.* Many of the factories, offices, and shops located in the reception areas before the outbreak of war can employ additional workers by introducing more shifts and by increasing the use of man power in other ways. However, there are many problems involved in this type of re-employment. First, not all facilities are flexible in the sense that an increase in man power with substantially the same capital equipment will lead to

an increase in production. For example, factories operating on a twenty-four-hour basis cannot introduce additional shifts. Furthermore, an expansion in labor force frequently requires an increase in all levels of skill, creating special managerial and engineering problems, and increased production necessitates an increased supply of raw materials and semifinished products. In many cases the source of semifinished products may be in devastated cities, and the supply will then be cut off.[38] Finally, not only will the transportation of raw materials from their sources in the reception areas entail great difficulties, but also the shipping of processed goods from the reception areas to the consumers will be more difficult.

(3) *Employment in agriculture.* Food shortages and the comparative safety of rural areas will encourage some urban evacuees to seek agricultural employment. However, the possibility of employing many additional workers profitably on farms is limited. In countries like the United States and Great Britain only a small proportion of the total labor force works in agriculture to begin with, and this proportion cannot be increased substantially without lowering the productivity per worker. In other words, if too many evacuees should seek employment on farms, there would not be enough work for them to earn a livelihood.

In summary, existing industrial facilities in reception areas will offer the principal opportunity for re-employing evacuated workers, whereas only a small fraction of the displaced urbanites will find jobs at newly constructed plants, and employment on farms can serve only as a last resort in case of a temporary collapse of the national economy.

Industries in reception areas are capable of absorbing a large

[38] Theoretically, the amount of raw materials needed in the devastated cities will be smaller, and the increased production in reception areas could be adequately supplied. However, it will be difficult to divert these raw materials quickly to new destinations.

Long-Term Evacuation of the Whole Population

increase in man power primarily because additional shifts can frequently be used in plants ordinarily operating with a single shift. In the United States during World War II, even in 1942 only about 40 per cent of the wage earners in war production were on evening and night shifts.[39] If need be, probably at least as many workers could be employed in these two shifts as on the day shift.[40] Of course, such arrangements would require expert organization to reallocate man power and raw materials over all the reception areas which offered opportunities for industrial employment.[41] The United States Employment Service or the Employment Exchanges in England could provide the administrative core for such gigantic relocation programs. Indeed, the Employment Exchanges were used widely during World War II to allocate scarce labor to war industries throughout Great Britain.

A device which can greatly facilitate the employment of evacuated workers is the linking of companies, whereby a firm in a target city makes a working agreement with another firm in the same industry in a reception area. Such an arrangement, for example, might lead to a merger of the firms after evacuation, with combined operations at the facilities in the reception area. Some preparations in this direction have been made in Great Britain: important industries in vulnerable areas have been encouraged to plan the removal of workers and light equipment to dispersed

[39] The industries here considered are metal work, chemicals, smelting and refining, and ordnance. In 1941, only 20 per cent of the workers were employed on the second shift, and 8 per cent were on the third shift. Morris Levine, "Shift Operations in Selected Defense Industries," *Monthly Labor Review*, Vol. LIII, No. 2 (March, 1941), 355–65.

[40] Harrison F. Houghton, "Working Hours in War Production Plants, February, 1942," *ibid.*, Vol. LIV, No. 5 (May, 1942), 1061–65.

[41] There are approximately 320 counties in the United States which do not contain a large target city (as defined by the federal Civil Defense Administration on July 1, 1953), but which have more than five thousand manufacturing employees (according to the U. S. Census of Manufacturers of 1947). These 320 counties would thus be the principal reception areas for the re-employment of evacuated workers. In 1947, they contained roughly one-third of all manufacturing employees in the United States.

sites where they could combine forces with firms of the same industry.[42]

Evacuated workers will not only need work useful to the national economy, but will also need transportation, housing, and food. To distribute the load of evacuees among reception areas, many evacuees may have to travel a great distance in search of a safe place where they can find both housing and employment. The housing of large numbers of evacuees presents many problems, especially when the evacuation may extend over many months or even years.

The outstanding feature of any large-scale evacuation lasting more than a few days is the need for billeting in private homes. All other accommodations are either insufficient or inadequate. Vacant dwellings, resort hotels, tourist homes, and similar facilities can absorb only a small fraction of all the evacuees. The rest will have to be billeted either in mass shelters or in private homes. While both of these alternatives entail social disadvantages, the disadvantages of billeting in mass shelters are infinitely greater than those of billeting in private homes.

Mass shelters, such as movie theaters, convention halls, and tents, are useful as collection and rest centers for the first night or two, but they are entirely unsatisfactory for a prolonged stay. Thus, private houses remain by far the most important form of billeting for large numbers of evacuees. Through an increase in the number of persons per dwelling, the evacuees can be accommodated in the private homes in reception areas. This process is analogous to the reaccommodation of homeless city dwellers in the undestroyed dwellings within a city. The size of the increase in housing density depends on the total number of evacuees, on

[42] During World War II the British government tried to concentrate various industries into fewer firms, not so much for the purpose of total evacuation but in order to save man power, floor space, and supplies. Great administrative difficulties were encountered by this concentration policy. Cf. E. L. Hargreaves and M. M. Gowing, *Civil Industry and Trade* (Hancock [editor], *op. cit.*), 202-33.

Long-Term Evacuation of the Whole Population

the way in which they are distributed, and on the number of dwellings in the reception areas. With some idea of the cities likely to be targets, it is a simple procedure to compute the increase in housing density in the reception areas which would result from any given number of evacuees.[43]

An equal distribution of all evacuees over all reception areas in a country would minimize the degree of crowding. However, on account of transportation difficulties or a lack of employment opportunities, equal distribution would not be feasible. Areas which lie closer to the target cities and which offer better employment opportunities will probably experience a higher than average increase in housing density.

Findings from various natural disasters indicate that the gravity of the emergency as perceived by the population contributes to the willingness of both evacuees and hosts to accept the deprivations of billeting. During Holland's flood disaster a few years ago, a dramatic presentation of the emergency through radio and newspapers evidently helped to make billeting more acceptable. In a survey of four small towns in the state of Washington, householders were asked how many refugees they could take in case of emergency.[44] The average for four towns was 3.6 persons per household. However, from 13 to 27 per cent said they could take "more if necessary" or "others in the event of a real emergency." This again illustrates that the perception of the emergency affects the hospitality of homeowners.

---

[43] The capacity of private houses outside of target cities is very large, provided evacuees can be distributed over the entire country. If two-thirds of the population from all target cities in the United States should be billeted in private homes in the reception areas, the resulting increase in housing density would be well within the limits that were frequently experienced in World War II without serious repercussions. For example, the density in white housing would increase from 3.48 to 4.08 persons per dwelling and in nonwhite housing from 4.16 to 5.06 persons per dwelling (see Iklé and Kincaid, *op. cit.*).

[44] "Project Revere" (Washington Public Opinion Laboratory, University of Washington, 1952).

The lack of alternative courses of action is the decisive influence leading to the high increases in housing density. Housing density in a reception area cannot be arbitrarily limited. It will vary with the severity of bomb destruction. A predetermined standard of housing density does not make sense if there are no better alternatives than to live with densities in excess of the "standard." Consider, for example, the following situation. A reception area is filled with evacuees whose homes are demolished, and all available accommodations have been utilized. After a while it may be felt that the housing densities are "unacceptable." There are, in theory, two alternatives left: either the evacuees will be forced out of their billets and left to camp in makeshift tents, huts, or shacks (the shortage of building materials will probably rule out construction of sufficient emergency housing), or they will be moved into another reception area. The first alternative seems grossly unjust to the evacuees, even though it may suit a few inhospitable homeowners, and it would probably not be tolerated by the public. The second alternative exists only if the housing density is lower in other accessible reception areas. If the housing density has already been approximately equalized over all the reception areas, then there remains no alternative but to accept the allegedly "unacceptable" housing density.

The new British civil defense plans take cognizance of the fact that it is futile to establish definite standards for maximum housing densities. It is felt that the densities will have to depend on the extent of evacuation.[45] However, it is planned to distribute evacuees equally in order to avoid excessive crowding in certain areas. During World War II some communities experienced a much larger increase in population than others. In particular, districts more readily accessible from London absorbed proportionately many more evacuees than districts farther away. In many such areas nonessential evacuees occupied housing that was ur-

[45] *Manual of Basic Training, op. cit.*, I, Welfare Section, Pamphlet No. 2, p. 39.

Evacuee-Host Relationship

gently needed for war workers. As a result, the government tried to divert evacuees from such places and ceased to give financial assistance to persons wishing to move there.[46] Furthermore, official evacuation was stopped, and the railroad and bus companies were urged to discourage travel to these "closed" areas.[47] These World War II measures are interesting because they reflect an effort to regulate the distribution of evacuees. Similar problems would certainly arise in connection with long-term evacuation of city dwellers after nuclear bombing.

In Japan there was the same tendency for evacuees to crowd disproportionately into reception areas close to the target cities, especially into those adjacent to Tokyo.[48] Generally the evacuees did not move to smaller cities but to rural areas, since many small cities also became targets of the Allied attacks. For example, the city of Nagoya in the Aichi Prefecture lost 56 per cent of its population between 1944 and 1945, and the population in all other cities in Aichi also declined. But the population in the rural districts (the so-called *guns*) increased on the average by 28 per cent.[49]

Evacuee-Host Relationship

The floods in Holland in February, 1953, provide a particularly instructive example of a long-term evacuation of a whole population and of the problems of human relations between evacuees and hosts. The British and German World War II experiences are mainly limited to the evacuation of nonessential persons, but the Dutch floods suddenly forced the entire population of large areas to evacuate within one night.[50]

[46] Titmuss, *op. cit.*, 367.
[47] Great Britain, Ministry of Health, *Report on Conditions in Reception Areas*, 11.
[48] The Saitama and Chiba Prefectures. Data from *Japan Statistical Yearbook, 1949*, 40–41; and *USSBS*, unpublished records to Pacific report No. 41.
[49] Data from *Aichi-ken Tokei-sho, 1949* (Statistics of Aichi Prefecture), 45–50.
[50] No exact figures are available concerning the maximum number of evacuated persons in Holland. On January 1, 1952, the total population of all the com-

The Social Impact of *BOMB DESTRUCTION*

The refugees from the flood were first brought, primarily by buses, to schools, community halls, churches, and other public buildings, which served as collection centers. Then the evacuees were rapidly assigned to private homes; hence, the billeting in emergency centers lasted only one or two nights at the most. The British plan to use mainly public buildings as collection or rest centers in case of wartime evacuation. The homeless would not be left there longer than a day or two because, on the basis of past experience, it has been found that billeting in emergency centers should be as short as possible. Thus, "A prolonged stay in a rest centre has a very undesirable and demoralizing effect on the occupants, who are apt to settle down to a most unsatisfactory type of existence and are then difficult to move. All billetable persons should be removed from the rest centres and billeted within, at most, a few days of their arrival."[51]

The floods in Holland were of great concern to the entire population of the country. Special news bulletins were broadcast in dramatic fashion throughout the first few days. Evidently they created a general atmosphere of co-operation and helpfulness and facilitated the billeting of flood victims in private homes. A great number of families volunteered to take in evacuees, and many collection centers received more offers to accommodate homeless persons than were needed. Frequently the volunteering hosts drove to the centers and waited with their cars to take the evacuees to their homes. In Rotterdam and several other places, the allocation of evacuees among the potential hosts was organized by the churches. The churches set up their own booths within the general collection centers and prepared lists of member-families who had

---

munities which were flooded was 580,814. But not all inhabitants of these communities were rendered homeless. (The Netherlands Central Bureau of Statistics, *Het Rampgebied Zuid–West Nederland* [February, 1953], 9; *Statistisch Bulletin*, No. 37 [1953]; and press releases).

[51] Great Britain, Ministry of Health, Government Evacuation Scheme, "Notes for Billeting Officers and Voluntary Welfare Workers" (August, 1941), 17.

offered their hospitality. Through this procedure, evacuees and hosts were automatically matched in religion.

Defense plans in Great Britain include provisions for compulsory billeting and special tribunals to whom the householders can appeal to change or cancel a billeting order. The World War II instructions to billeting officers stressed that the burden of accommodating evacuees should be distributed equally among the householders in the reception areas. Billeting officers were told not to hesitate, "in the interests of fair play, to use their compulsory powers if any particular householders are standing out and refusing to accept evacuees for no good reasons."[52]

Compulsory powers, however, were not used very vigorously during World War II. They are obviously of little value if children alone must be billeted, for children should not be left with foster parents who lack willingness and sympathy. Thus the burden of caring for evacuated children was distributed quite unequally in some reception areas. The poor and congested parts of reception towns, according to British reports, were convinced that they should accept children while the wealthier and roomier parts were left undisturbed.[53] In the case of homeless adults compulsory billeting can be more widely used, since adults can be accommodated in households even though they are not willingly accepted by the hosts. As has been said previously, the development and revisions of British evacuation plans since the beginning of World War II have led to increasingly greater support for private arrangements. Evidently experience has proved the great value of encouraging people to select their own billets.

In Holland, there were sufficient voluntary offers of hospitality to provide for all the flood victims the very first day. The Dutch authorities did not have to make use of compulsory billeting. In view of the large masses of homeless people, this is an important

[52] *Ibid.*, 5.
[53] Titmuss, *op. cit.*, 375.

finding, since, of course, voluntary billeting leads to infinitely more congenial arrangements.

After the flood disaster, regulations were passed providing small daily billeting allowances for board and lodging. If the evacuee was billeted in a boardinghouse, the allowances were higher. Payments were usually made directly to the evacuees, who in turn paid their hosts according to a fixed rate. The payments to the evacuees were somewhat higher than the billeting rates in order to allow for pocket money.

Clubs which were organized among evacuees in Holland gave the former neighbors of the flooded villages an opportunity to meet and discuss problems of common interest. The authorities employed social workers to visit the reaccommodated families and see whether any difficulties had developed. In some rare instances, hosts were relieved of the billeted evacuees who proved to be too troublesome; occasionally these problem families could be located in vacant apartments or hotels.

Actually, the evacuees in Holland came from rural areas and moved into towns or cities—a direction exactly opposite to that of wartime evacuation. But many of the social problems of billeting were the same. The inconveniences of billeting will always create problems in personal and family relationships, even if evacuees and hosts can be perfectly matched. However, the largest target cities, and hence those supplying the majority of evacuees, characteristically contain extremely heterogeneous populations in terms of economic, social, and ethnic characteristics. The influx of such a conglomerate population, for billeting in private dwellings in the reception communities, will almost certainly lead to hostility and conflict.

Interpersonal relations in reception communities have been studied extensively by the British on the basis of their experiences in World War II. The consensus is that, in order to reduce the incidence of hostility and conflict, evacuees and hosts should be

Evacuee-Host Relationship

matched with regard to religious, ethnic, and social characteristics. But there were many exceptions to this rule; evacuees and hosts of completely different backgrounds often got along better than those who were of the same class, religion and income group. As would be expected, friction and tension increased with time. In England, it was found progressively more difficult to locate new billets which were necessary to change existing arrangements or to accommodate new children because the hospitality in reception areas had worn off.[54] The same increase in social tension is borne out by studies of the Dutch evacuation in 1953. Apparently, people can adjust remarkably well to great hardships if an early end is in sight. Furthermore, the initial adjustment between host and evacuee is aided by an outburst of altruism and sympathy on the part of the hosts and by a prevailing feeling of solidarity in times of national crisis. However, when the prospect of long inconvenience appears and when the original hospitality wears off under the continuous inroads on privacy and the daily occasions for friction, social tensions will gradually increase. The factors which seemed to be particularly related to the incidence of tension between hosts and evacuees in Holland were differences in religious beliefs and income levels. The latter became important only in the long run. Furthermore, evacuated families with children experienced significantly more tensions than those without children, probably because the children placed a great burden on the hosts.[55]

[54] Great Britain, Ministry of Health, *Memorandum on Evacuation*, No. 8, Government Evacuation Scheme (London, H. M. Stationery Office, 1940).

[55] The number of households in which tension was reported increased sharply during the first three months and then remained roughly the same (Lammers, *op. cit.*, 110). Lammers distinguishes different stages in the evacuee-host relationship. After the spontaneous reception, occasional friction develops, and then mutual adjustments are made to establish a *modus vivendi*. Eventually, however, evacuation fatigue leads to tension (*ibid.*, 95–114). The part of this study which bears on the billeting tensions is based on 880 interviews in April, 1953, and on 490 questionnaires mailed in October, 1953; hence, the changes over that time can be statistically determined.

The Social Impact of BOMB DESTRUCTION

Summary

It is evident that the complications and repercussions of long-term evacuation are many and diverse. Long-term evacuation of the whole population is only one of the three principal types of evacuation. There are also the pre-attack short-term exodus to reduce casualties and the long-term evacuation of nonessential persons to mitigate the impact of bombing upon children and women.

In times of nuclear war all three types are likely to occur in various combinations. Long-term evacuation of the whole population will occur as a consequence of past nuclear destruction and will constitute the principal adaptive response of urban populations to a threat of repeated attacks. It is not likely to be total, but it may include the majority of exposed city dwellers, excepting only a small core of die-hards and highly essential maintenance workers. People who have witnessed nuclear destruction in the past, whose homes and workplaces may have been demolished, and who seriously fear future attacks will be impelled to retreat—not so much out of cowardice but rather as a natural attempt to survive. If the evacuated workers can be re-employed in the reception areas, they will be better able to support the national economy than if they had stayed in the bomb-scarred target cities. Opportunities to re-employ the evacuated workers can be created through a more intensive use of existing industrial facilities in the reception areas. This re-orientation of the national economy in a time of all-out emergency will require great feats of organization if the industrial production outside of target cities is to compensate in part for the lost production within the large cities.

The tribulations of evacuation, which seemed so serious in World War II, will be accepted more readily in an era of nuclear warfare. Personal hardships will be dwarfed by the appalling fatalities, the widespread incidence of radiation sickness, and the sheer terror of the enormous destruction.

Chapter V

TRANSPORTATION COMMUNICATIONS, AND OTHER UTILITIES

FATALITIES, HOUSING DESTRUCTION, and evacuation all reduce the population of a bombed city. Selective evacuation, furthermore, changes the composition of the remaining population by encouraging the exodus of non-essential persons, leaving those who are in the labor force. The next problem to be considered is how this remaining population can function and carry on its daily activities or, more precisely, how the aftermath of bombing destruction affects the productivity of the workers who remain in the city. This problem can best be studied in terms of the consumer-resources relationships which are crucial for the functioning of a city. Foremost among resources are transportation and communication facilities, the media which tie a city together and maintain its organizational integrity. In addition, other utilities are necessary for the operation of transportation and communication facilities, for the maintenance of productive machinery, and for the continuance of urban housekeeping.

Intra-urban Transportation

The majority of urban workers travel daily between home and workplace. In larger cities, commutation generally depends on the urban transit system because most workers live at a consid-

The Social Impact of *BOMB DESTRUCTION*

erable distance from their factories or offices. Hence, if the transit system is disrupted by bombing, workers will find it difficult or impossible to reach their workplaces (either their own places of work which survive or can be repaired or new ones). This will result in a man-hour loss additional to that arising from the decline in the total labor force on account of casualties, homelessness, or evacuation.

The effect of bombing upon urban transportation will be analyzed in terms of a consumer-resources ratio. The "consumers" are those who use the transit system; the "resources" consist of two components, the material system and the personnel who keep it functioning. Thus we must consider three components: the consumers — commuting workers, shoppers, persons traveling for recreation, and other passengers; the physical resources—vehicles, tracks, power supply, repair shops, etc.; and the human resources —drivers, engineers, switchmen, repairmen, and other personnel.

The three components of the transit system are all interrelated with the rest of the urban complex. The power for the transit system is provided by electricity, coal, or gasoline; hence it depends on workers in other utilities and industries. The transit workers have to be housed and fed, and the consumers of transportation, too, need housing, food, and clothing.

The most immediate and apparent effect of bombing upon transportation is the direct destruction of physical resources. To obtain perspective, we may compare the percentage loss in transit vehicles with the percentage loss in housing units for a few selected cities, using World War II data (see Table 8). These losses varied from city to city and with the intensity of the bombing attacks. Thus subways are much less vulnerable than surface transit facilities, and an accidental hit on a bus garage or on a streetcar switchyard will reduce the number of available vehicles disproportionately. To minimize the risk, certain English cities during the

Intra-urban Transportation

months of repeated German night raids moved their vehicles to the outer areas and parked them there for the night.[1]

TABLE 8
DESTRUCTION OF TRANSIT FACILITIES COMPARED WITH HOUSING DESTRUCTION

City	Type of Vehicle and Terminal	Dates	Vehicles Percentage Decline	Housing Percentage Decline*
Cologne	Streetcars	(1937–47)	65.0	57.4
Frankfurt	Streetcars	(1936–46)	69.4	
	Buses	(1936–46)	72.6	38.6
Kobe	Trolleys	(1941–45)	42.2	
	Buses	(1941–45)	43.7	50.5
Osaka	Streetcars	(1943–45)	40.9	
	Subway cars	(1943–45)	0.0	55.4

*As a percentage of the pre-destruction number of housing units. For the German cities the units are rooms; for the Japanese cities the units are houses; the terminal dates are 1939–46 and 1941–45, respectively.

As illustrated by the examples in Table 8, in Germany, the percentage decline in vehicles was usually larger than the housing loss. The discrepancy was even greater during the first days after a raid. As time went by, part of the loss in vehicles could be recovered through repairs. In Hamburg, for example, one month after the heavy air raids which left 51 per cent of the dwellings undestroyed only 32 per cent of the streetcars were still usable. Nine months later, 49 per cent of the original total were operating. Recovery in the number of elevated railroad cars was even more marked; 24 per cent were in use immediately after attack, and 69 per cent were in use nine months later.[2]

[1] Titmuss, *op. cit.*, 308.
[2] *USSBS*, European report No. 32, p. 24.

The Social Impact of BOMB DESTRUCTION

The human resources of the transit system will suffer losses from bombing because of casualties, absenteeism, and—perhaps unauthorized—evacuation. Among the operating personnel, such as drivers, engineers, and conductors, there is likely to be a smaller percentage of casualties, however, than there is loss of vehicles, because people can take refuge in shelters while vehicles are left unprotected. But evacuation and absenteeism may temporarily deplete the working force of a city's transit system. Thus, of the 10,000 employees of Hamburg's elevated railroads, only 10 per cent reported for work a week and a half after the heavy raids.[3]

The shortage of personnel for repairs will be more acute. Damage to tracks, switches, power lines, and vehicles will require an enormous increase in repair work over the customary peacetime level. Even without actual destruction there is much more repair work in wartime because obsolete rolling stock cannot be replaced. After bombing, the shortage of repairmen will constitute the principal bottleneck in the restoration of the transit system. However, if the repair crews are well staffed in peacetime, they will be in a better position to cope with their task after attack. Analogous to the housing situation, a margin in resources provides elasticity to cushion the effects of destruction.[4]

Private automobiles augment the physical resources of urban transportation, but in most cities outside of the United States their passenger capacity is too small to accommodate a substantial number of commuters. For purposes of comparison, in 1950 there were 249 passenger cars in San Francisco per one thousand inhabitants,

---

[3] Gauwirtschaftskammer (official Chamber of Commerce), Hamburg, minutes of the meetings of August 3–11, 1943.

[4] Actually, the number of repairmen is small in relation to their importance to a city. The subways of New York City, which transport approximately five million passengers on a weekday, have about twelve thousand repairmen and maintenance workers. In addition, there are some eighteen thousand workers operating the system. (Data for 1952, supplied by the New York City Board of Transportation.) This group of skilled people is of paramount importance for the rehabilitation of a city after a bombing attack.

Intra-urban Transportation

184 in Washington, D. C., and 119 in New York City, but only 52 in London (in 1953), 24 in Hamburg (in 1953), 12 in Warsaw (in 1948), 2.5 in Tokyo, and 1.8 in Kobe.[5] In cities of the Soviet Union the number of passenger automobiles per capita is also very small. During a war, the carrying capacity of private automobiles will be substantially reduced by the destruction of vehicles, shortage of gasoline, and lack of repair parts or new cars. For example, registration of private passenger cars in Hamburg dropped from 23.4 per thousand inhabitants in 1938 to 5.0 in 1947; in Munich it declined from 34.6 to 4.9, and in Essen from 13.1 to 2.5 in the same period.[6]

The capacity of taxicabs in a large metropolis should not be overestimated. If all the taxis in New York City were pressed into commutation service (with seven passengers per taxicab), they could carry only about one-tenth of the rush-hour load on subways.[7]

Bicycles were of great importance after the World War II bombings in European and Japanese cities, for of all means of transportation, bicycles are least affected by air raids. They need no gasoline and can be operated even if streets are partly damaged or blocked by debris.

The effects of bombing upon the physical and human resources of urban transportation are important, but the effects of bombing upon the consumers of transportation, must also be considered, especially the commuters who use the urban transit system to reach their workplaces—other types of passengers lose their importance in an emergency economy. Inhabitants who remain in a bombed city will commute considerably more than before the attack for two reasons: first, the needs of the war economy will

---

[5] Data for the American cities from *Automobile Facts and Figures* (published by the Automobile Manufacturers Association, Detroit, 1950), 23; for London (county area) from the Automobile Association; and for the other cities from municipal statistics.

[6] Frankfurt am Main, *Statistische Monatsberichte,* 1948, 49.

[7] Data on taxis from 1948, supplied by the New York Police Department.

The Social Impact of BOMB DESTRUCTION

lead to the employment of many persons who were formerly not in the labor force (and who will be prevented from moving closer to their places of work because of the wartime housing shortage); and second, the reaccommodation of homeless workers in undestroyed dwellings inevitably increases the distances between home and work.

That there is an increase in commutation is borne out by exceptionally detailed statistics from Hamburg which provide a cross tabulation of place of residence and place of work for forty districts for the entire labor force in 1939 and 1946.[8] These data make it possible to compare the length of commutation trips of the prewar and reaccommodated (postwar) working population. For the workers who commute to the central area of the city[9] (46 per cent of all commuters), the average distance traveled increased from 1.8 to 2.5 miles. This increase in the length of trips is shown in further detail in Table 9. The figures emphasize the transportation difficulty which is bound to arise after bombing: fewer vehicles will have to carry more commuters. Assuming that distances up to 3 miles can be traveled daily on foot,[10] the percentage of workers in Hamburg who were able to do without transportation declined from 75 to 58 per cent during the war.

Complementary evidence of the increase in commutation after partial destruction of a city can be found in the data on ticket sales of the suburban rapid-transit railroad in Hamburg.[11] These

[8] Kinder, "Wandlungen in der Struktur des Berufsverkehrs in Hamburg seit 1939" (Landesplanungsamt Hamburg, December, 1949) (mimeographed).

[9] This area includes all the districts in which the number of workplaces considerably exceeds the number of residences (the districts No. 3, 5, 17, 28, and 36, including the secondary downtown area of Harburg).

[10] Five per cent of all workers who lived from two to three miles from their workplaces walked, according to commuting surveys made in Washington, D. C., and in Baltimore. (Douglas Carroll, "Home-Work Relationship of Industrial Employees," unpublished dissertation, Department of City Planning, Harvard University, 1950, p. 28.) This percentage could, of course, be greatly increased in case of emergency.

[11] *USSBS*, unpublished records to European report No. 32.

Intra-urban Transportation

TABLE 9
PERCENTAGE DISTRIBUTION OF COMMUTERS TO CENTRAL AREAS
OF HAMBURG BY DISTANCE TRAVELED FOR 1939 AND 1946

Distance Traveled in Miles	1939	1946
Below three	75.0	58.0
Three to six	19.0	28.0
Six and over	6.0	14.0
	100.0	100.0

figures are available for every month before and after the heavy raids, and thus reflect more immediate bombing effects than the above postwar data. During the year prior to the heavy raids the per capita revenue from tickets increased slightly from 1.03 to 1.28 reichsmarks. In the first month after the raids it showed no further per capita increase (and an absolute decline), probably because of serious disruptions of train service. But two months later the per capita ticket sales had increased to 2.15 reichsmarks, which is about double the pre-destruction figure. Ticket sales (and hence the absolute number of passengers) also registered an increase. In the following year per capita sales decreased slightly (to 1.88 RM) but still remained significantly above the pre-destruction level.

A post-destruction increase in commuting, relative to the population present, is further corroborated by data from other cities which were bombed during World War II. In Frankfurt and Warsaw the ratio of the number of passengers per total population on streetcars and buses more than doubled between 1936-37 and 1946. In Kobe, the annual number of trolley and bus passengers per total population increased by 37 per cent from 1940 to 1945, and on Osaka's streetcars and subways it increased by 26 per cent in the same period.[12]

[12] Sources for data on the number of passengers: Frankfurt am Main, *op. cit.*, 1949, 132, 134; Ville de Varsovie, *Bulletin Mensuel de Statistique Municipale*, *passim*; Kobe-shi Tokei-sho (statistical yearbook of Kobe City), 1948-49, part II, 5 and part IV, 30; and *Osaka Shisei Nenkan* (municipal yearbook of the City of Osaka), 1950, 202, 290.

The Social Impact of *BOMB DESTRUCTION*

The consumer-resources ratio in transportation is more difficult to determine than in housing. The "consumption" of urban transit consists not only of the total number of passengers but also of the length of passenger trips; the resources comprise not only the physical capacity of all vehicles but also their performance. The performance of the existing rolling stock depends partly on the size of the personnel, or the human resources, and partly on other physical resources such as the power supply, tracks, condition of streets, etc. A rough measure of performance is the average mileage traveled by each vehicle. Taking this as an index for the functioning of the rolling stock, it is possible to construct a consumer-resources ratio as follows: the total number of passengers times the average length of a passenger trip, divided by the product of total vehicle capacity (seats and standing room) and the average

TABLE 10

ELASTICITY OF THE CONSUMER-RESOURCES RATIO
OF HAMBURG'S STREETCAR SYSTEM

	1938	1950	Percentage Change
(1) Total number of passengers (in thousands)	165,590	281,974	+70.3
(2) Average length of a passenger trip (in miles)	2.8	3.2	+15.6
(3) Total capacity of all vehicles	59,072	50,875	−13.9
(4) Average mileage traveled by a vehicle	27,603	27,353	−0.9
(5) Consumer-resources ratio = $\frac{(1) \times (2)}{(3) \times (4)}$	0.284	0.652	+129.6

Source of statistics: Urban, "Die öffentlichen Nahverkehrsmittel für die Personenbeförderung in der Hansestadt Hamburg," *Hamburg in Zahlen*, No. 1 (1952), 5–7.

Intra-urban Transportation

mileage traveled by a vehicle. In Table 10 this consumer-resources ratio has been computed for the city of Hamburg before and after the war. These data illustrate the changes due to bombing destruction: the consumer component increases because there are more passengers (line 1), and the passengers, on the average, take longer trips (line 2). At the same time, the resources component declines because of destruction of vehicles (line 3), although by 1950 the loss of physical resources had been partly recovered through repairs and replacements. Moreover, the mileage per vehicle (line 4) was probably greater in 1950 than immediately after the raids. Hence these 1950 figures yield a much larger resources component (line 3 times line 4) than earlier post-attack data would. In spite of this, the elasticity of resources, through increased use of vehicle capacity, permitted a 130 per cent increase in the consumer-resources ratio.[13]

To interpret this consumer-resources ratio correctly, however, one must bear in mind that passenger trips are not evenly distributed through vehicle trips.[14] During rush hours the density of passengers per seating and standing capacity is much above average. In fact, the peaks in demand will then temporarily exceed the maximum capacity of the vehicles, and some passengers will have to wait. This queueing for transportation which occurs in all large cities in peacetime is seriously aggravated by bombing destruction. Extending the concept of elasticity to the consumer com-

[13] For other cities, where data on the average length of passenger trips are not available, a partial consumer-resources ratio can be computed, consisting of the number of passengers per vehicle-mile (this corresponds to line 1 in Table 10 divided by the product of lines 3 and 4). Obviously, this ratio reflects only part of the increase in consumption relative to resources, since it ignores the fact that passenger trips became longer after destruction. This ratio of passengers per vehicle-mile on Kobe's trolleys increased from 10.5 in 1940 to 15.4 in 1943 and 25.3 in 1945; on Warsaw's streetcars it increased from 8.0 in 1937 to 17.9 in 1946.

[14] In Table 10 the "total capacity of all vehicles" (line 3) includes the customary number of standing passengers, but is less than the maximum physical capacity under conditions of extreme crowding. Using the latter, the consumer-resources ratio (line 5) would be lower in 1938 and 1950, and it could never exceed 1.

ponent, one might say that an insufficient elasticity of resources in transportation can be alleviated by an "elastic consumption" in the form of staggered trips or queueing.

A further gain in elasticity is due to the fact that only a fraction of all trips on an urban transit system are for commutation or other essential purposes.[15] Hence restrictions on nonessential travel will make more room for commuting workers. In Hamburg, for example, workers obtained priority cards entitling them to board crowded transit facilities first, and the use of buses during rush hours was restricted to commuters.[16] Apart from regulating consumption, many damaged cities further improved their transit services after World War II bombings by borrowing buses, trolleys, or streetcars from undamaged cities and by employing army trucks for public transportation.

As a last resort, in case of a disrupted transit system, workers can live in dormitories within walking distance of their factories. The commutation difficulties in Osaka after the raids in June, 1945, led to the billeting of student workers in dormitories at the factories. But by the end of the war, some two months later, only 10 per cent of all the students who had stayed in the city actually lived in these dormitories.[17]

In some bombed cities the shipment of goods, particularly of fuel and food, became more difficult than passenger transportation. The lack of drivers, the destruction of trucks, and the gasoline shortage so severely disrupted freight transportation that the regular urban transit system had to take over part of the freight shipments during lulls in passenger traffic. In Berlin, for example, 12

---

[15] According to a sample survey of intracity travel in London in 1948, one-fourth of the regular users of public transport travel to theaters or cinemas. (*London Travel Survey, 1949* [London Transport Executive, London, 1950].) In ten cities in the United States, less than one-half of the passengers on public transportation facilities were commuting workers. (Carroll, *op. cit.*, 83.)

[16] Gauwirtschaftskammer, Hamburg, *loc. cit.*

[17] *USSBS*, Pacific report No. 58, p. 111.

per cent of the local freight was transported on streetcars by October, 1944.[18]

The effect of bombing upon the urban transit system and commutation can now be summarized. Destruction lengthens commutation trips and increases the percentage of the commuting population. Therefore the need for transportation will increase greatly, unless the working population of the city diminishes sharply because of casualties or evacuation. At the same time, destruction will reduce the physical and human resources of the transit system. The increased demand can only be met by the diminished and disrupted resources if the capacity of the remaining vehicles is sufficiently elastic to permit greater passenger loads through crowding, and if nonessential travel can be curtailed and essential commuting spread more evenly through queueing and staggered working hours. But if the elasticity is not sufficient, or if the actual increase in the consumer-resources ratio is smaller than the fully compensating increase, part of the workers remaining in the city after bombing will be unable to reach their workplaces, and their man power will be lost.

Communications and Urban Organization

The communication system within a city, and between a city and the rest of the country, is vitally important for the rehabilitation of the urban economy after bombing. As in the case of transportation, bombing destruction leads to an increased need for communications and at the same time reduces the available physical and human resources of the communications network.

In times of war, even before actual bombing attacks, the demand for fast communication will increase greatly because of the expanded economic activity and the many shortages and emergencies. The overloaded long-distance telephone facilities during World War II are well remembered in the United States. But after

[18] *USSBS*, European report No. 39, p. 26.

The Social Impact of *BOMB DESTRUCTION*

a city has suffered actual destruction, there will be another sharp rise in the demand for local and long-distance telephone connections and telegraph facilities.

First of all, the authorities will have to organize and control the civil defense efforts. Medical personnel and other rescue teams will have to be summoned. New suppliers for food, blankets, and repair tools will have to be located. The various administrative departments of the city, the suburban communities, and the national government will have to get in contact with each other frequently. Messages broadcast over surviving radio stations cannot match the value of personal telephone communications, for in order to organize rehabilitation efforts, top administrators should be able to appeal directly to colleagues or subordinates and to short-cut formal procedures through personal contacts. (Telephone conversations among high officials personally acquainted contributed a great deal to the efficient rehabilitation of Hamburg.)

Second, business and industry will suddenly have a much greater need for communications than before bombing. Replacements of personnel will have to be arranged, repairmen will have to be called, and many additional contacts will be necessary to find new office space, to search for raw materials, or to make new arrangements for the delivery of goods.

Finally, a third source of increased demand on communications after disaster will be the distress, anxiety, or curiosity of private citizens. Separated family members will want to get in touch with each other, and relatives or friends in town and out of town will be anxious to communicate with people in a bombed area to learn their fate.[19]

---

[19] Civil defense plans now generally include some procedures to assist citizens in tracing their relatives or friends after attack. Such schemes were organized in World War II. For example, a reporting office was established in Hamburg after the large attacks, and everybody who had lived in the city prior to the raids was requested through newspapers and radio broadcasts all over the country to report his new address to the police. All these reports were entered on standard forms

Communications and Urban Organization

The resources of urban communication systems suffer not only from direct bombing destruction but also from general wartime shortages, much the same as the transit system. Scarcities of labor and materials restrict expansions of the communications network (e.g., new telephone lines) and necessitate the postponement of replacements and repairs. Mail service in wartime deteriorates because of labor shortages and overloaded transportation facilities. Actual bombing destruction will demolish aboveground telephone lines, radio stations, central telephone exchanges, and post offices within the radius of housing destruction, because aboveground communication facilities are as vulnerable as houses, if not more so. Even underground communication facilities will be destroyed close to the center of a nuclear explosion. If a central telephone exchange or a radio station is destroyed, it may not be repaired for a long time because reconstruction would require so much skilled labor and scarce equipment. Therefore, physical protection of the telephone exchange offices in a city should have high priority in civil defense preparations. Mail service after destruction will be hampered by the many address changes caused by evacuation and reaccommodation. In fact, the hasty changes of addresses after World War II bombings made delivery of mail at times almost impossible.

In Nagasaki, the number of private telephone sets shortly after the end of the war amounted to only 13 per cent of the pre-bombing total. However, more than half of this loss was not due to destruction by the atomic bomb but to requisitioning by the city government and occupation forces.[20] In Kobe, the number of telephone sets per 100 inhabitants had declined from 4.07 to 1.97 between 1936

---

and filed alphabetically for the whole city. Inquiries about persons for whom no address was available were also filed, in case the missing person could be located later. (Hamburg Police President, *op. cit.*)

[20] By June, 1950, there were more telephone sets in Nagasaki than before the bombing. Source: *Nagasaki Shisei Yoran* (Nagasaki statistical outline), *1950*. p. 155.

and 1948;[21] percentagewise, this decline was greater than the loss of houses. In Hamburg, as a precaution, the city hall had been connected with three different telephone exchanges and with the police telephone system. However, after the third big raid, all four of these alternatives had been destroyed. In addition, the prepared messenger service with bicycles failed at first, because all of the bicycles had been destroyed (having been stored in one place).

A loss of communications facilities can be partly or fully compensated for by the elasticity of resources and by restrictions in nonessential consumption analogous to the post-destruction adjustments in transportation. Partial destruction, therefore, might be completely absorbed so that consumption would not decline, much as when housing destruction is below a certain percentage it does not produce a population loss. This was probably the case in Wuppertal, a city of some 300,000 inhabitants in the Ruhr district, which lost between 20 and 30 per cent of its residential housing during the heavy raids in May and June, 1943. Its postal and tele-

TABLE 11

EFFECT OF DESTRUCTION ON COMMUNICATIONS IN WUPPERTAL: PER CAPITA NUMBER OF TELEPHONE CALLS AND LETTERS

Period	Outgoing Long-distance Calls	Local Calls	Outgoing Letters
Pre-destruction			
March, 1943	2.7	7.6	13.8
April, 1943	2.6	7.0	14.2
Post-destruction			
August, 1943	3.0	3.3	8.3
October, 1943	3.6	5.6	12.1
December, 1943	3.6	6.3	11.7

Source: *USSBS*, unpublished records to European report No. 33.

[21] *Kobe-shi Tokei-sho, 1948–49, op. cit.*, Part IV, 52.

Communications and Urban Organization

phone services measured in per capita ratios, recuperated close to the pre-destruction level within half a year after the raids (Table 11). By contrast, Osaka, Kobe, and other Japanese cities were virtually without mail service after the bombing raids later in the war. Couriers maintained the most vital contacts.

For the more immediate effects of large bombing raids during the first few days after attack, the records from the city of Hamburg again provide illuminating examples. Four days after the last heavy raid the telegraph service again functioned normally. Mail service, on the other hand, was badly disrupted at first because many post offices had been destroyed; but eight days after the raids mail could be obtained at a few post offices, and on the twelfth day outgoing mail was being dispatched as usual. Newspapers, which are important communication media for any large city, were equally hard hit. The *Hamburger Zeitung* appeared on the eighth day after the raid, but in an edition of only about four hundred copies.[22]

As emphasized at the beginning of this section, the organization of a city depends almost entirely on its communications system. In addition to radio, newspapers, telephone, telegraph, and mail services, other media of communication or organizational mechanisms are important for the integration and co-ordination of economic activities. Most of these are also vulnerable to bombing, either because they rely on the primary communications services or because their office buildings, records, and personnel are subject to destruction. In this category belong such distributive or service institutions as banks, commodity markets, transportation services (e.g., moving firms and shipping brokers), employment agencies, and so forth. Stock exchanges and part of the insurance business would have less importance in times of an all-out emergency (ordinary insurance would not apply to war risks).[23]

[22] Gauwirtschaftskammer, Hamburg, *loc. cit.*
[23] During World War I the large stock exchanges in the United States and in

The Social Impact of *BOMB DESTRUCTION*

The records from Hamburg indicate that monetary credit for the retail trade became a serious problem as early as the fourth day after the main destruction. But on the seventh day the German central bank (Reichsbank) was reopened and supplied with banknotes,[24] and on the thirteenth day the stock and commodity exchanges were reopened. However, the postal money order organization (which in Germany largely takes the place of the United States' system of bank checks and the central clearing system through the Federal Reserve Bank) had to be transferred to the clearing offices in such faraway cities as Dresden, Leipzig, and Breslau.[25]

These organizational services are about equally vulnerable, whether they are run completely by the government (as in the Soviet Union) or partly by private concerns (as in most Western countries), because in case of emergency the elasticity of physical and human resources is more decisive than the formal administrative structure. In addition to the traditional mechanisms of economic organization, a great many new organizational tasks arise after bombing which have to be handled by the government. Billeting, rationing, damage compensation, and allocation of man power and scarce materials are all severely affected by the destruction of communications facilities and office records and by casualties among personnel. As a safety measure, the city of Hamburg prepared substitute administrative centers, equipped with the necessary forms and other office materials. These aid centers were suggested by Lübeck's experience in the earlier air raids. They could be used to give administrative help to the population through

---

Europe were closed at the outbreak of war. The New York Stock Exchange remained closed for four months without any serious financial disturbances. Cf. H. G. S. Noble, *The New York Stock Exchanges in the Crisis of 1914* (New York, The Country Life Press, 1915).

[24] In recent years old bank notes have been stored in the United States for such emergency use.

[25] Gauwirtschaftskammer, Hamburg, *loc. cit.*

Maintenance and Housekeeping Utilities

the provision of such things as rationing cards, money, departure certificates, and advice on the repair and safety of damaged buildings. The evaluation and processing of claims for compensation of bomb damage was a gigantic task, and long queues formed in front of these offices.[26]

Maintenance and Housekeeping Utilities

The urban transportation and communication systems tie a city together and sustain the organization of its complex economy. But additional utilities or services are necessary to maintain transit and communications systems and to facilitate housekeeping for city dwellers, or—in extreme situations—to make life in a large, modern city at all possible. These maintenance and housekeeping utilities are grouped together here because the vulnerability of their physical resources is rather similar, and, collectively, they all have a manifold impact upon the network of other urban functions. The group includes the supply of water, electricity, gas, and other fuels and the sewage and garbage disposal systems.

Partial housing destruction is likely to disrupt the system of distribution of water, electricity, and gas. Consequently, many dwellings, even though still serviceable, will be deprived of these essential utilities. If these services, especially the water supply, cannot be quickly restored, the inhabitants will either waste man-hours because of housekeeping difficulties (e.g., fetching water at some communal emergency supply), or they will abandon the city entirely. The electrical system is particularly vulnerable if it is aboveground and a shortage of labor and materials delays repairs. This is illustrated by data from Hiroshima in Table 12.

During the immediate aftermath of a bombing attack the urban water supply may be severely depleted because of the many leaks in damaged mains and the huge consumption for fire-fighting. In Hamburg the water supply was seriously disrupted, because

[26] Krogmann, *loc. cit.*

The Social Impact of BOMB DESTRUCTION

TABLE 12
THE EFFECT OF THE ATOMIC BOMB UPON ELECTRIC UTILITIES IN HIROSHIMA

(Number of units after the war as a percentage of the prewar figure.)

	After Atomic Bomb Attack, August, 1945	August, 1946	August, 1949
Number of electric lights	26.0	29.9	63.2
Number of houses with electric lights	26.8	32.6	73.7
Number of poles	40.0	45.4	64.6
Length of lines	48.8	59.2	117.8
Number of transformers	20.6	74.0	137.4

Source: *Shisei Yoran Hiroshima, 1949,* (*Statistical Outline of Hiroshima City*), p. 93.

many pumping stations were either destroyed or cut off from their power supply. The wells which had been dug in many parts of the city did not yield a sufficient amount of drinking water, and all available sprinkling cars and tank cars had to be marshaled to distribute water to the public. Destruction of all pipe-cutting machines impeded the repair of water mains.[27] The water supply in Hiroshima declined by about 30 per cent after the atomic explosion, but five months later the supply was back to the predestruction level (restoration of the distribution system, of course, took much longer).[28] In Tokyo, the water supply for the city as a whole did not suffer from the World War II bombings.[29] A prolonged lack of water would render habitation of a city or an urban district impossible. Such a calamity did not occur in any city bombed during World War II, except where the authorities decided to abandon a totally damaged area and accordingly made

---

[27] Hamburg Police President, *op. cit.*, and Krogmann, *loc. cit.*
[28] *Shisei Yoran Hiroshima, 1949, op. cit.*, 97.
[29] *Tokyo-to Tokei-sho, 1950, op. cit.*, 65.

Maintenance and Housekeeping Utilities

no attempt to restore any utility services. This was the case, for example, in Hamburg's completely devastated St. Georg district. The sewerage system is the least vulnerable of all utilities because it is completely underground. The large raids in Hamburg caused occasional damage to sewers, and because of the hot summer weather it was feared that epidemics might develop. But no serious effects from damaged sewers are reported either for Hamburg or for any other city bombed during World War II.[30] A disrupted water supply, however, will put flush toilets out of service—seemingly a minor inconvenience, yet World War II records point out correctly that this can be a problem of major concern in densely built-up areas.[31] The collection of garbage will also create difficulties after a major attack, mainly because collection vehicles are vulnerable to destruction.[32]

Industrial consumption of electricity and gas will drop immediately after attack because destruction of machinery and manpower shortages will curtail production. In combination with the disruption of the system of distribution, this can actually lead to an unused surplus of electric power or gas in a bombed city. This was the case in Hamburg. Nine days after the raids, production of electricity exceeded consumption. The urban supply of electricity, gas, and other fuels in times of war may be disrupted not only by the direct destruction of power stations or gas plants within the city, but also by a nationwide coal or power shortage.

A complete interruption of the supply of electricity, even for a

[30] Many breaks occurred in the sewers of German cities, only part of which could be repaired because of labor shortage (*USSBS*, European report No. 65, pp. 250–55).

[31] In Hamburg, the population of areas where the water was cut off were advised to build privies, and calcium chloride was made available (Krogmann, *loc cit.*).

[32] Of Hamburg's eighty-seven garbage-collection cars, seventy were destroyed in the big raids, and seven of the seventeen remaining ones subsequently broke down because of excessive use. Hence, garbage had to be deposited in temporary dumps among the ruins. (*Ibid.*)

The Social Impact of BOMB DESTRUCTION

short time, has far-reaching consequences for the entire technological system of a modern city. Streetcars and subways cannot run, traffic signals fail, elevators are stopped, radio stations, telephones, and telegraph lines cannot operate, pumping stations for drinking water (and, in some cities, pumps for sewage) stop working, and valuable food stocks spoil because refrigerators and cooling houses require electricity.[33] Yet, if there is only a partial loss in supply, rationing and curtailment of nonessential consumption can save the important mechanisms of a city from paralysis. Generally maintenance and housekeeping utilities are cushioned against the effects of partial destruction because they, too, have an elastic consumer-resources relationship.

We have seen that transportation, communication, and housekeeping utilities show varying degrees of adaptability to partial destruction. More nearly total destruction—such as would result from nuclear bombings—would probably break up the central network of utility systems, and surrounding regions would then have to reorganize their utility services on an independent basis. But complete failure of any of these services would certainly delay rehabilitation and might even jeopardize the lives of those who survive the bombing. Ingenuity and co-ordination in the effort to restore these utilities would be of great importance in the post-disaster period, even more so than the repair of housing, which can be done on a more gradual and individual basis. For the repair of utilities, skilled workers and highly specialized tools and parts are essential; hence this is an area where civil defense preparations can make significant contributions.

[33] Such an interruption of electrical service occurred in Leningrad in 1941, during the first winter of the siege (mainly because of the fuel shortage). This led to a paralysis of the industrial activity in the city and caused a progressive breakdown of the water and sewage systems (Leon Gouré, *Soviet Administrative Controls during the Siege of Leningrad* [The Rand Corporation, Santa Monica, Calif., RM–2075, 1957], 18, 44–45).

Chapter VI

FOOD SUPPLY AND OTHER ESSENTIALS

BEFORE DISCUSSING the effect of bombing upon consumer goods, it is necessary to consider the substantial changes in consumption and supply which generally occur in times of war even when there are no air raids against cities. The background upon which the bombing effects are superimposed changes in relation to the war economy as a whole. Consequently, bombing attacks at the very beginning of a war produce effects quite different from those produced by attacks coming later in a war.

It can be stated as a simple, leading rule that practically all consumer goods become scarce during a war and that scarcity increases with the length of the war. The principal reason for this is that labor and materials which normally serve civilian production have to be diverted to war production. As peacetime stock piles become exhausted and the demand for labor in war industries grows stronger, the scarcity of goods for civilian consumption becomes more acute.

In times of war, man power declines in the food trades as well as in nonessential civilian production. The government will, of course, attempt to maintain the production of sufficient basic foodstuffs and curtail the production of luxury food items. In Great Britain, for example, the number of bakers declined by only 33

The Social Impact of BOMB DESTRUCTION

per cent from July, 1939, to July, 1944, in contrast to the number of workers dealing with cocoa, chocolate, and candies, which declined by 63 per cent in the same period.[1] Table 13 shows the decline in the supply of many consumer goods during World War II. Some of these items—civilian radio sets and automobiles, for example—almost disappeared from the market because production facilities could be readily converted to war goods. Similar

TABLE 13

WARTIME DECLINE IN THE SUPPLY OF CIVILIAN GOODS IN GREAT BRITAIN

	1943, in Per Cent of 1935
Woolen blankets	34.0
Wool carpets and rugs	4.0
Brushes and brooms	42.0
Table knives	17.0
Spoons and forks	11.0
Radio sets	3.0
Trunks	11.0
Watches	5.0
Matches	61.0
Automobiles	0.0
Motorcycles	4.0
Bicycles	34.0

Computed from Great Britain, *Statistics Relating to the War Effort of the United Kingdom*, 28.

changes in civilian production occurred in the other industrial nations which fought in World War II.

These wartime changes in the supply of consumer goods are

---

[1] Computed from estimates in R. J. Hammond, *Food*, I (Hancock [editor], *op. cit.*), 398.

Food Supply and Other Essentials

accompanied by important changes in latent demand and actual consumption. Increased employment, higher wages, and a lack of capital goods available for investment purposes all strengthen the demand for consumer goods, while changes in actual consumption are dictated by shortages. For example, expenditures for goods that are not rationed or scarce tend to rise either relatively or absolutely since they provide an outlet for the inflated income of the population. In Great Britain, personal expenditures for consumer goods and services declined by 14 per cent from 1939 to 1944, in terms of 1938 prices. The proportion of expenditures for alcoholic beverages increased relatively from 6.6 to 7.4 per cent, for tobacco from 4.1 to 5.5 per cent, and for entertainment from 1.4 to 2.4 per cent. On the other hand, expenditures for clothing declined from 10.0 to 7.4 per cent of the total spent on consumer goods, the percentage for household goods decreased from 6.7 to 2.7 per cent, and that for operating private automobiles from 3.0 to as little as 0.2 per cent. Expenditures for food, being the least elastic, amounted to 30 per cent in 1944 as well as in 1938.[2] In general, the latent demand for food is greater in times of war because of higher incomes, yet it cannot be met by the supply. This leads to rationing, which equalizes the consumption for the entire population at a level dictated by the supply.

How and where food is eaten changes considerably during a war, although the total amount consumed remains relatively stable. The number of meals served in restaurants increases because more women are employed in industry and working hours are longer, thus making home cooking less feasible. A rationing system favoring restaurant meals (as was the case in England) and a shortage of favorite, easy-to-cook foodstuffs further increase the demand for restaurant meals. According to British data, shown in Table 14, the number of meals served in restaurants more than doubled

---

[2] Source of the data: W. K. Hancock and M. M. Gowing, *British War Economy* (Hancock, *ibid.*), 76.

during the war, part of the increase, of course, was prompted by the destruction of homes.

TABLE 14

RESTAURANTS AND MEALS SERVED IN GREAT BRITAIN

	May, 1941	Jan., 1942	July, 1943	Dec., 1944	Aug., 1945	Jan–Feb., 1946
Number of restaurants (in thousands)	111.0	114.1	137.5	147.2	149.5	143.2
Number of meals served in restaurants weekly (in millions)	79.0	144.0	170.5	170.5	181.7	157.1

Source: Hammond, *Food*, I (Hancock [editor], *op. cit.*), 399.

Food Supply after Bombing

Bombing reduces the supply of food for a number of reasons: damage to the transportation system by which food is brought to the city; destruction of food-processing factories; losses in food stocks within the bombed city because of destruction of storage rooms, magazines, and cooling houses, or through radioactive poisoning;[3] disruption of the distribution system because of the destruction of shops, markets, and intracity transit facilities; and impeded preparation of food on account of demolished restaurants and kitchens in private homes or because of an interruption in the supply of water or cooking fuel.

Fatalities have two opposite effects: they deprive the city of personnel in the food-supply distribution system, and they reduce the number of consumers. Evacuation also causes a decline in the total number of consumers who have to be fed within a city; but, on the other hand, it suddenly inflates the demand for food in re-

---

[3] The absorption of long-lived radioactive substances from the fall-out in plants used for human consumption is more important for the post-war period and will be dealt with in the last chapter.

Food Supply after Bombing

ception areas. Since reception areas are physically intact, the elasticity of their catering facilities can absorb a great increase in consumers if there are sufficient stocks of staple food items. Such food stocks in the vicinity of target cities, moreover, are exceedingly useful to cushion losses of stocks within cities because they can be shipped quickly into the bombed area.[4] Food depots which had been prepared outside the city of Hamburg proved of great value after the heavy raids in World War II.

Since destruction of housing and utilities drastically curtails the opportunities for cooking in homes and restaurants, mass feeding becomes necessary after an attack. In case of very heavy raids, food supplies will have to be shipped to the bombed areas from undamaged regions. Properly organized mass feeding can make a great contribution towards the rehabilitation of a bombed city and can enable the survivors to maintain industrial production.

Immediately after the large raids in Hamburg, an ample supply of food was either brought into the city from other areas of Germany or salvaged from destroyed warehouses within the city. The distribution was organized efficiently by the army and the National-Socialist Welfare Agency (NSV), using field kitchens of the armed forces and other mass-cooking equipment. Thus, about 200,000 persons were served both hot and cold food after the first big raid, and even more were served after the second and third raids.[5] For about a week rationing was virtually abolished, and foodstuffs which before the raids were unavailable even for coupons were distributed free to those who had stayed in the city.[6]

---

[4] In the United States, food stock-piled by the Department of Agriculture for purposes of price stabilization could make a substantial contribution to the feeding of survivors of bombing attacks if the stock piles are properly protected. Thus, these large stock piles—undesirable as they may be for other reasons—should be most welcome for civil defense purposes.

[5] Allegedly, some 1,200,000 people were served food after the second raid. This seems an exaggerated figure, however, for it is almost equal to the total population (*USSBS*, European report No. 65, p. 352).

[6] Gauwirtschaftskammer, Hamburg, *loc. cit.*

The Social Impact of *BOMB DESTRUCTION*

This naturally bolstered morale and encouraged the working population to carry on. By contrast, the post-raid organization of the food supply in Kobe was much less efficient. The difficulties "forced the immediate evacuation of air-raid victims. Over 12,000 tons of rice—the complete stock of Kobe's emergency supplies—were destroyed in the March and June attacks. After the June attack, food distribution was completely disorganized and never got back to anything approaching normal. As a consequence, black market activities and absenteeism due to the necessity of foraging became extremely serious despite efforts to mitigate the problem at key factories by direct food distribution."[7]

In English cities, mobile canteens kept ready-to-cook food for the population. These proved very useful, for example, after a heavy raid in London when 20 per cent of the consumers of cooking gas had their supply cut off and some boroughs were without normal water supplies for three days.[8] How the feeding of a whole city can be jeopardized by an extensive air raid is described in the following passage, which refers to Coventry, England, a city of over 200,000 inhabitants:

> The notorious raid . . . on the night of 14–15th, November 1940, was the first of a series that, while they never produced a breakdown of food supplies, caused officials to reflect upon the narrow margin of safety they possessed, not indeed in food stocks, but in the help that was available to a community temporarily reeling under a blow. In Coventry, gas, electricity, and water supplies were all interrupted in whole or in part; all bakeries, except one that relied on oil fuel, were therefore out of action, as were milk-pasteurizing and bottling plants. Bread, to the extent of 100,000 loaves in a single day, had to be brought from Birmingham and Stoke-on-Trent; milk from other towns. So many people had lost both ration book and retailer that ra-

[7] *USSBS*, Pacific report No. 58, p. 166.
[8] Titmuss, *op. cit.*, 267.

Food Supply after Bombing

tioning had to be suspended. (It had to be restored ten days later because of the influx of visitors.) Many local tradespeople, including the chairman and vice-chairman of the Ministry of Food area provisions and groceries committee, were killed or missing; of those that survived nearly all, reported the Divisional Food Officer, were stunned for a couple of days and dazed for some days afterwards.[9]

After the explosion of the atomic bomb in Nagasaki, the demand for emergency feeding was enormous. Meals were prepared in near-by towns and villages and brought to Nagasaki. According to available records,[10] some 25,000 lunches were served on the day the atomic explosion occurred (August 9, 1945). On the same day, 75,000 dinners were served, enough to feed more than half of all the survivors. The next day about 67,000 meals were served at breakfast, lunch, and dinner. Thereafter the feeding scheme was reduced rapidly, so that six days later only 1,400 meals were prepared. If these figures are correct, this represents a remarkable feat of organization that illustrates the great possibilities of mass feeding.

The relaxation or suspension of food rationing in Germany after bombing attacks had to be curtailed during the later years of World War II because of the heavy attacks on German cities and the increasing food shortage. Ration cards could be dispensed with for no longer than three days after a heavy raid. Mass feeding without coupons was restricted to those whose cooking facilities had been destroyed and who held special air-raid-victim certificates. This restriction could be lifted only if the supply of cooking gas or electricity was interrupted or if a great many restaurants had been destroyed. In case of heavy raids, extra rations could be granted by the Ministry of Food, presumably for the purpose of improving morale.[11] All of these restrictions emphasize that bomb-

[9] Hammond, *op. cit.*, 156.
[10] *USSBS*, unpublished records to Pacific report No. 10.
[11] *Ibid.*, unpublished records to European report No. 65.

The Social Impact of BOMB DESTRUCTION

ing destruction affects consumption more severely if it is superimposed on general wartime shortages than if it takes place at the beginning of a war when the elasticity of resources is greater.

In addition to emergency mass feeding immediately after a raid, German cities established "community kitchens" for the permanent feeding of part of the population. The data in Table 15 show that the percentage of a city's population that took advantage of these kitchens increased as the war continued. As home feeding became more difficult a growing number of persons apparently availed themselves of public meals.[12] Commutation difficulties may also have contributed to a greater demand for meals outside the home, since it is customary in German cities (and in

TABLE 15

INCREASE IN THE PERCENTAGE OF THE TOTAL POPULATION SUPPLIED BY COMMUNITY FEEDING IN SELECTED GERMAN CITIES, 1943–45*

Date	Hamburg†	Cologne‡	Darmstadt§
1943: January	2.3	6.3	—
February-March	—	—	7.0
June-July	6.1	8.1	6.3
October	5.0	6.9	—
November-December	—	—	7.7
1944: June-July	7.0	7.4	—
August-September	7.6	7.2	8.5
October-November	9.5	7.8	9.9
November-December	10.1	11.1	10.0
1945: March-April	10.9	—	10.3

*Computed on the basis of the number of people remaining in the city at each date (those supplied with rationing cards).
†*USSBS*, European report No. 32, p. 6a.
‡*Ibid.*, unpublished records to European report No. 41.
§*Ibid.*, European report No. 37, p. 3a.

[12] The reason could not have been a rationing advantage since those who ate at community kitchens had to surrender their cards (in contrast to restaurant meals in England).

Food Supply after Bombing

other Continental European cities) to take the midday meal at home if at all possible.

In Great Britain, organizations similar to the German community kitchens grew out of improvised facilities set up to fill the need for emergency feeding after air raids. These were first called "communal feeding centers," and later, "British restaurants." It was rather difficult to set them up during the war as the necessary equipment was in short supply.

The "British restaurants" gradually became well organized and not only took care of post-raid emergencies but also increased the restaurant capacity throughout the country, which was heavily taxed during wartime. To be ready for an emergency at any time, the "British restaurants" were equipped with boilers heated by solid fuel, so that they could operate without gas or electricity, which were often unavailable after heavy bombing raids. Also, where possible, they were furnished with water storage tanks. It is said that "the value of these precautions has been seen in many places where British Restaurants have been able to carry on during and after raids and render great service to the homeless. Inevitably a few Restaurants have been actually destroyed by bombs."[13]

The British restaurants, however, were numerically less important than Germany's community kitchens. In terms of the number of meals served, they accounted for only a small percentage of all restaurant eating: 1.5 per cent in January, 1942, and 3.0 per cent in March, 1944. More important were the industrial canteens, which, by March, 1944, provided 33.6 per cent of all meals served in restaurants.[14] As shown above (in table 14), the total number of restaurant meals increased considerably during the war.

The feeding of an urban population can be considered as a

---

[13] Sir Thomas G. Jones, *The Unbroken Front, Ministry of Food, 1916–44* (London, Everybody's Books, 1944), 127.

[14] The National Council of Social Service, *British Restaurants* (London, Oxford University Press, 1946), 10.

The Social Impact of BOMB DESTRUCTION

functionally homogeneous relationship between consumers and resources, analogous to a city's housing or transportation system. Since foods are consumable goods, however, there is a time factor which complicates the consumer-resources relationship so that it cannot be expressed in a simple formula like that for the housing relationship. The number of consumers is, of course, identical with the number of survivors, but the resources consist of two components: the pre-destruction food stocks minus destruction losses and the current post-destruction production (or import). The latter component, it will be recalled, can be ignored in the case of housing.

The short-term elasticity in this consumer-resources ratio arises primarily from two factors. First, the stock piles remaining after destruction cushion the loss from disrupted production and destroyed processing facilities. Second, for a few days or weeks, the daily per capita consumption can fall substantially below the normal level without serious effects on the health of the population. Of course, the larger the undestroyed stock piles and the wider the margin between pre-destruction per capita consumption and the physiological short-term minimum, the greater is the short-term elasticity. Hence the great importance to civil defense programs of locating food stock piles in places relatively safe from destruction yet near enough to target cities to be readily transported in spite of disrupted transportation. Furthermore, a city has a relative advantage whose normal per capita food consumption is so high that partial destruction of food-processing facilities (bakeries, milk-bottling plants, flour mills, meat-packing houses, etc.) still leaves enough for the population's minimum daily food requirements.

In the long run, however, the elasticity of food resources is more limited. The stock piles will be gradually exhausted without replenishment from current production, and a prolonged subnormal per capita consumption will lower health and man-power

Food Supply after Bombing

efficiency. By contrast, an urban population can be housed for a long time with only half, or even less, of the city's dwelling houses left, and people can still commute despite substantial destruction of transit facilities; but the daily consumption of food must, in the long run, be almost as large as under normal conditions.

Thus maintenance of a sufficient food supply in a bombed city is more decisive for the efficient functioning of man power than any other type of resource. A plentiful food supply, more readily obtainable within the city than outside, is one of the most effective incentives for workers to remain in a partially damaged city in spite of other deprivations and the danger of future attacks. This was an important factor in the remarkable recuperation of Hamburg. On the other hand, authorities will hardly be able to keep essential workers in a bombed city if the supply of food is not sufficient. During the later years of World War II, food became so scarce in German cities that workers resorted to week-end trips to the country to round out their food rations through purchases or foraging in farm areas. This caused absenteeism and increased the load on the overtaxed transportation system. The food scarcity in Japanese cities was generally worse than in German cities. It is reported from Kobe that day laborers, badly needed in the war industries, fled to the country after the heavy raids because of food shortages in the city.[15]

It has been emphasized that limited alternatives restrict the voluntary behavior of air-raid survivors. The daily need for food is the paramount limitation to such alternatives. This fact can be utilized by the government to influence the public, if it still controls the nation's food supply after bombing attacks. An evacuation policy or rehabilitation program after heavy attacks can be enforced most effectively by withholding ration cards from unauthorized evacuees and by increasing rations and special allow-

[15] *USSBS*, Pacific report No. 58, p. 158.

ances of hard-to-get foods for workers engaged in the recuperation effort.[16]

The Supply of Other Consumer Goods after Destruction

When there is widespread housing destruction, the distribution system of consumer goods will suffer because of the loss of retail shops, wholesale markets, and vehicles for the shipment of goods. In the city of Remscheid, Germany, for example, bombing affected primarily the shopping area; 56 per cent of the city's food-shop capacity (in terms of annual sales) was destroyed, 85 per cent of the tobacco shops were lost, and 90 per cent of the textile, hardware, and stationery shops were ruined.[17] In England, the department stores lost over 20 per cent of their floor space during World War II, primarily because their downtown locations made them vulnerable to bombing destruction. Of course, the small shopkeepers encountered greater difficulties than the larger stores in securing the goods and labor they needed.[18]

The British government attempted to concentrate business in the retail trade in order to save labor for war industries, but the closing down of small stores became ensnarled in administrative difficulties and provoked strong opposition from the owners in spite of financial compensation. More successful was the concentration of establishments in the cotton, hosiery, shoe, and pottery industries, which resulted in substantial savings in factory floor space and man power.[19]

During the immediate aftermath of a large air raid, the reorganization of the supply of consumer goods requires administrative

---

[16] At the height of the famine during the siege of Leningrad, the ration system provided the Soviet authorities with a very effective means of control. In this case, however, unauthorized evacuation was out of the question, because the city was cut off (Gouré, *op. cit.*, 66–67).

[17] *USSBS*, European report No. 36, p. 30.

[18] Hargreaves and Gowing, *op. cit.*, 265.

[19] *Ibid.*, 231.

The Supply of Other Consumer Goods after Destruction

assistance from the government. In England, so-called "area distribution officers" visited the bombed city to explain to the merchants the mechanism for replacing their stocks and insure that shopping facilities were kept open. Portable booths were stored regionally to be rented as temporary stores to merchants whose shops had been destroyed, but it turned out that they were not needed, since the merchants could move into empty premises or quickly repair their damaged shops. Thus a crisis in the distribution system was always avoided.[20] After the heavy raids in Hamburg, emergency food stores were set up in suburban towns under the supervision of the mayors.

The demand for consumer goods increases strongly after bombing. Destruction of homes creates a need for the replacement of household goods and clothing and all other personal effects. Thus, in Hamburg, long queues formed in front of the clothing shops after the heavy raids, and the situation was aggravated by a lack of sales personnel. Similarly, the urgency of repairs all over the city leads to an unprecedented demand for tools and other hardware appliances. A week after the raids in Hamburg tools had to be imported from other provinces because the wholesale hardware shops were largely destroyed.[21]

Household goods, particularly furniture, saved from partly damaged buildings or from buildings later destroyed by fire will still be serviceable if it is possible to store such items or to protect them against the weather. Salvaging operations are simple in peacetime when houses have been destroyed by fires, but after a major bombing attack, they become almost unmanageable because of the lack of moving equipment and storage space. It is remarkable that the moving and storage of salvaged furniture was still possible after the many raids on London.[22] And even in Hamburg, the

[20] *Ibid.*, 295, 299.
[21] Gauwirtschaftskammer, Hamburg, *loc. cit.*
[22] Titmuss, *op. cit.*, 282, 295–96.

army and private moving firms organized the transportation of furniture to storage places outside the city. Ironically, however, part of this furniture could not be returned because it was not identified even though all homeowners had been advised to mark their property long before the raid.[23]

In summary, bombing destruction has a threefold effect upon durable consumer goods and clothing. First, it destroys existing stocks and reduces current production of civilian goods (in wartime, civilian production is further curtailed because of shortages). Second, bombing disrupts the distribution system for consumer goods. And third, it suddenly creates an enormous increase in demand, far in excess of the highest demand ever occurring in peacetime, because housing destruction necessitates replacements in the entire range of household goods and personal effects. Consequently, everything will be in short supply, from kitchen utensils to personal apparel and from sewing needles to mattresses. Bedding is particularly important for the reaccommodation of homeless survivors, for wherever there is an increase in the number of persons per dwelling there is a corresponding demand for additional beds. The size of this new demand for consumer goods is proportional to the number of homeless survivors; hence it would be very large in case of nuclear bombing unless fatalities from radioactivity should substantially decimate the number of homeless. The government policy for financial compensation of bombing losses can regulate the effective demand, but it cannot change the latent demand for replacements.[24] Thus, during World War II, usually only a percentage of the bombing loss was compensated in cash, while additional compensation was credited to the owners but could not be spent until later (especially compen-

[23] Krogmann, *loc. cit.*
[24] Private property insurance would not cover bombing losses, since war damages are exempted in practically all policies.

Salvaging personal belongings after a World War II raid on Berlin. Note new addresses of former occupants written on wall.

COURTESY USSBS, NATIONAL ARCHIVES

Mobile soup kitchens in Berlin after World War II bombings.

COURTESY *USSBS*, NATIONAL ARCHIVES

The Supply of Other Consumer Goods after Destruction

sation for destroyed buildings).[25] However, if the cash compensation is too small, there will be resentment and distress among the bombing victims.

[25] After the Holland flood disaster of 1953, compensation for property losses could be granted on a more generous scale because the peacetime economy provided a large enough supply of consumer goods. The owners were compensated for their destroyed household goods on a piece basis according to a standard scale. A higher scale was applied for property owners in a higher income bracket, on the presumption that their household fixtures averaged a higher value per piece.

Chapter VII

THE TOTAL EFFECT ON URBAN MAN POWER

BOMB DESTRUCTION affects urban populations in many different ways. Some consequences of destruction are direct and immediate; others result quite indirectly. The preceding chapters have traced the principal ways in which bombing losses, both material and human, disrupt the functioning of urban society. The total effect of destruction on society, however, cannot be assessed simply by summing up all the losses sustained. There are subtractions from the urban system in the form of physical destruction and casualties, but there are also compensating additions, since a city is a living system capable of extensive readjustments.

In order to draw the balance between losses and compensations we must find a common unit of measurement. Since most of the social effects of bombing can be related to urban man power, the balance of losses and gains can be conveniently summarized in terms of the effect of bombings on the number of man-hours devoted to industries and activities essential for survival.

The present discussion of the total effect of bombing on man power will be confined to single cities or urban regions. In the next chapter the discussion will be extended to include nations as a whole, thus combining the situation in the bombed regions with that in the undestroyed remainder of a country. Such an over-all

Factors Reducing Man Power

balance for the final effect of bombing upon a people and the war effort will necessarily be very conjectural. Even the topic of this chapter, confined as it is to bombing effects upon city-wide or metropolitan man power, presents enormous difficulties, and all conclusions necessarily permit wide margins of error.

Factors Reducing Man Power

CASUALTIES

There is a distinction between direct and indirect man-power losses from casualties, as was pointed out earlier. The former is the numerical reduction in the number of workers who survive and are able to work, and the latter is the diversion of labor from productive activities to the care of casualties. Both types of losses were negligible under the conventional bombing of World War II. But nuclear bombing results in a much greater number of fatalities, more injured people, and many serious illnesses from initial and residual (fall-out) radiation. This triple man-power loss from fatalities, mechanical and heat injuries, and irradiation sickness constitutes one of the most important effects of nuclear bombing upon a nation's war or recuperation effort.

The assumption is frequently made that nuclear attacks upon the large cities of a country would somehow automatically result in a nationwide "breakdown," a paralysis of the whole country which would end the war immediately. No proof is given for this assumption, and nothing is said about what would happen to the war if this instantaneous "paralysis" occurred on both sides. It should be pointed out here that there is a very simple causal relationship between nuclear attacks and a nation's capacity to continue a war. This is the sheer numerical reduction in urban man power which results from casualties (i.e., death, injuries, and sickness). Until this clear-cut effect has been more carefully explored, there is no reason to accept such vague concepts as "breakdown of society" or "national collapse," which have an all-embracing, almost mystic connotation, and hence are not useful for an objective study.

The direct effect of casualties on manpower depends on two factors: the actual personnel effect of a bombing attack (i.e., the number of persons killed, wounded, or seriously affected by irradiation) and the compensating adjustments of the city or the country. The former are largely determined by the physical conditions of the explosion, and, a nation can introduce protective measures, such as pre-attack evacuation or shelters, which may substantially reduce the physical effect on personnel.

The indirect man-power effect of casualties will be serious in the event of widespread irradiation sickness. Those who are seriously ill from irradiation will require extensive nursing care for perhaps a year or even longer. This not only will tie up all available nursing facilities, but will keep family members who are unhurt from working full time or with full efficiency. Many healthy persons from the fringe areas of nuclear destruction will have to make a choice between nursing their sick and injured family members or working for the war or rehabilitation effort. Such a conflict exists even in peacetime disasters.[1] Its resolution depends on the strength of family ties as opposed to patriotism or fear of government coercion. In our society, it is likely that immediately after bombing a large segment of the surviving labor force will be preoccupied with the care of family members or close friends who are casualties. Later the government may be able to organize large emergency hospitals for the prolonged treatment of those suffering irradiation sickness and other serious injuries.

Fatalities also impose an indirect man-power drain, but this is much less than that caused by the sick and injured. Disposal of the dead must occupy some of the time which could otherwise be employed for repairs and other rehabilitation activities. Normal peacetime forms of burial, however, will have to be dispensed with,

[1] Killian, *loc. cit.*, 309–14.

Factors Reducing Man Power

and the effect of burials on man power will not be very important. In Hamburg, some 30,000 bodies—about three-fourths of all the fatalities—were buried in a mass grave prepared in the municipal cemetery with construction machines.[2]

HOMELESSNESS, EVACUATION, AND ABSENTEEISM

The man-power loss from housing destruction will be minimized if most of the bombed-out workers are able to find reaccommodation within the city and if those homeless people who do evacuate are largely nonessential to matters at hand. However, damage to private homes and the friction of reaccommodation will cause a loss in man-hours even if the number of workers in the urban area does not decline. The head of the family whose home has been destroyed will naturally want to help move his household to new quarters. In case of damage he undoubtedly will undertake the repairs himself because building workers are not available. Thus, damage to homes will cause absenteeism from

TABLE 16

AVERAGE NUMBER OF DAYS LOST PER WORKER DURING THE FIRST 17 DAYS AFTER A RAID

City	Date of Raid	Days Lost Because No Work Was Available	Days Lost Because of Personal Reasons (Work Available)
Coventry	November 14–15, 1940	2.5	2.0
Clydebank	March 14–15, 1941	2.2	6.5
Bootie	May 1–8, 1941	2.2	2.8
Creenock	May 5–7, 1941	2.2	3.0
Norwich	April 27–30, 1942	1.3	1.1
Exeter	April 23–26, 1942	2.5	1.1
Canterbury	May 31–June 1, 1942	1.2	1.3

Studies by the Ministry of Home Security, Research and Experiments Department. (Source: *USSBS*, unpublished records to European report No. 64b.)

[2] Krogmann, *loc. cit.*

The Social Impact of BOMB DESTRUCTION

work. According to a study made in England during World War II, a worker whose home was rendered permanently uninhabitable lost an average of six days from his job while seeking re-accommodation.[3] Table 16 shows that the British worker generally lost as many or more working hours after a raid because of damage to his home or other personal reasons than he did because no work was available on account of factory damage.

As a result, absenteeism after an air raid aggravates the labor loss which is due to evacuation and casualties. Only a reduced number of workers remain in the city, and those who do stay work less because they must repair their homes. In Osaka, factory payrolls declined by 40 per cent from January to July, 1945; in addition, average attendance rates among the 60 per cent of the workers who remained at their jobs declined from 79 per cent to 59 per cent.[4]

Evacuation of nonessential persons, by definition, leaves the urban labor force unaffected. World War II experience indicates, however, that visits to evacuated family members sometimes leads to absenteeism, and that workers whose wives have been evacuated become less efficient because of unsettled home lives and inadequate meals.

Short-term pre-attack evacuation of the whole population—the principal civil defense measure presently advocated in the United States—will, of course, interrupt the entire urban economy. But the short time loss in man-hours will be absolutely irrelevant in comparison with the number of casualties that may be prevented. In case of repeated attacks—or, rather, repeated threats of attack—this type of evacuation could eventually disrupt production—a small price to pay for the prevention of huge casualties. However, if attacks have materialized in some cities and there remains a sustained threat of additional attacks in other cities, short-term evacuation will probably be abandoned by the majority of city

[3] Titmuss, *op. cit.*, 341.
[4] *USSBS*, Pacific report No. 58, p. 104.

Factors Reducing Man Power

dwellers, and workers as well as nonessential people will resort to a more permanent long-term evacuation.

Long-term evacuation of workers leads to a loss in productivity because the employment opportunities for evacuees in the reception areas will be much less favorable than in the cities. Many evacuated workers will probably remain unemployed for a considerable period of time. Long-term evacuation of the whole population of a city is a likely consequence of nuclear warfare, especially if the devastated areas remain dangerously radioactive for some time. While this situation did not arise during World War II, some provisions for the re-employment of evacuees were introduced. In England, government-sponsored evacuees who were normally employed were ordered to register for employment if they were without work, thus enabling the authorities in reception areas to find the newly available workers who had come as evacuees.[5]

The prevailing type of evacuation in World War II was the long-term removal of nonessential urban residents; hence, the manpower loss from evacuation was relatively small. For example, one month after the heavy raids on Hamburg, employment in manufacturing industries had declined by only 1.8 per cent, but at the same time about 40 per cent of the population was still evacuated. The textile industry suffered a 55 per cent decline in employment, the largest loss for a single industry; and the food industry, with a decrease of 9 per cent, had the second largest loss.[6] Both of these industries employed a large percentage of women, who, apparently, evacuated to a greater extent than men workers.

The fear of future attacks was an important cause of absenteeism during World War II. In the last year of the war Japanese factory workers often stayed away from their jobs because they

[5] Great Britain, Ministry of Labor and National Service, *Report for the Years 1939–46*, 42. The regulation was called the "Evacuated Persons Employment Order."

[6] *USSBS*, European report No. 32, p. 34b.

The Social Impact of BOMB DESTRUCTION

feared the daytime raids on their plants. Under nuclear bombing, fear of future attacks will lead to evacuation rather than to absenteeism, since a person's home will be no safer than his factory or office. It has been stressed that the anticipation of future attacks is exceedingly important for motivating city dwellers to evacuate and remain in evacuation. Accordingly, in a situation where future attacks seem likely, the principal cause of the urban man-power decline, apart from casualties, will be this anticipation of further bombing.

Finally, there is absenteeism because of an increased sick rate among the workers. In several German cities, an excessive number of workers were absent on sick leave after the heavy raids.[7] This was due partly to minor illnesses induced by the bombing experience, such as shock, neurogenic heart and stomach disorders, and peptic ulcers.[8] But many of the absences represented malingering which had its roots in the fear of future bombing or in the desire to repair a damaged home.

LABOR NEED FOR CIVIL DEFENSE, REPAIRS, AND DISPERSAL

Civil defense will absorb a great many man-hours prior to an attack as well as after. Many civil defense tasks, such as the clearing of debris from the streets and the decontamination of radioactive objects, require skilled workers. In World War II it was

---

[7] *Ibid.*, European report No. 65, p. 108. It is interesting to note, however, that in spite of this post-bombing increase in the sick rate, there was a decline in the over-all number of disabled workers up to 1943 in the Krupp industries (and probably in other German industries). This overcompensation of the bombing losses was due to fewer industrial accidents or perhaps to better safety measures. On the other hand, German wartime statistics understate absenteeism, because many unauthorized absences were not reported by managers in order to avoid trouble for their workers and the factory. (*Ibid.*, European report No. 64b, Vol. I, 54.) In bombed German cities absenteeism seems to have been roughly double the normal rate (*ibid.*, 58-59).

[8] *Ibid.*, 99. A marked increase in the incidence of peptic ulcers has also been recorded in Great Britain and other countries after air raids (Janis, *Air War and Emotional Stress*, 90-91).

Factors Reducing Man Power

generally possible to rescue persons trapped in collapsed buildings and thereby save a great many lives. Under conditions of a nuclear attack, manpower and tools would not be available to rescue a significant number of trapped people. Unless self-rescue is possible, they would thus become fatalities.

In World War II many civil defense activities were carried out after working hours to allow personnel to remain regularly employed during the daytime. As the air raids in Great Britain became less devastating, civil defense workers were released, subject to recall in the event of a new emergency.[9] Only 1.3 to 1.7 per cent of England's working population was ever engaged in full-time civil defense activities, as compared with the 11 to 23 per cent who were in the armed forces.[10]

After an attack more labor will be required for repairs than for actual civil defense measures. In the event of war the building trade will be monopolized by defense work of top priority, such as the construction and repair of air bases, arsenals, communication centers, docks, and railroads. Hence the construction industries will have neither the man power nor the materials for the general repair of bombed cities. Furthermore, manpower in the building trade will decline much as does the population at large because of casualties and evacuation. One month after the heavy raids in Hamburg only 38 per cent of the building workers remained, and it took seven months for the building trade to recover 80 per cent of its pre-destruction strength.[11]

The shortage of construction workers and the gigantic needs for repairs will prompt the authorities to establish a priority system and to rationalize and expedite building activities. Preference will

---

[9] The peak in civil defense employment in Great Britain was reached by the end of 1941, when 400,000 people were engaged full time and a further 1,250,000 were employed part time (H. M. D. Parker, *Manpower*, 195).

[10] W. K. Hancock (editor), *Statistical Digest of the War* (London, H. M. Stationery Office, 1951).

[11] *USSBS*, European report No. 32, p. 18.

be given to construction and repair work which can salvage the maximum number of housing units with the available labor. This means that completely demolished buildings will be left untouched, unless the rubble has to be cleared from important thoroughfares. Similarly, no repairs will be made in habitable dwellings where the damage does not jeopardize the safety of the structure or the health of its occupants.

In Hamburg this priority system was regulated in great detail. Minor damage to roofs, doors, and windows was repaired by emergency squads. The building workers formed teams under the organization of the guilds to make the most urgent repairs according to minimum standards. These standards were specified minutely so that labor could not be diverted by bribes to unnecessary repairs.[12]

In London a special organization was set up to increase the labor force and expedite repairs of bomb damage. Building firms from other parts of England and Scotland were brought into the city. The districts within London exchanged their building workers according to the needs dictated by the attacks. It is said that:

> Labor was allotted in the first place to the various boroughs in proportion to the damage to be repaired. In some areas the work was exceptionally difficult and complicated, in others it was interrupted by new damage. At first the London Repairs Executive was determined to avoid the substantial movement of labour from one London area to another, but encouraged the transfer of small numbers of repair workers from some of the boroughs where the programme was far advanced to other boroughs where the work was going more slowly. At the end of 1944, however, when the labour forces in the different areas were reviewed, it became clear that if houses were to be repaired in the right order, and if the second-stage repairs were to be completed everywhere before the third-stage repairs were begun

[12] Krogmann, *loc. cit.*

Factors Reducing Man Power

anywhere, there must be movement of labour on a considerable scale.[13]

By December, 1944, there were about 130,000 men employed in the London civil defense region for the repair of bomb damage.[14] They constituted a very large portion of London's entire working force; about one out of every fifteen employed workers in Greater London was occupied with bomb-damage repair.

Decontamination of radioactive buildings, plants, railroad yards, and similar installations requires an enormous amount of man power and many special tools, such as measuring instruments, bulldozers, and water-hosing equipment. Clearly, such work would have to be confined to a few key installations or transportation arteries, since neither the labor nor the tools for clearing a large area would be available. If measuring instruments were plentiful it would be conceivable that householders could decontaminate their own homes—given the proper instructions—much as minor damage was repaired by the homeowners themselves during World War II.

Post-attack dispersal of plants may be desirable because of radioactivity or anticipated future attacks, but it will be feasible only to a limited extent since it would involve an additional drain on labor and especially on building workers. Underground construction in particular is expensive in terms of labor and building materials. In England, some aircraft factories were dispersed by breaking them into smaller units, and a few plants were put underground. Yet the labor shortage was such an impediment that altogether only seven underground structures were built in England during the war.[15] Germany succeeded in putting some oil

[13] C. M. Kohan, *Works and Buildings*, 226.
[14] By March, 1945, this figure had risen to 135,000, about 50,000 of whom had been recruited from the provinces. The housing of all these transferred workers in London was a major problem in itself. (Parker, *op. cit.*, 250–51.)
[15] Kohan, *op. cit.*, 316–17.

refineries underground during 1944, but after that a large-scale program could no longer be implemented.[16] A hasty dispersal of plants was initiated in Japan after the heavy attacks. This aggravated the existing labor shortage, placed an additional burden on the transportation system, and led to a further loss in production.[17]

TIME-LOSS AND LOWERED EFFICIENCY FROM AIR-RAID ALERTS

So far we have confined ourselves to the effects of actual physical destruction from bombing. This does not cover the entire impact of bombing raids upon urban man power. Air raids alone lead to a social disturbance, even if they are not accompanied by any physical damage. The loss of working hours because of daytime alerts and the loss of sleep because of nighttime alerts constituted serious problems during World War II. Nighttime alerts created fatigue and nervous tension which reduced the efficiency of workers and increased absenteeism and illness.

In case of air-raid alerts against nuclear bombing, these effects would be greatly accentuated. During World War II it was possible to have different degrees of air-raid warnings; if only a few enemy bomber planes were involved it was not necessary to disrupt all activities in a city. But with the threat of nuclear bombing one enemy plane could mean a great disaster, and the entire population would have to protect itself. Moreover, persons who had once witnessed an atomic explosion or had received graphic accounts of one from near-by cities would take each alert seriously. In World War II, urban populations became conditioned to smaller air raids, and most activities in a city continued during a minor air-raid alert without greatly endangering human life or creating anxieties. Alerts against nuclear bombing, on the other hand, would lead to an almost complete disruption of all urban activities throughout a country.

[16] *USSBS*, European report No. 112.
[17] *Ibid.*, Pacific report No. 57, p. 30.

Factors Reducing Man Power

INEFFICIENCY AND DISORGANIZATION DUE TO DESTRUCTION

It is frequently said that the most decisive effect of large-scale bombing destruction is chaotic disorganization of the national economy or of society in general. Here we are concerned with the loss of man-hours arising from the various organizational difficulties that are caused by physical destruction or casualties. Organizational aspects enter into people's lives in so many different ways that it is impossible to estimate all the losses in man-hours which arise because of less efficient or disrupted mechanisms of organization and co-ordination.

Some order can be introduced by separating the man-hour loss caused by increased friction or disorganization of the private lives of workers from the loss in man-hours caused by disrupted relationships within the production process.[18]

Some working hours will be wasted after a disaster because many of the daily activities of private life become more time-consuming. During World War II, transit difficulties in Japanese cities contributed greatly to absenteeism. The aftermath of bomb destruction will not only make the journey to work more time-consuming and thus reduce the possibilities for a longer working day, but many other daily chores will demand more energy from the worker and thus reduce his productivity. The purchase of food and clothing may require many hours instead of merely a short shopping trip on the way home from work. Visits to the doctor and the bank, laundry services, and car repairs will all take more time than previously. Housewives will be unable to spend as much time working in industries if they have to queue for food. During the last war, welfare officers in England tried to work out schemes to alleviate the shopping difficulties for working women. Neighbors who were not employed were urged to do the

---

[18] We will not deal with the loss in output which stems directly from demolished machinery or the destruction of factories, since this is more a question of engineering than of the social impact of bomb destruction.

The Social Impact of BOMB DESTRUCTION

shopping for working women, and systems for placing orders and collecting the goods at a given time and place were adopted.

Apart from these difficulties in the daily activities of the workers, an additional loss in man-hours results from the disruption of normal business relationships and the disorganization of production processes. This disruption springs from the physical destruction of communications facilities and the casualties among managerial or executive personnel. Administrators within different business firms or branch offices many lose time in making necessary contacts because telephone, telegraph, and mail service are less efficient or even completely disrupted. Since the normal procedures will have become invalid, a great number of managerial man-hours will be spent in reorganizing a firm after a bombing attack. Surviving managers will be faced with a host of cumbersome new tasks, such as finding replacements for employees who were casualties, getting in touch with workers who evacuated, locating new suppliers of raw materials, organizing rationing procedures, and working out new arrangements with shippers, wholesalers, brokers, and insurance companies.[19]

MOBILIZATION FOR THE ARMED FORCES

Mobilization is not a direct effect of bomb destruction, and it is mentioned here only to complete the catalog of the total labor force. Mobilization which takes place before bombing naturally reduces urban man power. After destruction has occurred, this loss may be keenly felt, especially in those occupations for which there is an excessive demand, such as construction work.

The percentage of the labor force absorbed by the armed forces tends to increase as the war is prolonged. In Great Britain the percentage of the working population in the armed forces and

[19] The possible disruption of large U. S. corporations is discussed by Margaret Bright Rowan and Harry V. Kincaid, in *The Views of Corporation Executives on the Probable Effect of the Loss of Company Headquarters in Wartime* (The Rand Corporation, Santa Monica, Calif., RM-1723, 1956).

Factors Increasing Man Power

auxiliary services (excluding civil defense) rose from 11 per cent in 1940 to 23 per cent in 1944. In Germany it rose from 14 per cent of the total labor force (including foreigners) in 1940 to 28 per cent in 1944.[20]

The great problem in times of nuclear bombing is, of course, to what extent mobilization for the armed forces may still be possible after widespread destruction has occurred in many cities. Apart from the casualty loss in potential military man power, there will be difficulties in the mobilization procedures because of disrupted communications and transportation. Furthermore, rescue, repairs, and rehabilitation will create strong competing demands for the surviving labor force.

Factors Increasing Man Power

EMPLOYMENT OF PERSONS FORMERLY NOT IN THE LABOR FORCE

During wartime, people who are normally not employed can be drawn into the labor force to compensate for the man-power losses sustained on account of bombing and mobilization. In World War II many housewives joined the ranks of workers, primarily in defense industries. Thus, in England the number of women in the metal industries was about three times as large in 1945 as in 1939. But in the textile industry the number of women decreased, since the industry as a whole was sharply curtailed. Thirty-eight per cent of the British industrial labor force were women in 1945, as compared with 27 per cent in 1939. On the other hand, in Germany the maximum number of women employed during the war was only slightly above the prewar level.[21]

---

[20] Source of data: Hancock, *op. cit.*, 8; and *USSBS*, European report No. 3, p. 207.

[21] Great Britain, Ministry of Labour and National Service, *op. cit.*, 128, 150; and *USSBS*, European report No. 3, p. 34. Excluding the increase in the labor force because of the population rise, Germany did not have more females at work during the war than before, while the United States added 35 per cent and Britain 21 per

The Social Impact of *BOMB DESTRUCTION*

Other sources of urban man power include old people in retirement and young persons not yet in the labor force. In Japanese cities after the heavy raids, when the labor supply became very short, students were conscripted and put to work in war factories. This form of conscription was fairly successful because students could be drafted and put to work in class groups under control of their teachers. This procedure also simplified the organizational problem during a time when disrupted communications made it difficult to control conscripted labor. The attendance rates of conscripted students in Kyoto were persistently better than those of other conscripted or regular workers.[22]

In World War II considerable time elapsed until participation in the labor force reached its maximum. It took from one to three years for the maximum number of women, retired persons, and young people to become part of the labor force. After nuclear disasters the demand for additional workers would be much more urgent than it was during the rather gradual mobilization process of World War II, and the time required for persons formerly not employed to enter the labor force would depend on governmental organization and incentives. Extra food rations or tobacco allowances may be more important than wages for these marginal workers.

LENGTHENING OF THE WORK WEEK

While the recruiting and training of new or retired workers

---

cent to its female labor force (allowing for population increase). Germany had comparatively higher allowances for dependents of members of the armed forces than Great Britain and the United States (considering differences in income level). This probably reduced the incentives for German women to take wartime jobs. Cf. Clarence D. Long, *The Labor Force in War and Transition: Four Countries* (National Bureau of Economic Research, *Occasional Paper 36*, New York, 1952), 3, 41–43. A particular difficulty with newly recruited women workers is that they have less geographic mobility than men because of family obligations (Parker, *op. cit.*, 288–92).

[22] *USSBS*, Pacific report No. 58, pp. 11, 254.

Hamburg in August, 1943, after the big fire raids.

COURTESY *USSBS*, NATIONAL ARCHIVES

Hiroshima in October, 1945, two months after the atomic bombing. Main streets were cleared of rubble, but there was only pedestrian traffic.

COURTESY *USSBS*, NATIONAL ARCHIVES

COURTESY WIDE WORLD PHOTOS

Hiroshima, ten years later. The area is completely rebuilt.

Factors Increasing Man Power

takes time, the work week can be lengthened almost immediately and therefore would constitute the most important source of additional man-hours after sudden nuclear destruction in cities. In a country where the work week is relatively short before destruction, there is more leeway for adding hours than in countries with long working hours. The concept of "elasticity" applies here also: the man-power resources are not fully utilized where work hours are short and the participation rate of the population in the labor force is low (few women, young people, and old people employed). In such a case, expansion to compensate for a bombing loss is more readily possible, just as cities with a low housing density can better absorb destruction than those that are crowded.

For Germany the data on the work week during World War II do not indicate much of an increase over the average. But the average figures are misleading, because the increase of part-time employment lowered the average length of the work week. The work week in Germany in all industries increased from 47.6 hours in March, 1939, to 49.1 in March, 1943, and then declined again slightly.[23] In comparison, the work week in the United States increased from 42 hours to about 45 hours during the war.[24]

CONVERSION FROM NONESSENTIAL TO WAR PRODUCTION

Fatalities and evacuation will reduce the number of consumers in a partially damaged city. This will theoretically lead to a decrease in the demand for consumer goods and services; however, the number of workers who thus become available for war industries is rather small. The reduction in consumption on account of evacuation or fatalities is not likely to close down whole establishments, but it will lessen the work load. This gain is easily absorbed by the loss in time and efficiency which results from destruction.

[23] *Ibid.*, European report No. 3, p. 215.
[24] A. J. Jaffe and Charles D. Stewart, *Manpower Resources and Utilization* (New York, John Wiley Sons, 1951), 205.

The Social Impact of *BOMB DESTRUCTION*

A forced transfer of workers from civilian production or services to war industries was introduced in many cities during World War II. In Kyoto such a shift from nonessential to war production took place at the expense of the textile industry. From October, 1943, to February, 1945, the percentage of Kyoto's total industrial employment in metal manufacturing rose from 43 to 62 per cent, while the percentage engaged in textiles declined from 38 to 7 per cent.

In Osaka a special program was designed to enroll everyone not regularly engaged in essential industries for at least sixty days' emergency work during a year. But this reallocation of man power was not successful. The air raids had disrupted many of the neighborhood organizations which were supposed to recruit workers for emergency labor, and the authorities found it so difficult to evaluate the many conflicting requests for additional labor made by the war industries that it was impossible to allocate recruited workers efficiently.[25]

In Germany it was primarily the distribution services which were curtailed to make labor available for production work. In Hamburg, the number of firms and employees engaged in wholesale trade was reduced by over 50 per cent between 1939 and May, 1944. The retail trade, especially food shops, declined even more.[26] This decline was only partly due to physical destruction. A comparison of the dates for the successive reductions in the number of retail firms with the dates of air raids shows that a large part of the decline in retail trade was the result of official curtailment policies rather than the direct effect of destruction.

During the latter part of the war the German authorities organized special drives to augment the labor supply. Persons still outside of the labor force were to be recruited, and nonessential enterprises were to close down or reduce the number of their em-

---

[25] *USSBS*, Pacific report No. 58, pp. 110, 112, and 253.
[26] *Ibid.*, European report No. 32, pp. 29, 30.

Factors Increasing Man Power

ployees. But while the number of retail shops declined, the labor force did not increase correspondingly. A principal cause of failure was the discrepancy between the registration of workers and their actual placement in war industries. Many of the recruited workers could not be placed in a job, presumably because they lacked the necessary skill or because there were organizational difficulties.

The forced expansion of the labor force necessarily involves many administrative measures, any one of which may easily break down in a bombed city since the whole administrative apparatus is impaired by destruction. The additional man power has to be located and registered, and then the registered workers have to be classified and grouped according to their abilities, skills, and location. Next, the claims and demands from the various industries require evaluation, screening, and matching with the new labor supply. Finally, the allocation of new workers has to be supervised; many a worker may fail to report for work or may quit after a short try.

The discrepancy between registration and actual placement of labor is well demonstrated by statistics for Berlin's man-power recruiting drives (see Table 17). These figures, furthermore, show that each successive drive had to draw from increasingly depleted resources. Therefore the means of enforcement had to be strengthened and the range of nonessential activities widened. Altogether, these recruitments added about 12 per cent to Berlin's labor force.

Since the transfer of workers from essential occupations to war production evidently meets with considerable administrative friction and takes a long time it cannot relieve the man-power shortage in the event of sudden attacks. However, evacuated workers who remain in reception areas will find themselves divorced from their former jobs and will thus be more readily available for new assignments in emergency activities than persons who are somehow able to maintain their former positions in the nonessential labor force. The very severity of the disruption caused by nuclear attacks may

The Social Impact of *BOMB DESTRUCTION*

TABLE 17

DRIVES TO INCREASE THE LABOR FORCE FOR WAR INDUSTRIES IN BERLIN

Measures used and date	Number of workers registered		Number of workers placed	
	Men	Women	Men	Women
January, 1943—Compulsory labor registration law for persons not fully occupied	28,045	209,111	4,442	90,723
March-July, 1943—Closing down and restricting commercial enterprises	13,872	15,750	7,984	9,840
August-November, 1943—Combing out the civilian production and services for nonessential workers	—	—	14,773	38,553
1944—"Voluntary honor service"	108	4,527	71	1,720
1944—Declaration of total war (primarily reducing personnel in civil administration)	13,674	54,018	8,376	42,999
Total: absolute	55,699	283,406	35,646	183,835
In per cent of the total labor force	19.0		12.0	

Source: *USSBS*, unpublished records to European report No. 39.

overcome a certain inertia in the reallocation of man power. But this will be the case only with unskilled labor; the reallocation of skilled man power will be slowed down severely because of disrupted organizational mechanisms.

SUMMARY

There are several factors which decrease urban man power in

Factors Increasing Man Power

the event of bombing, and there are other factors which partly or fully compensate for this loss. In a great many cities that were severely damaged during World War II, the man-power loss was almost completely compensated. Through selective evacuation, the decline in man power was significantly less than the total population loss. Accordingly, an increasing percentage of the total population was in the labor force. In Hamburg the proportion of inhabitants in the labor force increased by 9 per cent between 1942 and 1945, and in Berlin, Düsseldorf, and Darmstadt it increased by 12 per cent.

Figure 10 illustrates how a potential man-power loss could be cushioned successfully in a partially damaged city, not causing any decline in its important war industries. Forty per cent of Berlin's housing was destroyed, and the city lost 33.3 per cent of its population. As housing elasticity permitted the reaccommodation of its homeless workers, evacuation could be confined largely to persons who were not in the labor force, and the labor force decline was much smaller than the population loss. Major productive industries suffered no loss at all; conversion from less essential occupations probably helped to replace the relatively few workers who had evacuated or were casualties.

It must also be remembered that a large portion of the urban labor force is engaged in providing goods and services for the city's inhabitants and in maintaining the city's physical apparatus and administration. According to A. J. Jaffe's estimates, these maintenance activities amount to about 73 per cent of the total labor force in large American cities (over 100,000 inhabitants).[27] By curtailing civilian consumption, labor can be converted from maintenance activities to war production. This must have been the case during World War II in the United Kingdom as well as in the

[27] "Urban Manpower and Problems of Mobilization" (unpublished [mimeographed] report, Bureau of Applied Social Research, Columbia University, October, 1951).

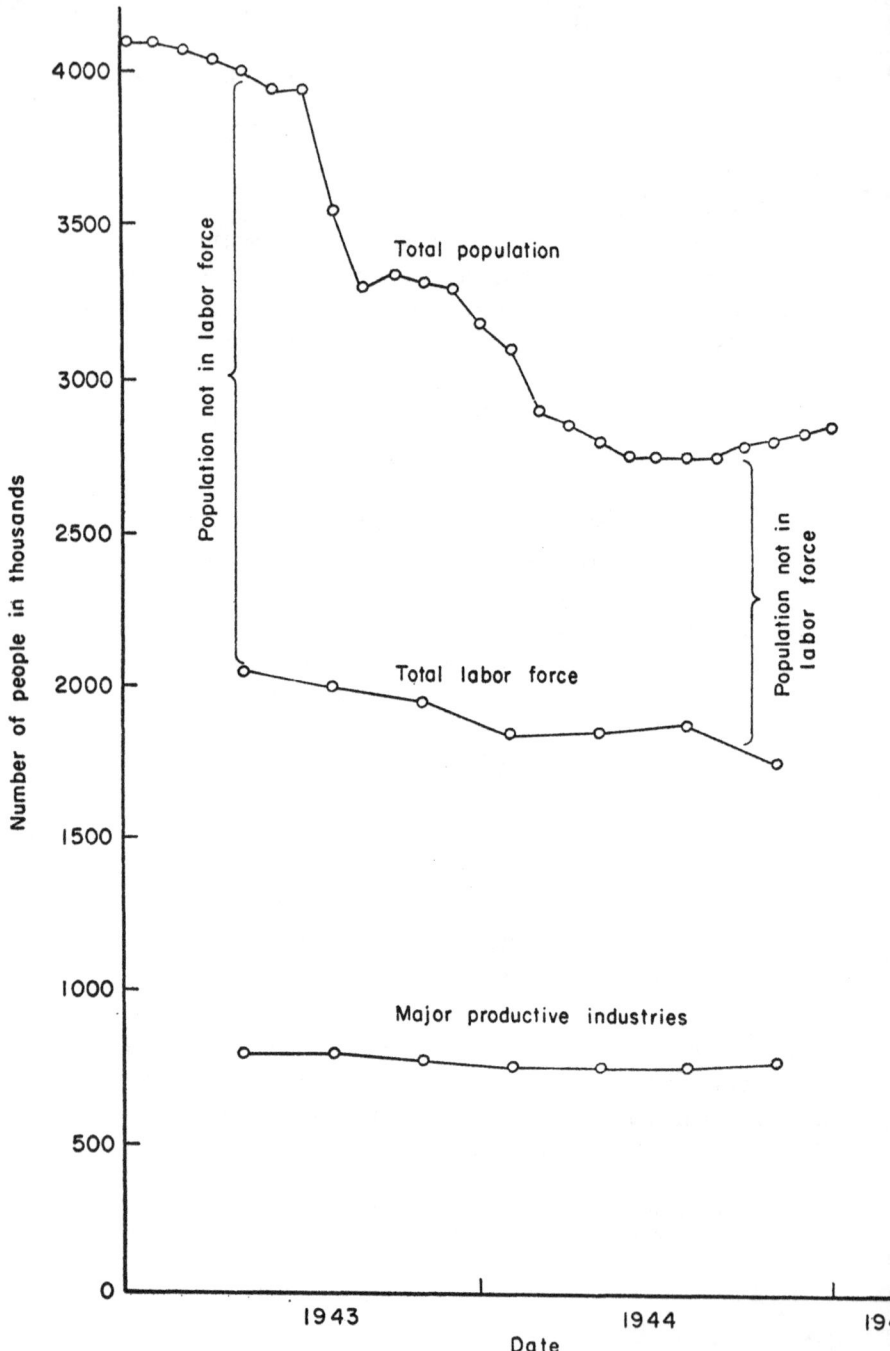

Fig. 10.—— Population and manpower loss in Berlin

Factors Increasing Man Power

United States, because the labor force statistics show a decline in maintenance activities.

The most significant facts about urban man power can now be recapitulated. First, after nuclear attacks, casualties constitute by far the most important loss in labor force. They reduce the number of able-bodied workers, and they cause a prolonged drain on man power through the attendant nursing needs of people with nonfatal injuries, particularly radiation sickness. Second, long-term evacuation removes workers from the urban industrial sites (but many of those would be physically destroyed anyway), leaving, however, the possibility of some re-employment in the reception areas if industrial towns and smaller cities remain free of serious damage. Third, a further loss in productive man power is caused by repair and decontamination activities. And lastly, there is widespread disorganization, which leads to a waste of man-hours and lowered efficiency, especially immediately after attack.

The measure which can compensate some of this man-power loss most rapidly is the lengthening of the working week. In the long run, an increase in labor force participation (i.e., adding young people, women, and retired workers) will further augment the man-power resources. However, transfer from nonessential to essential activities is administratively cumbersome and takes considerable time to become effective.

Chapter VIII

THE CUMULATIVE IMPACT
ON THE NATIONAL WAR EFFORT

IT IS NOW technically feasible for the great world powers to cause stupendous destruction anywhere on the earth. This threat alone has a decisive influence upon war and peace. The impact of the latent power of nuclear weapons will be felt increasingly as the stock piles of weapons and means of delivery grow larger and more efficient. It imposes a potent ultimate constraint upon international politics and military actions. Thus nuclear bombs may alter the course of history by their mere existence. Indeed, the potential devastation that nuclear bombing could cause gives rise to the hope that an all-out war may be forever avoided. This idea was eloquently expressed in Sir Winston Churchill's speech on defense and the hydrogen bomb, in which he said that we may reach a stage "where safety will be the sturdy child of terror, and survival the twin brother of annihilation."[1]

The actual effect of the use of nuclear weapons upon the outcome of a war seems to be a more remote problem, fortunately, than the deterrent effect of unused nuclear capabilities. However, since we are concerned here with the social impact of actual bomb

[1] Address in the House of Commons, March 1, 1955. For recent discussions of the problems of deterrence and limited warfare, see William W. Kaufmann (editor), *Military Policy and National Security* (Princeton, Princeton University Press, 1956); and Henry A. Kissinger, *Nuclear War and Foreign Policy* (New York, Harper & Brothers, 1957).

The Cumulative Impact on the National War Effort

destruction and not with the political and military implications of potential destruction, we must consider the effect of actual bombing on war and peace in order to evaluate realistically what bombing might do to people and society.

One must remember that the social effects of bombing, such as the losses in population, man power, and other urban resources, together with the subsequent readjustments, can occur only in the political context of aggression and defense. The disaster forms an integral part of an international war, and its social effects are inseparably connected with the termination or continuation of hostilities.

Strangely enough, the relation between nuclear bombing and the termination of war has received little public attention, possibly because of two obstacles: first, most people encounter an emotional block when they try to imagine the aftermath of horror and misery in the context of continued hostilities and with the prospect of further devastation and terror; and second, there is an intellectual difficulty of comprehending a world in which war continues amid widespread nuclear destruction. It is difficult enough to picture a nuclear disaster's occurring in a society whose only effort is to mitigate its effects—as in the case of natural calamities—and the additional task of relating bombing effects to a continued war effort seems almost insurmountable. As a result, public discussions of nuclear bombing have generally left the impression that a war would end as soon as nuclear attacks have been launched. The heritage of death and destruction is then pictured as a part of the postwar period, and the way in which the thermonuclear war would be terminated remains unexplained.

It is significant that the bombings of Hiroshima and Nagasaki did not cause the survivors to lose interest in the outcome of the war. Indeed, to many citizens the fate of the nation and the hoped-for victory seemed more important than their own individual survival. Whether such a reaction was peculiar to the Japanese

The Social Impact of *BOMB DESTRUCTION*

is hard to say, but all accounts confirm their continued concern about defeat or victory. Most striking is an incident reported from one of Hiroshima's hospitals, where patients, severely wounded or ill and without adequate care, were suddenly cheered when they heard the false rumor that Japan also possessed the superweapon and had retaliated in kind, bombing San Fancisco, San Diego, and Los Angeles. Thus, "the whole atmosphere in the ward changed, and for the first time since Hiroshima was bombed, everyone became cheerful and bright. Those who had been hurt most were the happiest."[2] The desire for vengeance might prevail over the desire for victory, especially if nuclear destruction should be more nationwide than was the case in Japan and if the survivors could be better informed about the true extent of destruction and casualties. But if the survivors should begin to feel that the substance of their nation is lost, many of them might become mainly interested in saving their families and their own lives.

The Economy of the Remainder

Hydrogen bombs can cause destruction in such a large area that a single bomb could demolish nearly all the resources of a large city or even of a metropolitan region. Only the resources located underground could escape obliteration. Protective measures, such as evacuation and deep shelters, could save a substantial part of the population, but there would not be sufficient physical resources left to revitalize the city while the war continued. Furthermore, residual radioactivity near the site of the explosion might necessitate long-term evacuation of all the survivors. Hence the compensation and recuperation processes discussed in the preceding chapters would have to take place on a nationwide scale. The elasticity of housing, for example, would quickly be exhausted within the metropolitan region, and urban survivors would have to be billeted in other areas of the country.

[2] Michihiko Hachiya, *Hiroshima Diary*, 48.

The Economy of the Remainder

A disaster of this magnitude cannot be comprehended in terms of its local effects on single cities, but must be assessed within a larger framework. Basically, the post-attack situation is determined by the resources which remain to the country as a whole. Foremost in importance, of course, is the size of the total national population that survives the urban attacks and escapes the possible fall-out effects. Next in importance are the total food and housing left in the nation and the ability of the transportation system to bring survivors to the remaining billets and food to all the people. These are the prerequisites for the survival of the nation and of any economic or military potential.

A more detailed estimate of what would remain of a country's economy after nuclear bombing requires specific assumptions about the extent and nature of the attack. Because we do not intend to speculate here about present and future capabilities of weapons, we can deal with this problem only abstractly.

The population remaining after attacks consists of those people who escape death or serious injury because they were either sufficiently far away from the nuclear explosion or protected by shelters. A combination of shelter and distance may constitute the most important form of protection for the population of a whole country. It is theoretically conceivable that the area of total mortality for persons not protected by specially equipped, deep shelters could cover an entire country. Considering the lethal range of one of several hydrogen bombs, this becomes a real possibility in the case of very small countries. But excluding this extreme, the following components would remain after an attack: the rural population, which would not suffer serious harm from fall-out, and the total physical resources of farms and mines; the inhabitants of small towns (if they are not affected by or are protected against fall-out) and the total physical resources in these towns; and probably a large number of urban refugees and possibly a number of larger and smaller cities which, for one reason

The Social Impact of BOMB DESTRUCTION

or another, escaped destruction. The economic, military, and political functions of this remainder would determine the war effort of a nation that has suffered a nuclear attack.

Throughout the areas affected by bombing, the economy will at first be totally disrupted because of the casualties, the physical damage, and the tremendous fall-out hazard. Before anything else, the people will have to satisfy their most urgent needs for food and housing. In the long run, food will be more critical than housing because all evacuees can eventually find billets by doubling up in the undestroyed houses in small towns and villages. However, enough food will be left in the country because the destroyed cities are consumers rather than producers of food. In a country like the United States, which has large stock piles of food the effects of radioactive contamination of livestock and crops could be cushioned until new crops were available—provided, however, there would not be renewed or lingering contamination affecting the next crop. The threat of starvation among the survivors will arise not from a basic lack of foodstuffs within the nation as a whole, but from the difficulties of transporting and distributing food to all the people. If food has been stock-piled in widely separated places throughout the nation, no area will be entirely without food after an attack in spite of disrupted transportation.

Following urban destruction of great magnitude, it is inevitable that many commodities will be scarce and some will be missing entirely. A number of factors will be responsible for the great gaps that will appear in what remains of the economy. Reserves of certain types of goods in undestroyed areas are likely to be very small and the time required to put them into production again very long. There will be a shortage of man power for building factories where none existed before; component products and raw materials will be lacking or scarce; and the high casualty rate may leave practically no survivors with the necessary specialized skills

National Organization and Decision-Making

in fields in which the training of new specialists may require several years.[3]

Examples of the urban concentration of skilled executive personnel and technical experts can readily be found. In the United States in 1950, for instance, 80 per cent of all the aeronautical engineers were located in seventeen standard metropolitan areas, and 80 per cent of all the metallurgical engineers were found in sixty metropolitan areas. The concentration is even greater among business executives: 90 per cent of the top officers in the 180 largest American corporations were located in less than forty metropolitan areas.[4]

National Organization and Decision-Making

Our analysis of the partial destruction of cities in World War II has shown that the losses in current production were proportionately smaller than the losses in urban resources. We attributed this outcome to the elasticity of the physical resources and to the relatively small number of casualties. Predictions about the possible effects of nuclear destruction, on the other hand, frequently suggest that the losses for the country as a whole would be larger than the total amount of actual destruction. It is argued that disorganization would spread over the undestroyed remainder of the country and that the extensive devastations would deprive the national economy of many irreplaceable components. As a result, the parts of the country that remain intact would also suffer serious disruptions or cease to function altogether.

[3] A case of high casualties among specialized experts caused the delay of an important military effort during World War II. Hans Rumpf (in *Der Hochrote Hahn*, 101) reports that an American day raid on August 17, 1943, destroyed the guided missile research institute at Peenemünde, killing almost the entire research staff and thus causing a delay of "more than six months" in the weapons program.

[4] Margaret B. Rowan and Takuya Maruyama, *The Concentration of Essential Personnel in American Cities* (The Rand Corporation, Santa Monica, Calif., RM-1722, 1956).

The Social Impact of BOMB DESTRUCTION

It is, of course, impossible to predict to what degree disruption would ensue from nuclear attacks because this depends on the size and nature of the destruction. It is known, however, that with the kind of damage that occurred in World War II certain forms of nationwide disruption were discernible, especially in transportation. Therefore, it seems justified to assume that nuclear destruction would lead to very substantial disorganization and economic disruption in those parts of the attacked country which remain intact and unharmed.

Since it is impossible to describe comprehensively the nationwide disorganization resulting from nuclear attacks, we must confine ourselves to some of the crucial elements in a country's organizational system and examine the extent to which they would be vulnerable to disruption. The area in which disorganization would have the most immediate effect on the outcome of the war is that involving the co-ordination of those components of the armed forces already in existence before the initial attack took place. If urban destruction is widespread, the total defensive and offensive position of the country will hinge on these existing forces since effective mobilization of new forces and resumed war production will have to be discounted for a considerable time. Hence the organization of the existing military forces is obviously decisive.

There arises the question of whether or not the co-ordination and direction of these military forces would necessarily be seriously disrupted by the physical and social effects of large-scale nuclear attacks. It is conceivable that the technical apparatus and the personnel necessary for military organization will have been completely separated from the urban communications network and physically protected against the anticipated bombing effects. Immediate military disorganization, therefore, is not a necessary consequence of disruptions in the urban economy from nuclear attacks. Whether the military organization of a country will actually be divorced from the urban structure and physically protected will

National Organization and Decision-Making

depend on the advance preparations of the armed forces themselves. The fact that this separation and protection is possible—in comparison with other defense measures it is actually quite cheap—does not, however, guarantee that a particular country will have made adequate preparations.

The continuity of the national government depends on the survival of the principal government officials (or the effective designation of successors) and on a communications system which permits these officials to maintain contact with each other and to retain control over the military and local authorities.) The problem of survival and succession has been dealt with earlier, and we shall now examine the question of communications and control.

It may be useful to approach the problem from the bottom of the governmental hierarchy. In areas which have suffered no severe physical destruction, the offices and facilities of the local government will remain serviceable. If there is a danger from fall-out, the local government personnel may be forced to remain in shelters for several days. But it is readily conceivable that important offices could be rendered perfectly safe against fall-out radiation. Thus the mayor's office, the headquarters of the police, civil defense, local army commands, and so on could continue to function effectively during the crucial days after a nationwide attack. The extent to which protective preparations have been made will determine the continuity of local government in the fall-out areas. However, failures in electric power may extend into areas which are otherwise intact and disrupt telephone and radio communications.

The most urgent task of the local authorities in undestroyed areas which are not subject to fall-out will be to accommodate evacuees and to send relief in the form of food and medical help to the stricken cities. In areas where there is a fall-out hazard, however, decontamination and other safety procedures must take precedence over outside relief work.

In the days immediately following large attacks on urban areas, most people in undamaged areas where they cannot perceive the effects of the bombing will not be paralyzed by panic or chaos, and the local government officials will be entirely capable of fulfilling their usual duties. Sheer inertia and the lack of alternative courses of action will help to maintain order and will induce many persons to continue their daily routine. There will be nothing for the small-town housewives or farmers to do but continue looking after their children or working on their farms. If informed of the dangers from bombing, some may build or improve their shelters or evacuate to areas which are considered still safer. Changes will surely occur, but they will be brought about gradually by the influx of evacuees and the increasing shortage of all the goods that formerly came from the cities.

Law and order will be maintained by the inertia of cultural traits and the persistence of people's habits. The great devastations may offer opportunities for looting, but law-abiding citizens will not suddenly turn into criminals. There is absolutely no evidence from past disasters of a precipitate increase in crime, although a gradual rise in the delinquency rate usually occurs during prolonged wars. It is quite likely that some looting will take place after bombing attacks, especially in the partially damaged areas, but it will be completely overshadowed by immensely more serious problems, such as the huge casualties, the fall-out hazard, and the food and water shortages.[5] Such an inordinate amount of attention has been given to the possibility of looting and other crimes

---

[5] Michihiko Hachiya mentions that looting occurred in Hiroshima about three weeks after the bombing and one week after the surrender (*op. cit.*, 117). The surrender undermined the authority of the police and army and probably contributed more to the lawlessness than the bombing itself. However, it is evident from Hachiya's diary that these instances of looting made little difference in a disaster of such magnitude. The unimportance of looting in natural disasters is well documented in Charles E. Fritz and J. H. Mathewson, *Convergence Behavior in Disasters: A Problem in Social Control* (Committee on Disaster Studies, National Academy of Sciences, National Research Council *Publication No. 476*, Washington, 1957), 52-55.

National Organization and Decision-Making

after nuclear bombings that this bias deserves to be corrected; in comparison with the other consequences of nuclear devastation, looting will be truly insignificant.

A likely target for bombing attacks attempting to bring about nationwide disruption is the site of the national government. In the event of a successful nuclear attack on the capital, the continued functioning of the government will depend on strongly sheltered offices or on the evacuation of the staffs before the bombing takes place. But surviving officials cannot operate in emergency headquarters if they are cut off from the rest of the country. They must re-establish contact with the military forces and the local authorities in undestroyed parts of the nation. Conversely, the local authorities and military commanders must be told that parts of the national government have survived. They must accept the emergency government as legitimate, know its location or contact points, and be able to receive and issue communications. Disruption of communications between the local and national authorities will arise not only from the destruction of the capital but also from misunderstanding and confusion at the local level.[6] Local officials are not normally prepared to take orders from out-of-the-way emergency headquarters and from unfamiliar officials in high government positions.

The delegation of decision-making to regional and local levels will greatly facilitate the continuity of administrative functions at a time when the traditional hierarchy of the government has been disrupted,[7] but independent action of local government officials cannot lead to a co-ordinated national policy without directives from a central authority.

[6] After the heavy raids in Hamburg, city officials believed false rumors that the national government in Berlin had been evacuated. As a result, a delegate was sent to Berlin to find the new location of government offices. (Gauwirtschaftskammer, Hamburg, *loc. cit.*)

[7] Decentralization of decisions is recommended by Walter E. Todd, Willard S. Paul, and Val Peterson in "National Defense against Atomic Attack," *The Scientific Monthly*, Vol. LXXX, No. 4 (April, 1955), 240–49.

The Social Impact of *BOMB DESTRUCTION*

The continuity of an effective national government and the implementation of policy decisions on a nationwide scale are very intricate processes even under normal peacetime conditions. Problems of authority, power structure, and public administration are involved; these are complex phenomena which differ from country to country. Therefore, one cannot glibly predict that national paralysis will follow from a given level of destruction or postulate that the governmental structure will be disrupted after the capital has been hit. Neither can one foresee whether the co-ordination of the military forces will cease after widespread urban devastation or whether anarchy will prevail throughout the stricken country. The possibility of such consequences cannot be denied, but many qualifications must be considered, and it would be difficult to make any general predictions without knowing the situation in great detail.

Nationwide Transportation

Protective measures could be quite effective in preventing disruptions from nuclear attacks to a country's communications system and its governmental machinery, but the nationwide transportation network is more vulnerable and more difficult to protect because it depends on extensive, physically exposed resources which are largely concentrated in cities. In the early years of World War II, well-organized emergency crews repaired the bomb-damaged railroad yards in Hamburg, and through traffic was resumed only a few days after the raids had destroyed half of the city's housing. The number of outgoing freight cars amounted to half the predestruction figure during the first month after their raids, and three months later it had nearly reached the pre-raid level.[8]

However, serious disruptions in the German and Japanese railroad systems occurred later in the war, when the lines were cut repeatedly at many places and fuel became short and a large per-

[8] *USSBS*, unpublished records to European report No. 32.

centage of the rolling stock was damaged or destroyed. The repair crews then could no longer keep up with the rate of destruction, and the disruptions had a cumulative effect.[9]

Multiple attacks with nuclear weapons would disrupt a nationwide transportation system much more severely than did the final stages of the bombing campaigns against Germany and Japan. Damage to the highway system and airports would aggravate the effects on the railroads. There would be physical destruction of highways in the bombed cities, and an acute shortage of gasoline would result because of damaged refining and distributing facilities. After thermonuclear attacks, bomb craters and highly radioactive spots could render important traffic centers impassable for a long period of time. Undamaged airports and highways that by-pass bombed cities might be the only facilities for nationwide transportation, and the available stocks of gasoline would permit only a small volume of traffic. Furthermore, large casualties would decimate the ranks of transportation workers and divert man power from repair work.

As a result of disruptions in the transportation system, the whole country might be economically divided into islands of undamaged rural areas or cities. These islands might still contain valuable resources, but would probably have an unbalanced economy. Hence the economic worth of the remainder would be less than the total of the nation's undestroyed resources would suggest. To use a familiar example, if iron ore and coal cannot be brought together, there can be no steel production in spite of undamaged mines and some undestroyed steel mills. Widely distributed stock piles of raw materials could cushion the disruptions caused by severed traffic connections, but the movement of finished goods to the consumer would have to wait until means for bulk transportation had been restored. Some regions might remain unable to exchange goods with other parts of the country until the end of

[9] *Ibid.*, European report No. 200, *passim.*

The Social Impact of BOMB DESTRUCTION

the war. Thus, havoc in the nationwide transportation system is a further reason why the mobilization of armed forces and war production cannot be very effective after multiple nuclear attacks.[10]

"Broken-backed Warfare"

The British White Paper on defense for 1954 employed the term "broken-backed warfare" to describe the conduct of hostilities after intense atomic attacks.[11] Although this term has since come into general use, little has been added that clarifies its original implication. The prevailing assumption is that a nuclear war, if it should come, would begin with massive initial attacks by the aggressor, rather than more gradual attacks which would forego the advantage of surprise and permit stronger retaliation. These nuclear surprise attacks would then be met by immediate counterattacks with nuclear weapons—provided capabilities to mount counterattacks survived. Their purpose would be to stifle the military power of the aggressor, particularly his power for further nuclear attacks, and also to inflict heavy damage on the enemy country as a whole.

---

[10] Hornell Hart's discussion of the cumulative effects of a sudden raid on many cities in the United States also stresses the disruption of transportation as one of the most critical causes of the breakdown of the national economy. ("The Remedies versus the Menace," *Bulletin of the Atomic Scientists*, Vol. X, No. 6 [June, 1954], 197–205.)

[11] *Statement on Defence, 1954*, Cmd. 9075 (London, H. M. Stationery Office, 1954). The key passage reads: "If, by some miscalculation in Communist policy or by deliberate design, a global war were to be forced upon us, it must be assumed that atomic weapons would be employed by both sides. In this event, it seems likely that such a war would begin with a period of intense atomic attacks lasting a relatively short time but inflicting great destruction and damage. If no decisive result were reached in this opening phase, hostilities would decline in intensity, though perhaps less so at sea than elsewhere, and a period of 'broken-backed' warfare would follow, during which the opposing sides would seek to recover their strength, carrying on the struggle in the meantime as best they might." The more recent British White Papers on defense are more concerned with deterrence than with the "broken-backed warfare," thus reflecting the true objectives of the defense effort. But the term remains a useful name for hostilities that continue after deterrence has failed.

"Broken-backed Warfare"

However, instead of the intense initial atomic attacks, one can visualize a less precipitate beginning of nuclear warfare. Localized or peripheral hostilities may spread and eventually lead to nuclear bombing—rather by accident than by design—perhaps after there has first been a limited tactical use of atomic weapons. In an era of mutual deterrence this may be a more serious danger than the dreaded surprise attack[12] because a strategy which is based on an initial nuclear onslaught would almost certainly provoke retaliation in kind and thus jeopardize the very purpose of the strategy and threaten to destroy all its political objectives.

However a nuclear war begins—whether gradually or with a surprise attack—the question remains: How will the destruction and its social and military consequences lead to a termination of the war? There are basically two alternatives: either the end comes about immediately—that is, the initial nuclear attacks are quickly decisive—or there is a transitional period between the initial attacks and the termination of the war. In the latter case, the hostilities conducted during this period may be called "broken-backed warfare."[13] The transitional period can only be avoided if the government of one of the belligerents surrenders at once or if both belligerents immediately accept a cease-fire and later negotiate a truce.

A government which considers surrendering to the enemy after

---

[12] Hans J. Morgenthau considers dispersal of atomic capabilities among many nations as a factor that may in the future increase the risk of a nuclear war ("Has Atomic War Really Become Impossible?" *Bulletin of the Atomic Scientists*, Vol. XII, No. 1 [January, 1956], 7–9).

[13] There has been a tendency to picture "broken-backed warfare" as a form of terminal military operations conducted primarily with conventional weapons. This concept seems unrealistic since the conventional weapons system would be more vulnerable than nuclear capabilities—especially in an era of large nuclear stock piles, guided missiles, and submarines capable of launching nuclear bombs. Hence, according to our interpretation, "broken-backed warfare" will be significant because nuclear weapons can still be employed. Conventional military operations, however, will be unfeasible or unimportant. Cf. Bernard Brodie, "Nuclear Weapons and Changing Strategic Outlooks, *Bulletin of the Atomic Scientists*, Vol. XIII, No. 2 (February, 1957), 56–61.

its country has suffered nuclear attacks will have to evaluate a combination of highly uncertain and incommensurable factors.[14] These include: the chances that a continued war effort will be successful, the political and territorial gains this effort would bring if successful, the destruction and casualties that would be incurred during continued hostilities, and the chances of obtaining a stalemate or truce instead of surrender. And, unless the military superiority of the enemy power is quite obvious, the government leaders will also wish to consider the possibility that the enemy may surrender first. Hence they must evaluate how all these factors look to the enemy from his vantage point. If the leaders then conclude that the enemy must consider his situation hopeless, they may prefer to await his surrender. The issue, therefore, depends critically on the government's estimate of the military and political strength and capabilities of the enemy as compared with its own. But with all the disruptions and upheavals from nuclear destruction it will be very difficult to assess the remaining national capabilities, let alone estimating the enemy's capabilities.

It is possible that the surviving leaders of a bombed country will neglect these intricacies and decide to surrender without attempting such complex estimates, impelled solely by the magnitude of destruction and suffering in the country. However, even with such a short-cut decision, there will still remain the difficulty of putting the surrender into effect, against the opposition, perhaps, of dissident die-hards.

Finally, surrender—like a truce—is a two-sided decision, depending on some agreement and co-operation between the two belligerents. It is difficult enough to arrive at such an agreement in conventional wars, where the belligerents have plenty of time to arrange for diplomatic representation through a neutral country and where international communications function uninter-

---

[14] For a general discussion of the mechanisms of surrender, see Paul Kecskemeti, *Strategic Surrender* (Stanford, California, Stanford University Press, 1958).

"Broken-backed Warfare"

ruptedly. The history of Japan's surrender from late in 1944 until its consummation in August, 1945, illustrates how difficult it is for a government to surrender as long as the homeland remains unoccupied, even if the military superiority of the enemy is undeniable. In the case of Japan the difficulties were due partly to die-hard militarists, partly to inadequate communications, and partly to tragic misunderstandings about Japan's minimum conditions for surrender in contrast to the political objectives of the United States.

In spite of these obstacles to a quick surrender or a truce, hostilities would cease immediately if the nuclear attacks destroyed nearly all of the men and materiel necessary for further fighting. This, indeed, may be one of the main objectives of the attacks; but if the existing military forces have been properly protected and separated from the urban system, some part of them may continue to function after attack. In this case the hostilities would not cease without a truce agreement.

Although the idea that there could be "broken-backed warfare" after massive nuclear attacks seems rather unlikely at first glance, it appears more likely after we have considered the alternatives. The fact is that none of the alternatives—surrender, truce, or a technical cessation of hostilities—may materialize quickly enough to prevent "broken-backed warfare." This type of warfare is surely not part of the original strategy upon which an aggressor would deliberately embark, but it may develop by default because the belligerents cannot find any other course of action. It then will become the decisive transition from the original nuclear bombings to the termination of the war. As such, it will shape the political situation of the postwar world. Although it is totally unpredictable and scarcely imaginable, it may determine the boundaries of entire continents, it may lead to the formation or disappearance of states, and it may bring a monopoly or abolition of nuclear power in the future.

The Social Impact of *BOMB DESTRUCTION*

We have previously concluded that widespread nuclear bombing damage would practically put an end to war production and make the mobilization of troops temporarily impossible.[15] Although this conclusion seems plausible, one must not be absolutely certain of it, since the actual outcome would depend largely on the magnitude of destruction in relation to the total national resources. For short-run military operations, however, the direct impact of bombing on existing land, naval, and air forces would be more important than the destruction of the mobilization potential.

How the surviving population and the remnants of the urban economy will bear up during the period of "broken-backed warfare" depends not only on the initial casualties and destruction but also on the prospect of repeated attacks. If the first raids appear to be the only substantial bombing attacks, the survivors can focus their energies on a continuous repair and recuperation program, and, more important, they can expect that things will get better rather than worse. In the event of widespread radiation injuries there will be a wave of increased sickness after two or three weeks, and many of those who become ill will die within the next month or so. But once the acute radiation syndrome has run its course the impact of bereavements and personnel losses will subside. We can judge from World War II evidence that the evacuees from destroyed or damaged cities will then tend to return rather quickly since the threat of additional attacks will seem remote. The gradual recuperation of the urban industrial areas will be one of the most important developments during a "broken-backed" war in which there are no further heavy bombing attacks. Prerequisite to urban

---

[15] As early as 1946 Bernard Brodie expressed this proposition with regard to the atomic bomb. "The idea which must be driven home above all else is that a military establishment which is expected to fight on after the nation has undergone atomic bomb attack must be prepared to fight with the men already mobilized and with the equipment already in the arsenals." (*The Absolute Weapon: Atomic Power and World Order,* 88). If one reckons with thermonuclear bombs and fallout effects, there can surely be little quarrel with this proposition.

recovery, of course, will be the survival of a substantial portion of the city dwellers.

It is perhaps more realistic to assume that there will be other nuclear attacks during the period of "broken-backed warfare," especially if the termination of the war is further delayed and if some means for delivering nuclear weapons remains after the initial assault. In this case the situation for the survivors will change radically: the threat of additional attacks will keep the evacuees from returning and will result in the evacuation of other areas which the inhabitants consider to be likely targets. The threat of bombing will assume an immensely stronger aspect of reality for those who have witnessed a nuclear attack. To a large extent, this sense of reality concerning the threat will also arise even though the attacks took place in other parts of the same country if news reports and eyewitness accounts reach the unbombed cities. This heightened fear of bombing among the survivors of an atomic attack is seen in reports from Hiroshima and Nagasaki. According to Irving L. Janis' study of the Hiroshima records, "one of the most frequent types of sustained emotional disturbances appears to have been a phobic-like fear of exposure to another traumatic disaster. This reaction consisted in strong feelings of apprehensiveness accompanied by exaggerated efforts to ward off new threats."[16]

Our imagination is appalled when we try to visualize the state of a society which is exposed to additional nuclear attacks during a period of "broken-backed warfare." As a result of the initial disaster all reception areas around the target cities will be crowded with refugees, many of them sick or injured. Radiation sicknesses

[16] Janis, *Air War and Emotional Stress*, 46. Grinker and Spiegel, in their study of pilots in World War II, found that the actual experience of a danger contributed greatly to the fear of future threats: "Fear of enemy activity is seldom concrete until the flier has seen a convincing demonstration of what damage can be inflicted, and how little can be done to avoid it. After a series of such demonstrations, the men are fully aware of what can happen, and the expectation of a repetition produces a drag of fear which is difficult to shake off." (Roy R. Grinker and John P. Spiegel, *Men Under Stress*, 34.)

may claim a large toll, not only among urban evacuees but also among the rural population. Many who are exposed to fall-out radiation will linger through weeks of sickness and depend on relatives for nursing help unless they can find space and care in the overcrowded emergency hospitals. Evacuees who are able to travel will generally leave the distressed areas around target cities and seek refuge with friends or relatives elsewhere in the country. Thus streams of evacuees will crisscross the country, moving as best they can—on foot, in buses, trains, or private cars if they have gasoline. And all will compete for the nation's diminishing resources.

The elasticity of housing within the nation as a whole will probably be sufficient to absorb all the homeless survivors, although billeting conditions will naturally be poor. But additional attacks, or the threat of them, will prevent reaccommodation within those urban areas from which the evacuees came. This will constitute the basic difference between the population displacement due to repeated nuclear disasters and the reaccommodation that was possible in World War II. There will not only be the quantitative difference of an immensely greater amount of destruction, but also the qualitative difference from the fact that the urban refugees will remain removed and cut off from the urban industrial areas. Hence the recovery of industries will not take place as long as the threat of further nuclear attacks prevails, regardless of the amount of damage to factories and transportation facilities.

Under repeated bombings the chances of survival and useful work in the cities will appear so slim that the evacuees will prefer to accept the hardships and discomfort of continued evacuation. Under such conditions the government will be in no position to enforce a return to the cities. It will probably not wish to do so, since it must prevent additional casualties so that the nation as a people may survive. In fact, the government will probably be more concerned than the individual citizens, who may have ceased to care about their own lives. There will be difficulties enough

"Broken-backed Warfare"

with the fall-out hazard without exposing concentrated population groups to blast and fire effects.

The hardships of the survivors will certainly be great. Masses of refugees will trek across the country, avoiding, if possible, the cities that may be attacked in the future. Some will move with a definite destination in mind; others will seek food and shelter wherever they can. Many will forage on farms or form queues at soup kitchens and other relief points. Many will search for relatives, nurse family members who are sick, or simply mourn the loss of their kin. A lack of money or shortage of goods will leave them unable to replace their clothing and household utensils. For a new job and for their means of sustinence they will depend on the government or on the relief provided by local authorities and helpful fellow citizens. Friction will soon arise between the invading refugees from the disaster cities and the old inhabitants. But the numerical strength and pressing needs of the refugees will be so overwhelming that they will overcome the resistance of the natives and force them to share their homes, their kitchens, and their household goods. Thus, the small-town inhabitants will be forced to share the deprivations and distress of the city dwellers and may fare little better than survivors from devastated cities. And worst of all, both evacuees and native residents will live under the constant fear that their town or small city may also be attacked. If that happens, the terror will begin afresh—heralded by the lightning-like, terrifying explosion, covering vast areas with blast, fires, and the insidious threat of radiation, and leaving a wake of dead, burned, maimed, or sick.

With this picture of terror and tribulations in mind one might be inclined to think that the suffering people would want the war to end at almost any price, just to put a stop to the fearful attacks. But any desires of the civilian populations will not stop enemy attacks. In an intercontinental war only the government or military commanders can arrange a capitulation. Civilians may try to influence their leaders to give in, but even this is a difficult and slow process with communications disrupted, parliamentary procedure suspended, and the government itself hidden in secret headquarters. Actually the civilian populations who have suffered from bombing attacks are powerless to speed up the end of the war. They cannot surrender by themselves because the enemy is separated by oceans and continents. Thus the continued effort and struggle of the civilians is not so much an exhibition of fortitude as the result of the hard fact that there are no other alternatives.

The effect of bombing upon civilian morale is now less misunderstood than it was prior to and during World War II. Before the end of World War II it was thought that bombing destruction would lower civilian morale and that low morale would lead to lessened war production or even to a revolt against the government, forcing it to surrender. The fallacy of this premise lies in the fact that two quite different types of "morale" are involved in these two alleged consequences of bombing. The German language has a different word for each kind of "morale"; consequently the German intelligence reports in World War II concerning the civilian home front always clearly distinguished between the two. These reports correctly showed that bombing destruction lowered *Stimmung,* the "passive morale" or the way people felt. But the low *Stimmung* did not destroy *Haltung,* the "active morale" or the way people actually behaved under stress.[17] Habits, discipline, the fear of punishment, and the lack of alternative courses of action left the behavior (*Haltung*) of the civilian population unaffected by the low feelings and depressed mood (*Stimmung*). This distinction, which was so important during World War II, must also be maintained to approach the problem of civilian morale during "broken-backed warfare."

The morale effects of nuclear disasters may be more important for soldiers on the front than for civilians. Most civilians have no

[17] *USSBS,* European report No. 64b, p. 42.

other choice but to try to live through the disaster, regardless of their "passive morale."[18] But the soldiers can show greater variation in their actual behavior under stress depending on their "passive morale." Soldiers may fight effectively, but they may also retreat, evade, or even desert. Their actual behavior may therefore deteriorate if they learn that their homes were demolished and their families killed and that their country is becoming increasingly devastated.[19]

In this discussion of the cumulative effect of bombing on the national war effort we have argued that repeated nuclear attacks, or the threat of them, would prevent the rehabilitation of industrial areas, even if the initial attack left a large portion of the national resources intact. At the same time, however, important military capabilities could survive the bombing if they have been properly

---

[18] P. E. Vernon ("Psychological Effects of Air Raids," *Journal of Abnormal Psychology*, Vol. XXXVI [October, 1941], 457–76) has discussed the relative advantages of civilians over soldiers in the preservation of emotional and mental stability during wartime. Civilians are at a disadvantage, for instance, with respect to their lack of corporate spirit and disciplined training and their inability to release emotion through attacking the enemy. On the other hand, they have the advantage of remaining in the home environment and retaining greater freedom, initiative, and autonomy of action. They can express fear without shame. Above all, they are not burdened with the conflict between the present danger and the imagined security of a hospital or of the home country. They are not prone to see advantages in being sick or wounded (as means of returning home).

[19] Arnold J. Toynbee has made it clear that the fundamental threat of nuclear warfare to the survival of a nation as a people shakes our old concepts of heroism and valor: " 'Who dies, if England live?' was a question to which, in a pre-atomic age, a noble soul had been able to give only one answer; but this time-honoured challenge had undergone a disconcerting mutation since the explosion at Hiroshima on the 6th of August, 1945, and the question had now come to read: 'Who can die to make England live, if England has to die with him?' While few might be found to dispute that *pro patria mori* was *dulce et decorum*, it was not indisputable that to die *with*, instead of *for*, one's country would be either gratifying or even meritorious.—No doubt this reformulation of the question does not dispose of the problem for there is an element in heroism which is beyond Reason because it is above it." (*A Study of History*, IX [London, Oxford University Press, 1954], 521.)

The Social Impact of *BOMB DESTRUCTION*

protected and readied in advance. The belligerents would therefore be faced with the task of reducing the residual capabilities of the enemy without being able to start or resume a real mobilization at home. During this struggle against the residual military forces additional bombing attacks would lead to further heavy losses among the remaining national resources. But sooner or later the military operations would be likely to reveal that one belligerent has considerable superiority in his remaining forces. This would set the stage for surrender negotiations, and the prospect of additional population losses would provide the government of the militarily weaker country with a particularly compelling reason to surrender.

Some of the residual military capabilities may be formidably powerful weapons, and they may be very difficult to destroy in spite of a strong enemy superiority. For example, there could be a fleet of submarines capable of launching thermonuclear missiles. The need for a political truce or capitulation agreement will therefore be much more imperative than it was in wars of the past, when a last-ditch fight by the loser could not jeopardize the survival of the winning nation. At the end of World War II, for example, while Japan's residual forces could still have caused heavy battle casualties among the American forces, they could not endanger the survival of the American people as a residual nuclear capability might have done.

The side which emerges with stronger residual forces during the period of "broken-backed warfare" may be tempted to try to knock out the enemy by attacking his surviving population and remaining cities since the residual military forces may be much more difficult to destroy. But by doing so it may irrevocably close the door to a political termination of the war, and then it will have to annihilate all the residual forces of the enemy. Such a prolonged agony may well lead to desperate counterattacks and repercussions that could practically eliminate the national population of the

"Broken-backed Warfare"

stronger power as well. If the enemy is losing the last substance of his population, his residual military forces will have nothing left to fight for, nor will they have any reason left to surrender, and they could perhaps be without any government that could order them to surrender. It has often been said that if an atomic bomb had been dropped on the Imperial Palace in Tokyo instead of on Hiroshima and Nagasaki, the war against Japan might have been prolonged for many months.

It is a fallacy to assume that every additional increase in civilian destruction will speed up surrender. There is no quick and direct cause-and-effect relationship between destruction and the kind of political action that is required for a truce or surrender. As we have seen earlier, the survivors of bombing attacks follow certain behavior patterns and adaptive processes which are dominated by their habits of the past and their immediate problems of physical survival. These processes take place in time; the task of biological survival comes first, the interest in the family next, and organized political action last—if at all.

There are many examples from World War II where the stronger force wanted to speed up the enemy's surrender by delivering the last knock-out blows. It is now quite clear that this additional destruction contributed very little to hastening the surrender, but it brought a heavy legacy for the future that has proved to be invariably detrimental to the winner. One of the most tragic and absurd examples of this is the German attack on the city of Rotterdam on May 14, 1940, which was actually carried out after capitulation had already taken place. According to German accounts, the news of the capitulation did not reach the attacking bombers in time to forestall the raid.[20] Another example is the heavy raid by the British on the city of Dresden on the night of February 13–14, 1945. Over eight hundred bombers caused tremendous fire storms in this city, which was packed with

[20] Rumpf, *Der Hochrote Hahn*, 29.

refugees from the east. So huge were the casualties that about thirty thousand bodies were found during the next two months.[21] Even now, more than a decade later, the Communist authorities in Dresden are still exploiting the memory of this formidable event to stir up hatred against the West. Finally, with regard to the atomic bombings in Japan, strong arguments have been advanced that these attacks, too, did not produce the enemy's surrender; it is said that simple political arrangements could have accomplished the same end much sooner and at an immensely lower cost to both sides.[22]

The final conclusion is somewhat paradoxical. After widespread nuclear attacks, war production and mobilization would be practically halted, and, with further attacks or the threat of them, there would be no recuperation. But this alone would probably not end the war because residual military capabilities—especially nuclear weapons—could prolong "broken-backed warfare." Therefore, a political settlement would be imperative to save the remainder of the belligerent nations from ultimate destruction. Additional bombing alone might not accomplish the termination of the war because the residual military capabilities could be made almost invulnerable to bombing attack and the social effects of bombing would accrue much too slowly to lead to political action. The means to end the destructive agony would thus belong almost exclusively to the political sphere.

[21] *Ibid.,* 131–32.
[22] Cf. Robert J. C. Butow, *Japan's Decision to Surrender* (Stanford, California, Stanford University Press, 1954), 130–35, 231.

Chapter IX

POSTWAR RESULTS OF BOMB DESTRUCTION

THERE ARE MANY possible long-range effects of bombing destruction which would outlast a war and alter the lives of the people and the structure of society for decades or even generations. Much attention and publicity has been given to the so-called genetic effects of radiation following a nuclear war, but, in fact, they constitute just one of many consequences of such a war. Indeed, there is no scientific justification for attributing greater importance to genetic effects than to other effects that appear to be more serious and can be expected with much greater certainty.

Just as the military outcome in a war in which nuclear weapons bring destruction to cities and civilian populations is unpredictable, so any discussion of postwar results must be largely conjectural. Here we shall speculate about what could be expected in the postwar era if nuclear war should ever become a reality.

The Heritage of Death and Disease

All postwar results from vast nuclear bombing destruction would be dominated by the long-term effects of casualties. The number of people who survive without being permanently incapacitated is the most significant factor in the postwar world. No other question about thermonuclear bombing is more important than

The Social Impact of *BOMB DESTRUCTION*

how many people in a nation or in the world at large could survive such a war.

Many of the factors which would determine the number of healthy survivors are well known, but their quantitative evaluation is so difficult and there are so many unknown details in connection with them that it seems impossible to estimate, or even to guess, how large a population would ultimately survive. A small selection of these unknowns may suffice to illustrate the complexity of the problem. Of utmost importance—and something that can scarcely be estimated—are the number and size of bombs that would be dropped and the actual location of the explosions. Next is the nature of the explosions—whether ground or air bursts—which would have a substantial effect on the fall-out hazard.[1] In addition civil defense preparations and the extent of advance warning would have a decisive influence on the size of the postwar population after the war, as well as the length of the war and the possibilities for escape from areas with residual radioactivity. Finally, there are delayed medical effects from certain fall-out products which still are not very well understood: some long-lived radioactive isotopes, such as strontium-90, might be ingested by large numbers of people, which could seriously impair their health.[2]

Thus, depending on many unpredictable factors, the proportion of a nation's population which would survive and escape serious health damage could be as large as 95 per cent or as small as 5 per cent of the prewar population. Since this percentage is the gauge of well-being in a postwar world, obviously no firm predictions can be made about it. If the problem is not to be abandoned entirely, it must be discussed in terms of alternatives.

Assuming first that the number of survivors is relatively large, we can examine the population effects on the basis of past bombing

---

[1] U. S. Department of Defense and U. S. Atomic Energy Commission, *op cit.*, 409.
[2] *Ibid.*, 450–54.

The Heritage of Death and Disease

experiences. During World War I the age-and-sex structure of the populations of belligerent countries was seriously upset because of casualties.[3] To a lesser extent this was also the case after World War II. This change in the demographic structure of nations was a result of battle casualties, the majority of whom were males, aged eighteen to thirty-five. Air-raid casualties, however, to a degree offset the selectiveness of battle casualties.

The age and sex distribution of air-raid victims shows that there was a higher proportion of deaths among older persons, probably because they were more vulnerable during attack and had less chance of survival if injured. In Germany there were more women than men among the air-raid fatalities,[4] because fewer men were exposed to city bombing on account of mobilization. For England the age and sex distribution of air-raid casualties can be ascertained from a sample survey of civilians admitted to hospitals for injuries from enemy action. Table 18 compares the incidence of these admissions in relation to the total population. To facilitate comparison, the rates are expressed as percentages of the relative incidence among females aged fifteen to sixty-four.

These statistics show that evacuation substantially reduced casualty rates among children. During aircraft bombing, civilian men under sixty-five suffered almost twice the casualty rate experienced by women—their civil defense duties exposed them to greater risk. But during the rocket attacks, when missiles arrived

[3] Compared with the normal number of deaths, the loss of life owing to battles and war wounds was not as great in World War I as the absolute figures might suggest. This loss amounted to about one quarter of the deaths which would normally have taken place if the countries had not been at war. The death rates in Germany and France increased by about 40 or 45 per cent. In Britain the increase was a little less than 35 per cent, and in the United States it was only about 6 per cent. (William Fielding Ogburn, *American Society in Wartime* [Chicago, University of Chicago Press, 1943], 2.) Cf. also Warren S. Thompson, *Plenty of People*, Chap. V.

[4] Heinsohn, *loc. cit.;* and Hans Rumpf, "Die Verluste der westdeutschen Zivilbevölkerung im Luftkrieg," *Wehr-Wissenschaftliche Rundschau,* Vol. III (October, 1953), 493–97.

The Social Impact of BOMB DESTRUCTION

TABLE 18

AGE-SEX DIFFERENTIALS OF THE INCIDENCE OF AIR-RAID INJURIES IN ENGLAND DURING WORLD WAR II

	Boys Under 15	Girls Under 15	Men Aged 15–64	Women Aged 15–64	Men 65 and Over	Women 65 and Over
1st period—Air raids	49.0	41.0	185.0	100.0	177.0	172.0
2nd period—V–1 projectiles	35.0	35.0	92.0	100.0	162.0	211.0
3rd period—V–1 and V–2 projectiles	56.0	61.0	83.0	100.0	106.0	139.0

Source: Great Britain, *Report of the Ministry of Health for the Year Ended 31st March, 1947*, Cmd. 7441 (London, H. M. Stationery Office, 1948), 97.

without warning, male losses were no longer greater. Table 18 also shows that elderly people in England experienced relatively higher casualty rates, corroborating similar German evidence.

It may be said in summary that no appreciable demographic effect resulted from air-raid casualties during World War II, since the number of deaths was very small in relation to the total national population or in comparison with normal peacetime mortalities. Even for individual cities the numerical effect of deaths due to bombing was slight. As far as the age and sex ratio is concerned, air-raid casualties somewhat offset battle casualties since there was a generally higher incidence of bombing fatalities among females and older persons.

The number of casualties would be much higher in a future war than in World War I or World War II if nuclear bombs are exploded in or near cities. If the number of fatalities should amount to as much as one-fifth or one-third of a country's population,[5] the

---

[5] For the civil defense exercise "Operation Alert" on June 15, 1955, the hypothetical assumption was made that the enemy's attack had resulted in five million fatalities among the United States' population (*New York Times*, June 16, 1955). In the hearings of the Senate Armed Services Subcommittee on the Air

The Heritage of Death and Disease

demographic effects would be felt for two generations or more. The most recent example of such a huge population loss is provided by the war of 1865-70 in Paraguay.[6] As a result of battle casualties, epidemics, and famine, Paraguay lost about one-half of its entire population, and the losses in the male population alone were even more excessive. Before this war Paraguay's population was about 500,000, but a census taken the first year after the war found only 221,000 people in the country.[7]

In spite of these terrific losses Paraguay survived as a nation. But not until about 1900 did its population recover to the prewar size. It is difficult to ascertain more about the effect of these casualties on the nation and society, apart from the obvious finding that during many decades after this war Paraguay lagged behind other South American nations in development. Its population would probably be considerably larger today had it not been for this war, but the statistics are too unreliable and scarce to allow a more detailed statement about the social effects of this population loss.

Fatalities comparable to those in Paraguay in the nineteenth

Force in 1956, the question of the lethal effect of a United States Strategic Air Force assault against Russia in the event of nuclear war was answered by Lieutenant General James M. Gavin as follows: "Current planning estimates run on the order of several hundred million deaths that would be either way depending upon which way the wind blew. If the wind blew to the southeast they would be mostly in the U.S.S.R., although they would extend into the Japanese and perhaps down into the Philippine area. If the wind blew the other way they would extend well back up into Western Europe." (*New York Times,* June 29, 1956.)

[6] The war was against Brazil, Uruguay, and Argentina under the dictatorship of Francisco Solano Lopéz.

[7] The prewar figure of 1,337,439 for the year 1857 was a deliberate exaggeration of Lopéz I to make Paraguay appear one of the first powers in South America. More reasonable estimates for the prewar population are 500,000 or 800,000. The postwar census, on the other hand, may not be complete. It breaks the 221,000 inhabitants down into 106,000 women, 86,000 children, and only 29,000 men. Cf. Harris Gaylord Warren, *Paraguay: An Informal History* (Norman, University of Oklahoma Press, 1949), 243; Hector F. Decoud, *Geografía de la República del Paraguay* (Asunción, n.p., 1900), 43, 129; and Gabriel Carrasco, *La Población del Paraguay antes y después de la Guerra* (Ascuncion, n.p., 1905), 4-8.

century occurred in the medieval plague epidemics. The Black Death in the fourteenth century killed one-third or more of the inhabitants of many communities or entire countries. Exactly how great the mortality was is impossible to ascertain now except for a few specific institutions, such as monasteries or schools, which kept death records. The effect of population losses from the plague on the course of history is a matter of controversy. Some historians believe that the plague caused a definite change in medieval culture and economy.[8] In particular, it is pointed out that the population loss led to a labor shortage which resulted in an increase in wages and the decline of the landholding nobility.[9] However, somewhat more careful and detailed investigations of the records from that period reveal no abrupt changes or cultural and economic revolutions on account of the plague.

The medieval universities did suffer heavy losses in their teaching staffs and enrollments which probably slowed down the progress of learning. On the other hand, endowments increased, partly because of the plague deaths.[10] There were also vacancies in the clergy and in monasteries—a shortage of priests was reported four years after the Black Death. Land rent fell by one-half in some instances, and there were some uncultivated acres and idle mills during the first years after the epidemic.[11] However, an examination of pertinent manorial records in England shows no radical change in the rural economy. Land that became vacant because of the plague was taken up readily by new tenants, and many manors had no vacant tenements afterwards.[12]

[8] See Anna Montgomery Campbell, *The Black Death and Men of Learning* (New York, Columbia University Press, 1931), 4, for evaluations by various authors of the historical importance of the plague.

[9] According to Francis Aidan Gasquet (*The Black Death of 1348 and 1349* [London, Bell & Sons, 1908], 230), King Edward III ordered a wage freeze to combat the economic effects of the labor shortage.

[10] Campbell, *op. cit., passim.*

[11] Gasquet, *op. cit.,* 130–34, 203, and 240ff.

[12] Elizabeth A. Levett and A. Ballard, "The Black Death on the Estates of

The Heritage of Death and Disease

The impact of large population losses on our modern society cannot be inferred from events of the Middle Ages or experiences of the primitive agricultural economy of nineteenth-century Paraguay. These historical examples may caution us against quick presumptions about the end of civilization or the death of nations from fatalities amounting to one-third or one-half of the population. But in contrast to the plague epidemics, fatalities from nuclear bombing would be accompanied by destruction of capital. Hence goods would be in as much demand as labor, and the man-power shortage would not dominate, except in some skilled occupations and in reconstruction work. Since destruction and casualties would be concentrated in cities, there would probably be a world-wide surplus of agricultural goods, although local food shortages might persist in many areas for a few years after the end of the war.

A large number of fatalities would inevitably lead to broken homes. In many families there would be both survivors and fatalities because there is no sharp line between areas where people survive from nuclear bombs and areas where everybody is killed. Hence the first postwar generation would contain many orphans and many adults who had lost their children or spouses.

In addition to supporting children from broken homes, the postwar society would have to care for survivors who had been crippled. Even more serious might be an increase in sickness caused by delayed radiation effects. Under certain circumstances fall-out might contaminate large agricultural areas with strontium-90, which tends to be taken up from the soil by plants. If consumption of these contaminated crops were not avoided, some of the strontium-90 could collect in human bones in amounts large enough to cause bone cancer (osteogenic sarcoma). From what

Winchester," *Oxford Studies in Social and Legal History*, V (1916). See also John Saltmarsh, "Plague and Economic Decline in England in the Latter Middle Ages," *The Cambridge Historical Journal*, Vol. VII, No. 1 (Cambridge, England, 1941), 23–41.

is known of ingested radium—a substance with effects similar to those of strontium-90—this disease develops rather slowly, over perhaps ten years or more, and leads to incapacitation, crippling, and eventually to death.[13] Certain other delayed radiation effects might also be important. Among the survivors from Hiroshima and Nagasaki who had been exposed to nuclear radiation, it was found that the incidence of leukemia (a form of bone cancer that is generally incurable and fatal) was substantially above normal. However, less than 1 per cent of those with severe radiation exposures developed the disease.[14] There was also a marked incidence of radiation cataracts among these survivors,[15] but not all were serious enough to lead to an impairment of vision or to require surgery.

Finally, there are the genetic effects of nuclear radiation, about which so much has been augured but so little is actually known. Experiments with lower animals—primarily fruit flies and mice—have shown that radiation induces genetic mutations with a frequency that increases with the total dose of irradiation. It is believed by geneticists that sublethal doses—in fact, very low doses—could cause sufficient genetic damage to lead to an appreciable number of defective individuals in later generations.[16] Some of the defects may be barely noticeable, while others may be so gross that the affected individual would not be viable. However, genetic

---

[13] Joseph C. Aub, Rolley D. Evans, Louis Hempelman, and Harrison S. Martland, "The Late Effects of Internally Deposited Radioactive Materials in Man," *Medicine,* Vol. XXXI, No. 3 (September, 1952), 221–329. Cf. also Charles F. Behrens, *Atomic Medicine* (New York, Thomas Nelson & Sons, 1949), 137–45.

[14] William C. Moloney, "Leukemia in Survivors of Atomic Bombing," *New England Journal of Medicine,* Vol. CCLIII (July, 1955), 88–90.

[15] John C. Bugher, "Delayed Radiation Effects at Hiroshima and Nagasaki," *Nucleonics,* Vol. X, No. 9 (September, 1952), 18–21. Cf. also U. S. Department of Defense and U. S. Atomic Energy Commission, *op. cit.,* 480ff.

[16] Cf., for example, A. H. Sturtevant, "Social Implications of the Genetics of Man," *Science,* Vol. CXX, No. 3115 (September 10, 1954), 405–407; and H. J. Muller, "How Radiation Changes the Genetic Constitution," *Bulletin of the Atomic Scientists,* Vol. XI, No. 9 (November, 1955), 329ff.

theories based solely on animal experiments cannot take into account the peculiarities of human genetics, such as the selection of mates, deliberate control of fertility, and possibly eugenics.[17] Furthermore, mutations that seem harmful in animal breeding may not be so in a human society. For example, mutations that reduce only fecundity may not affect fertility since fecundity (the biological capacity to reproduce) is always much higher in human populations than fertility (the actual frequency of births among women of childbearing age). Even if fertility should be reduced as a result of mutations, it could prove to be beneficial for society, rather than harmful, in the many areas of the world that suffer from too rapid population growth or too high population densities.[18]

The Redevelopment of Cities

There remains the problem of the permanent effects of urban destruction upon the postwar development of cities and the future of urban living. The question is whether the character of cities would change so basically that perhaps a new form of metropolis would arise that would be better planned and more practical and beautiful than present cities. Or, one may wonder whether cities might not altogether disappear after a war with widespread bombing destruction, leaving only a few surviving urbanites who would permanently settle in rural areas and future generations who would be unwilling or incapable of resuming urban life.

[17] Cf. T. C. Carter, "The Genetic Problem of Irradiated Human Populations," *Bulletin of the Atomic Scientists*, Vol. XI, No. 10 (December, 1955), 362ff.

[18] At the present time about one-third of all pregnancies in Japan are being terminated by nontherapeutic induced abortions. Cf. Yoshio Koya, "A Study of Induced Abortion in Japan and Its Significance," *The Milbank Memorial Fund Quarterly*, Vol. XXXII, No. 3 (July, 1954), 282–93. However, while mutations would be beneficial if they reduced fertility, this benefit might be outweighed by their other debilitating and harmful effects. For a judicious evaluation of society's genetic risk from ionizing radiation(primarily in peacetime), see National Academy of Sciences—National Research Council, *The Biological Effects of Atomic Radiation: Summary Reports*, 3–30; and Great Britain, Medical Research Council, *The Hazards to Man of Nuclear and Allied Radiations*, Cmd. 9780.

The Social Impact of *BOMB DESTRUCTION*

Actually, both these extremes are unlikely. If a large segment of the urban population were killed, many cities would be smaller in size during the first postwar generation, and some urban areas might never be redeveloped; but if most of the urban dwellers should survive, the devastated cities would rapidly recover their prewar size and would be rebuilt essentially along the old pattern. The main differences would be greater crowding, poorer housing, and probably more uniformity and dreariness.

The period after World War II provides extensive evidence on the redevelopment of bombed cities where the majority of the urban population had survived in spite of great housing destruction. Even where casualties were relatively large, as in Hiroshima and Nagasaki, redevelopment followed the same pattern. National populations as a whole, however, did not decline appreciably during World War II; and a nuclear war with a high casualty rate might result in a much slower recovery of urban communities.

The bomb damage from World War II brought changes in the population distribution not only within cities but also within counties, and more people lived in small towns and villages after the war than before; but these changes proved to be neither spectacular nor permanent, as can be seen from Table 19 for West Germany and Japan.

The population increase in smaller communities in West Germany was partly due to the influx of refugees from East Germany and hence was not entirely the result of bombing. In England there was a similar decrease in the population of the largest cities between 1939 and 1951, while the population of smaller urban areas increased;[19] but this was not so much a result of war destruction as a continuation of the prewar trend toward suburban living.

Since these over-all changes in rural-urban distribution are so

---

[19] Great Britain, General Register Office, *Census, 1951, England and Wales, Preliminary Report* (London, H. M. Stationery Office, 1951), p. xix.

The Redevelopment of Cities

TABLE 19

PERCENTAGE DISTRIBUTION OF POPULATION IN JAPAN AND
WESTERN GERMANY BY SIZE OF COMMUNITY

Size Category	Germany*			Japan†		
	1939	1946	1950	1940	1948	1950
Below 20,000	53.3	61.9	58.5	58.0	60.2	57.6
20,000–50,000	7.8	8.5	8.8	7.4	9.2	9.2
50,000–100,000	5.5	6.2	5.4	5.2	8.0	7.6
100,000 and over	33.4	23.4	27.3	29.4	22.5	25.6
Total	100.0	100.0	100.0	100.0	100.0	100.0

*Source: *Statistische Berichte*, Statisches Bundesamt, Wiesbaden, August 16, 1952, p. 3.
†Source: *Japan Statistical Yearbook, 1950*, Prime Minister's Office, Statistics Bureau, 12; and *ibid.*, 1951, 12, 13.

slight, it is of greater interest to focus attention on the effects of bombing upon the internal pattern of cities. Convenient measures for these changes in bombed cities are the population densities of different urban districts. Changes in population density show whether decentralization resulted from bombing and whether some devastated districts remained permanently depopulated. However, it is necessary to take into account the prewar trends in urban densities because population densities in different parts of a city have never been stable. Furthermore, it is well to remember that the nighttime density of the resident population is not a true indication of the change, for the daytime density of people at their places of work is an equally significant index of urban land use. It is generally more difficult to find figures for the latter, but a few illustrative cases can be cited, together with the nighttime densities.

During the first postwar years some of the most severely damaged districts remained almost desolate in comparison with their prewar population. In Hamburg the district of St. George, for ex-

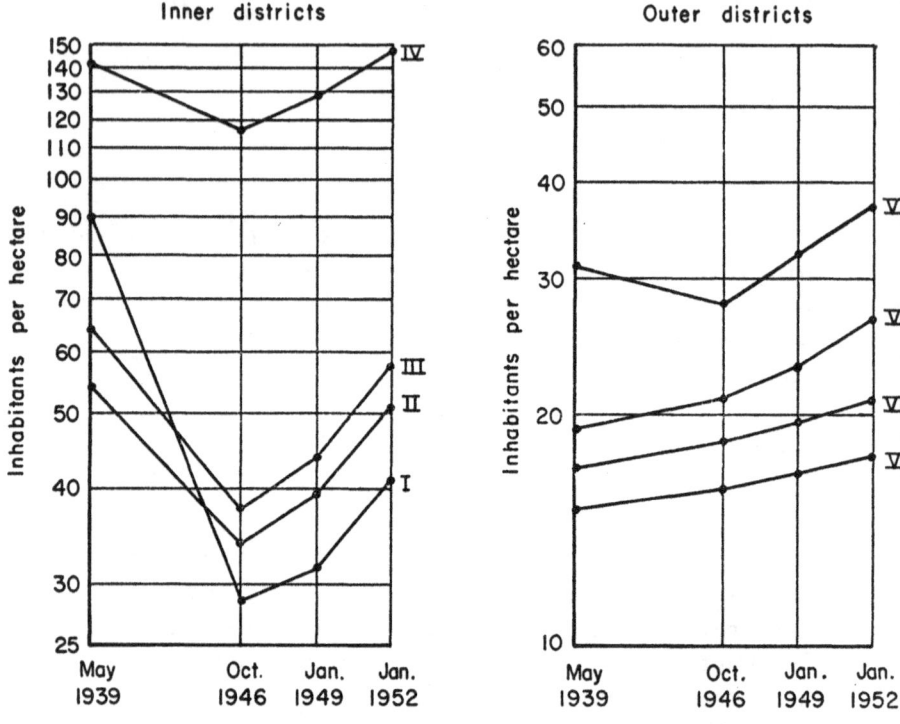

Fig. 11. —— Frankfurt, 1939 — 1952
Population density by districts.

ample, lost over 90 per cent of its 1939 population as a result of the big raids in 1943. The population of the borough of Chelsea in London declined by more than 50 per cent from 1939 to 1941, and the central area in Frankfurt (Bezirk 1 to 3) decreased from 15,270 inhabitants in 1939 to a mere 960 in 1946.

But for the bombed cities, particularly the less damaged districts, recovery set in quite rapidly, in many instances even before the end of the war. That was, of course, mainly due to the fact

The Redevelopment of Cities

that the number of bombed-out people greatly exceeded the number of deaths from air raids. As emphasized previously, this is one of the most significant aspects of World War II bombings. When practically all of the original inhabitants survived, reconstruction could proceed with great vitality. Hamburg, which had lost half of its housing, had recovered its prewar population by 1950, and Greater London's population in 1948 was only about 2 per cent below its prewar size.

A more detailed analysis of the changes in internal density indicates that this recovery was not merely due to doubling up in undestroyed areas but actually represented a reconstruction of the cities. This reconstruction largely followed the prewar pattern. The densely populated districts in the center of the city, which generally suffered the greatest damage, experienced also the most rapid recovery; and the lower densities in suburban areas—while increasing somewhat—remained well below the population density of the reconstructed city center.

Figure 11 illustrates this development for the city of Frankfurt. The districts of the outer zone suffered hardly any destruction and therefore did not lose in population density. The inner districts, on the other hand, experienced a marked decline in population during the war. After the war they all recuperated rapidly. It is particularly remarkable that the most densely populated district (District IV) attained a higher density after the war than before. Obviously war destruction did not lead to a deconcentration of population in Frankfurt.

A similar picture is given by Fig. 12, which shows the density trends in Nagasaki by different damage zones. The "area of destruction" is the region where most houses were demolished either by blast or by fire. The "surrounding area" includes the districts which largely escaped destruction by the atomic bomb but which are still urban in character, having a relatively high population density. The "outer area" comprises suburban districts

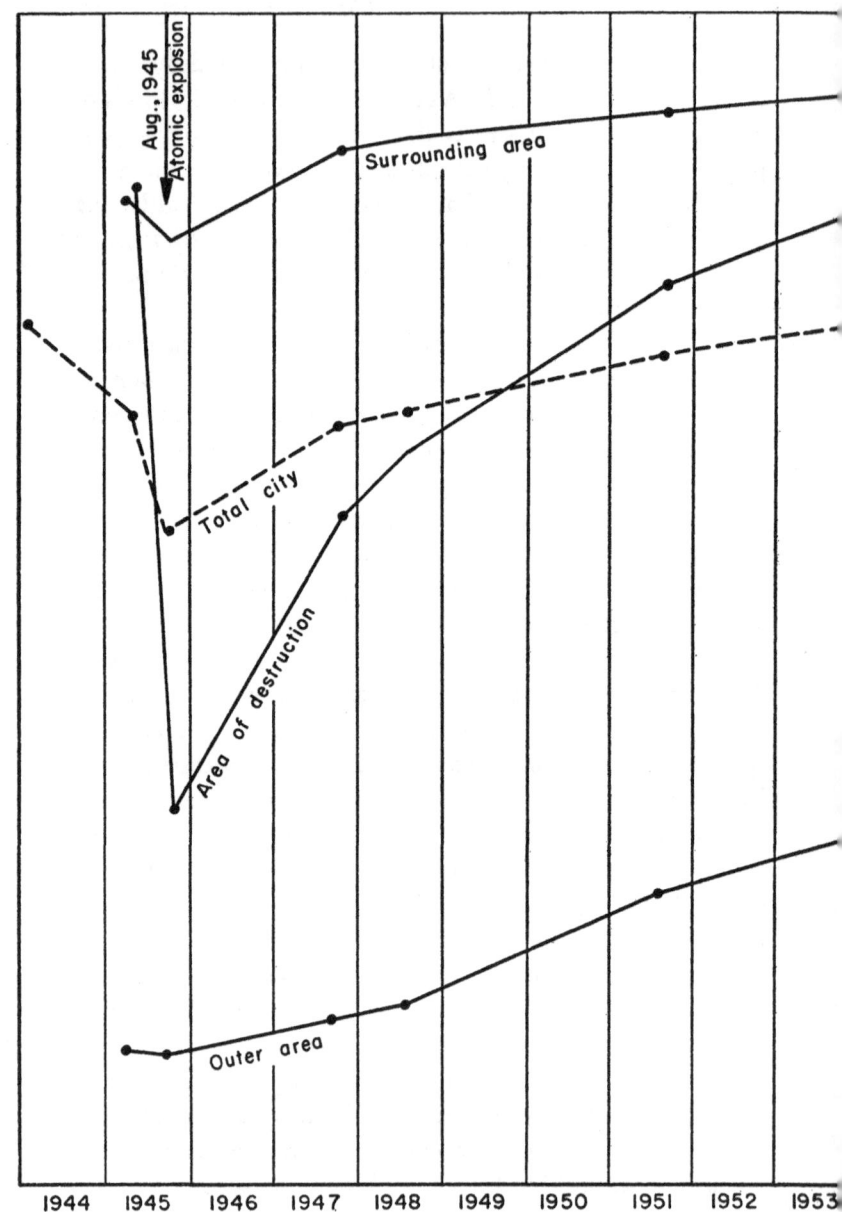

Fig. 12.— Nagasaki, 1944–1953
Population density for areas and total city.

The Redevelopment of Cities

of Nagasaki which are part of the political city but have a low population density.[20]

From the trend line for the "total city," it can be seen that there was a decrease in density during 1944 and early 1945 prior to the atomic explosion, primarily because of evacuation. For the city as a whole the density loss after 1944 had been almost recovered by 1953. As one would expect, the "outer area" attained a higher density after the explosion than before because people who lost their homes in the center of destruction moved to suburban districts.

The most revealing finding, however, is the rapid recovery of the "area of destruction." The density trend on the chart shows a continuous steep increase. Extending this trend into the future, one finds that sometime toward 1960 the pre-destruction density will have been recovered. In other words, the effect of the atomic bomb upon the density within the city of Nagasaki will have disappeared within ten to fifteen years after the explosion.

For the city of Hamburg we can place the war-born changes into a wider historical context since comparative data are available as far back as 1880. Thus we can determine how the effects of bombing have influenced the long-range trend in the city's development. In order to obtain a simplified over-all view of the changes in population density, the districts or census tracts have been combined into three concentric zones; namely, a small "inner zone" constituting the historic center and present business district, an "intermediate zone" surrounding the inner zone and consisting of continuous built-up areas, and an "outer zone" which contains

[20] The "area of destruction" includes these districts *(kus)*: Inasa, Shiroyama, Yamazato, Zeniza, and Nishizaka. The "surrounding area" includes Togiya, Shinkozen, Katsuyama, Kaminagasaki, Irabayashi, Kojima, Nita, Sako, Kita Oura, Minami Oura, Namino Hira, Tomachi, Tategami, Akumoura, Asahi, and Kosakaki. The "outer area"includes Kogakura, Dionokubi, and Nishiurakimi. Sources: *Nagasaki Shisei Yoran, 1951, op. cit.*, 9, 10; and data supplied by the Nagasaki Statistical Office.

217

The Social Impact of *BOMB DESTRUCTION*

the fringe of the built-up area, suburbs, and satellite cities (e.g., Harburg).[21]

The population changes for these three zones are shown in Table 20. On first inspection it seems that war destruction led to permanent changes in the city's internal population distribution. The "inner" and "intermediate" zones—where most of the damage

TABLE 20

NUMBER OF PERSONS BY PLACE OF RESIDENCE IN DIFFERENT ZONES OF HAMBURG

(in thousands)

	1880	1939	1950
Inner zone	171	66	38
Intermediate zone	474	784	429
Outer zone	134	848	1,039
Total	779	1,698	1,506

occurred—had a substantially smaller population in 1950 than before the war, although the city as a whole had recovered most of its prewar population. On the other hand, the "outer zone"—

[21] The boundaries of such zones necessarily have to be arbitrary. After 1939 an entirely new statistical division of the Greater Hamburg Region was introduced. Small areas have been combined into zones here in such a way that the zones based on areas inhabited prior to 1939 match as closely as possible with corresponding zones after 1939. Where a difference was unavoidable, this has been indicated by breaking the trend line in 1939.

From 1880 to 1939 the data on resident populations are based on censuses. Statistics for small areas were made comparable in *Allgemeine Statistik des Hamburgisch-Preussischen Landes-planungsgebietes* (Hamburg, 1930), I, 17–19; and in *Aus Hamburgs Verwaltung und Wirtschaft,* 1939. The data for July and October, 1943, and for April, 1944, are based on ration card records published in *ibid.,* Sondernummer 7 (June, 1944), 14–18. For assistance in making statistical areas comparable over time, we are indebted to Dr. Heinsohn and others at the Statistical Office of the City of Hamburg as well as to Dr. Kinder and Dr. Pause at the City Planning Office. (The publication by Kinder and Pause, *op. cit.,* was most valuable for this study.)

The Redevelopment of Cities

where there was almost no bombing damage—had gained in population.

Placed in the context of the long-range historical trends, however, the effects of the war appear much less drastic. In the long range they seem almost negligible. This is borne out by Fig. 13, which shows the density trends for the three zones from 1880 to 1950. For the "inner" and "intermediate" zones the density of the population at the places of work is given in addition to the density of total population at the places of residence (i.e., the nighttime population density).[22]

The density of the resident population in the "inner zone" shows a continuous decline since 1880, and the precipitate loss after the raids of 1943 merely accelerated this downward trend. Similarly, the resident population density in the "intermediate zone" began to decline around 1930, and the recovery after the war has restored the density approximately to the level which it would have reached without a war if the prewar trend had continued. Finally, the population density in the "outer zone" had been increasing steadily since 1880, and the further increase after the war is a continuation of the prewar trend. The development in the density of workplaces shows a similar picture, where the recovery after the war leads toward the level of the prewar trend.

Hamburg suffered about as many casualties as Nagasaki as a result of the atomic bomb, but the number of dwellings destroyed was much greater than in Nagasaki. Yet the postwar development of the city conforms to the pattern found for Nagasaki. The spacing of the population within this city is little different from what it would have been had there been no war. The redevelopment of Hamburg, Nagasaki, and Frankfurt, which has been discussed

[22] Data on number of persons by place of work are based on censuses for 1900, 1910, 1925, and 1939. For October, 1946, they are based on a commuting survey compiled from ration cards by the city planning office.

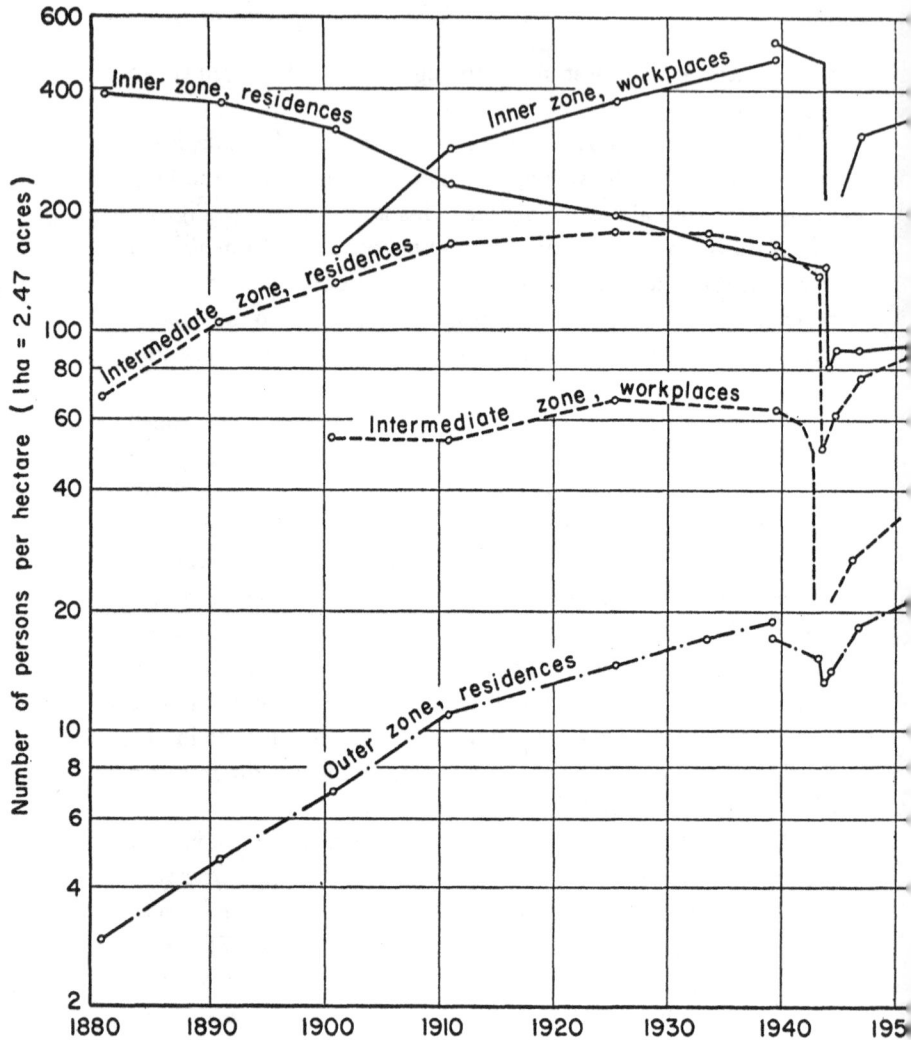

Fig. 13. — Hamburg, 1880-1950
Population density by places of work and by places of residence in different zones.

The Redevelopment of Cities

above, is in no way unique. Most cities bombed during World War II conform to this pattern.[23]

The density changes discussed so far convey the important outlines but do not tell the whole story of the redevelopment of cities. Other features that may have been variously affected by bombing destruction are the locations of different types of business establishments, land values, and social characteristics of the different neighborhoods. These features cannot be covered as easily as density changes; we are therefore confined to some limited observations and local data.

In general, business establishments showed a strong tendency after World War II to return to the same locations they had occupied before destruction. This is borne out by maps comparing business locations in two districts of Hamburg for 1939 and 1945.[24] The location of business establishments in these destroyed or damaged areas developed along the same pattern after the war. The newly constructed shops cluster in the same groups and on the same street corners or alleys as before destruction.

A study of districts in Berlin with high delinquency rates shows a persistence of the social characteristics in the city in spite of destruction.[25] The areas with high delinquency rates remained the same, even though many of these city blocks had been partially destroyed. Some interesting exceptions, however, can be found. An area which was totally destroyed ceased to be a district of prostitution after reconstruction. In a rooming-house district with high delinquency before the war, the dwellings or rooms became permanently occupied by bombed-out inhabitants, and the delinquency rate fell in this area.

[23] Further data can be found in the following publications by the author: "The Effect of War Destruction upon the Ecology of Cities," *Social Forces*, Vol. XXIX, No. 4 (May, 1951), 383–91; and "Reconstruction and Population Density in War-damaged Cities," *loc. cit.*, 131–39.

[24] Kinder and Pause, *op. cit.*

[25] *Sozialgeographische Karten* (edited by Helmut Winz and issued by the Hauptamt für Gesamtplanung, Magistrat von Gross-Berlin, 1950), 19–20.

The Social Impact of *BOMB DESTRUCTION*

The persistence of the social and economic characteristics of bombed districts after World War II was partly due to the attachment of persons to their former neighborhoods. Older inhabitants were especially anxious to move back into the areas where they used to live. The return to the pre-destruction location was due partly to land ownership and a desire to secure the good will and old clientele of the former location. Amos H. Hawley found that the land value pattern of Okayama remained the same in spite of large destruction. Since the land ownership remained intact, the many ownership claims created a strong inertia to any radical change.[26]

From the standpoint of city planning this inertia in the redevelopment of war-damaged cities may have been undesirable. There was a noticeable disappointment among the enthusiasts for garden cities and decentralization schemes, who had hoped that destruction would spur the decongestion of large cities and enhance planned improvements on a grand scale, because, as it turned out, destruction of houses did not remove the social and economic obstacles to far-reaching changes in the cities' internal patterns.

An important factor favoring reconstruction on the old sites was that practically all the destroyed houses retained much of their economic value. Frequently damage was only partial, and the old structure could be utilized.[27] But even where none of the above-ground structure remained intact, a large part of the construction cost could be saved by rebuilding on the old foundations. The excavations, drainage, utilities, and streets could all be salvaged by foregoing changes in the layout of the city. After a war it is

[26] Hawley, "Land Value Patterns in Okayama, Japan, 1940–52," *The American Journal of Sociology*, Vol. LX, No. 5 (March, 1955), 487–92.

[27] Only about 40 per cent of all new dwellings in Hamburg in 1948 were newly constructed buildings; the rest were repaired, reconstructed, or subdivided ("Der Wohnungsbau in der Hansestadt im Jahre, 1948," *Hamburg in Zahlen* No. 5 [1949], 5). In the city of Warsaw only 14 per cent of the residential buildings begun in 1947 and early 1948 were new houses; the remaining 86 per cent were reconstruction (data from *Statistical Yearbook of Poland, 1948* [Warsaw, 1949], 31).

The Redevelopment of Cities

particularly important to save building costs since the housing shortage is so great and war-damaged nations are impoverished. Municipalities are burdened with a heavy load of reconstruction, even if they avoid radical changes and make full use of the utilities and streets that are left. This is illustrated by data from Munich, where 35 per cent of all man-hours in construction work in 1948 were absorbed by public works, such as repairs of streets and sewerage systems, and only about 20 per cent of the man-hours were devoted to the construction of dwellings. (Of the remaining man-hours, 31 per cent were spent for industrial construction and 14 per cent for the removal of debris.)[28]

On a limited scale, however, the city authorities were able to improve the street pattern and zoning restrictions after World War II. More spacious layouts of streets could be introduced in small areas which suffered almost complete destruction. For example, in London the Stepney-Poplar Reconstruction Area is to be redeveloped so that it will house 58 per cent fewer people than before its devastation.[29] The central district of Plymouth has been rebuilt with a drastically changed and widened street pattern, and in the core of Frankfurt the total area given over to streets has been increased by one-third.[30]

Improved zoning, combinations of small parcels, and the widening of streets are city developments which occur apart from war destruction, as a result of economic changes and population growth. The devastations of World War II merely facilitated more radical and rapid developments of this type. The outstanding

[28] *Münchener Statistik*, January, 1949, 7.
[29] London County Council, *London Housing Statistics, 1948–49* (London, 1949), 9.
[30] Leo Grebler, "Street Changes in the Rebuilding of European Cities," *The American City*, Vol. LXX, No. 8 (August, 1955). Cf. also by the same author, *Europe's Reborn Cities* (Washington, D. C., Urban Land Institute, Technical Bulletin No. 28, 1956); and "Continuity in the Rebuilding of Bombed Cities in Western Europe," *The American Journal of Sociology*, Vol. LXI, No. 5 (March, 1956), 463–69.

The Social Impact of *BOMB DESTRUCTION*

lesson from the reconstruction period, however, is the over-all persistence of urban land use and the drive of the bombed-out city dwellers to return to their urban habitat. As long as large urban population groups survive, large cities are bound to remain, and the cities that are rebuilt after bombing destruction will look much like the old ones. There will be few completely different, beautifully planned, and spacious new forms of human habitation arising from the ashes. On the contrary, the rebuilt cities will, as a whole, be more crowded, of cheaper construction, with smaller apartments, and fewer amenities. During the tribulations of war the population may be promised that the world of tomorrow will bring a better life and better cities, but the enormous poverty resulting from destruction will not permit fulfillment of this wishful thinking.

Survival of Civilization

The social effects of bomb destruction become increasingly more difficult to estimate as one moves further away from the direct physical and biological consequences of the destructive explosions. We have so far been able to make relatively precise estimates of how destruction of dwellings affects housing conditions, and we have been able to show that partial destruction of a city's housing resources tends to be compensated by an increase in housing density in the undestroyed dwellings. Similarly, the loss of other physical resources, such as transit facilities, restaurants, shops, and consumer goods, leads to only a partial loss of the functions dependent on them (e.g., commuting, eating, and housekeeping), and the loss is partially made up by a more intensive utilization of the remaining resources or by substitutions.

Furthermore, we have determined some of the principal protective reactions of a population exposed to bombing. Excavation, for example, assumes different forms depending on the perception of the danger, the duration of the threat, past bombing expe-

Survival of Civilization

riences, and alternative courses of action that are open and known to the population. Social consequences vary with the different forms of evacuation, ranging from the strain of broken-up families and the urge to reunite them to a disruption of the urban labor force on account of unemployment and social tension in the reception areas. Other protective measures, such as shelters, fire-fighting, and decontamination, present more of a physical problem than a social one. But here, too, there are some predictable social consequences, such as loss in man power and conflicts in motivation.

Then we have drawn these threads together to show—at least qualitatively—how the various primary social effects of bombing combine to reduce industrial man power and to impair and disrupt the functioning of the urban economy (over and beyond the impairment which results from the destruction of factories and transportation facilities).

But our analysis becomes considerably more difficult and uncertain when we move to the political and cultural effects of bombing. The only realistic context of bombing destruction—in contrast to destruction caused by natural disasters—is an all-out war. The crucial problem is how the outcome of the war is affected by the social effects of bombing. Here our conclusions have been based largely on conjecture, since the specific political and military situation is of decisive importance and not amenable to generalization. Two conclusions, however, seem to emerge. First, partial destruction of cities, such as occurred in World War II, does not lead to a loss in war production commensurate with the loss of property. As long as the number of casualties is slight, recuperation and increased utilization of the remaining resources can keep the losses in current war production much smaller than the losses in industrial capital. Second, very large destruction combined with large casualties, such as might be caused by nuclear bombing, would probably bring industrial production almost to a standstill, but it would not by itself lead to termination of the war unless one belligerent should escape this destruction. In particular, repeated attacks could inhibit the kind of political action that is the prerequisite for the termination of war.

Still further removed from the primary physical and biological damage are the postwar social effects of bombing. In a way these are less unpredictable than the impact of bombing on the war itself because they are of a more statistical nature and not as dependent on unique circumstances as are political and military decisions. Thus the most important aftermath of bombing may be the demographic consequences of large casualties, and, given the number of casualties, these consequences follow relatively simple and predictable actuarial rules. Similarly, the most manifest effect of both conventional and nuclear bombing directed against nonmilitary targets is the destruction of urban areas. The redevelopment of destroyed cities follows fairly predictable lines and would bring fewer surprises than the immediate political and military consequences of bombing.

There is one exception to this relative predictability of the postwar results of bombing. This is the possible impact on civilization of extremely widespread destruction and huge fatalities, such as would follow an all out thermonuclear war. Such destruction, it is feared, might jeopardize the survival of civilization. (Nowadays there can be no doubt that civilization would continue after conventional bombing, although prior to World War II this was sometimes questioned.)

Obviously, a civilization must die if there are no persons left who can maintain it. The prerequisite for a living civilization is a society of living persons; hence, when a population is extinguished and not replaced from outside, all social phenomena will come to an end. But there are many historical examples of civilizations disappearing even though the populations on which they were based continued to survive. Historians have offered various explanations for such a downfall of civilizations, but even in cases that are

Survival of Civilization

exceptionally well documented the causes remain obscure. Several factors have been held responsible for the death of certain civilizations, yet one can always find other examples from history where the same factors were present and did not cause a cultural decline. Part of the difficulty lies in the complexity of the concepts "civilization" or "culture," which are more in the nature of assumed realities than observable phenomena. One of the major problems of sociological theory concerns the way in which social institutions and customs, art, science, technology, law, government, religion, and ideologies are woven together to constitute a civilization.

Some components of civilization are clearly less vulnerable to the effects of bombing than others. For example, language and the art of writing are more resistant to social catastrophes than are economic organizations or political structures. Technology and science may suffer no loss if a substantial number of scientists and engineers survive and if the postwar environment will permit research and teaching. But the state of technology and science would deteriorate if teaching were interrupted for many years or if a new cadre of scientists had first to train itself.

The fine arts also constitute a component of our civilization. The destruction of cities would undoubtedly demolish many art treasures that have been preserved from the past. During World War II the destruction of works of art was confined mainly to architecture since there was time to evacuate the most valuable items from museums and private collections.[31] It is not certain that the enormous loss of works of art from nuclear bombing destruction would impede the future development of the fine arts in a postwar civilization. The contrary may also be expected. Jakob Burckhardt, a historian famous for his study of the Renaissance, once wrote that the loss of great works of art in the past may have permitted a less encumbered creation of new art. Accord-

[31] For a pictorial record of the works of art destroyed by World War II bombings in Europe, see Henry La Farge (editor), *Lost Treasures of Europe*.

The Social Impact of BOMB DESTRUCTION

ing to him, Renaissance artists could not have created what they did had great masses of Greek sculpture and paintings been found in the fifteenth century.[32]

Another aspect of the survival of civilization is the possible impact of bomb destruction on the basic patterns of human relations and the social attributes of human personality. One may wonder, for example, whether the family would survive in its present form as the basic unit of human society. The transformation of the family during the last hundred years has been attributed to the trend of industrialization and urbanization—with its increasing division of labor, the separation of place of work and place of residence, and the impact of technology on housekeeping. In the period after a nuclear war family life would be affected by crowded housing conditions and a shortage of furniture and other household equipment. But if the postwar society could devote its energies and resources to reconstruction, the housing shortage would be largely alleviated within ten or twenty years, particularly if the population losses had been large in relation to the destruction of property. Thus the impact on family life of these changes in housekeeping and living conditions would be temporary, and since social institutions and customs change rather slowly, the structure of the family would probably survive practically unaltered. Since World War II no significant changes in the family have been observed that can be traced to the evacuation experience, although at the time the evacuation of children disturbed family life and altered the environment in which the children grew up.[33]

The psychiatric effects of the World War II bombing experiences proved less harmful than was expected. There was no in-

---

[32] Burckhardt, *Weltgeschichtliche Betrachtungen* (Bern, Switzerland, Hallwag, 1941), Chap. VI, "Ueber Glück und Unglück in der Weltgeschichte," 391.

[33] Helmut Schelsky, *Wandlungen der Deutschen Familie in der Gegenwart*, 192–218; and Gerhard Baumert, *Jugend der Nachkriegszeit*, 59. Both these studies point out that postwar family life in Germany was resumed in the prewar pattern.

Survival of Civilization

crease in mental disorders, and the number of suicides declined during the war in countries which suffered from bombing.[34]

The most seriously threatened elements of civilization are the political and governmental organization and the economic structure. In the aftermath of the bombing disaster the traditional forms of government would be inoperative, and this would lead to military control and emergency measures. After the end of the war, it might be a slow and difficult process to revert to the prewar situation, and many governmental innovations—for good or evil—might remain in force.

The economic structure that would evolve in the postwar era is of particular interest since it is so closely linked with political and ideological developments. Apart from the enormous loss in total national wealth, there are two especially serious problems for any postwar economic system. One is the unequal and largely fortuitous distribution of property losses among the survivors; the other is the destruction of many financial records that are necessary to determine property relationships.

Jack Hirshleifer, in a discussion of the economic structure after a bombing disaster, considers four possible ways in which this conflict might develop.[35] The major conflicting groups would not be the economic "classes" in the old Marxist sense, but the dispossessed who had suffered from bombing destruction and those who had retained their homes and other property relatively unscathed.[36] The four possibilities in this situation would then be: proportionate compensation for the war damage (i.e., shifting

[34] A decline in the number of suicides is usual during wartime; it was also observed in World War I. See Titmuss, *op. cit.*, 340–41; and Jean Daric, "L'Evolution de la Mortalité par Suicide en France et à l'Étranger," *Population*, Vol. XI (October, 1956), 673–700.

[35] Hirshleifer, "Some Thoughts on the Social Structure after a Bombing Disaster," *World Politics*, Vol. VIII, No. 2 (January, 1956), 206–27.

[36] The Soviet economic system would also be affected by the unequal distribution of bombing losses since clothing, furniture, and sometimes small houses are privately owned in the Soviet Union.

the loss from those whose property was destroyed to the nation's property owners in aggregate); acceptance and stabilization of the postwar distribution of wealth; an entirely "new deal" of wealth, presumably on more or less equalitarian lines; and abolition of private wealth (i.e., socialization) in greater or lesser degree.

If destruction had been very great, proportionate compensation would not seem feasible, especially since so many records of the former ownership relations would have been wiped out (in the absence of nationwide preparations for record protection). Hirshleifer expects that it would take special government interventions (such as moratoria on debts and the granting of emergency government loans) to prevent a wave of bankruptcies. Assuming survival of a functioning constitutional government, Hirshleifer concludes that a compromise solution would be likely. There would first be some minimal compensation, mainly to permit the maintenance of the survivors, and later a more or less compensatory reapportionment of property which would have strong equalitarian features and be directed primarily toward maximal restoration of production.[37]

The political climate after the war and the size of the surviving population in relation to the remaining wealth would have a decisive influence on the development of the economic structure. But there is no cogent reason to assume that very large property and population losses would permanently paralyze the economy. The survivors in war-damaged countries would, on the average, be much poorer, and during the first postwar generation life would probably lack many of its former amenities and its prewar security. The milieu of the postwar society would be dominated by ever-present shortages and material hardships, a feeling of helplessness as a result of the bombing experience, the importance of sheer

---

[37] Hirshleifer, *op. cit.*, 226. Even the compensation in the Philippines after World War II was somewhat equalitarian, replacing only losses up to five hundred dollars in full and 52.5 per cent of the losses over this amount.

Survival of Civilization

material survival as contrasted with the former regulated and secure life, and a high incidence of severe illnesses from delayed radiation effects. Such a pattern would resemble the violent tenor of life that J. Huizinga found characteristic of the Middle Ages:

> Calamities and indigence were more afflicting than at present; it was more difficult to guard against them, and to find solace. Illness and health presented a more striking contrast; the cold and darkness of winter were more real evils. Honours and riches were relished with greater avidity and contrasted more vividly with surrounding misery. We, at the present day, can hardly understand the keenness with which a fur coat, a good fire on the hearth, a soft bed, a glass of wine, were formerly enjoyed.[38]

But if we reason from this speculative picture that another Dark Ages would set in, we are presupposing that for many generations after the war there would be development of a most disruptive and chaotic nature, for which we cannot seek the cause in the bombing destruction alone. The pillaging of Rome in 408 and 455 and all the other destruction wrought in the Roman Empire by the barbarian invaders cannot be made responsible in themselves for the Dark Ages that followed.

Finally, there remains the ultimate and ghastly question of whether an extreme use of nuclear weapons could actually extinguish all human life on earth. Some writers have called this possibility a real threat and stressed it with a macabre fascination —as if the preservation of peace would really hinge on our fear of mankind's extinction. The misery and horrors of a nuclear war are beyond the power of human imagination and are not clarified by presaging the end of all human life. On the contrary, such prophecies deprive the threat of its realism.

---

[38] Huizinga, *The Waning of the Middle Ages* (London, Edward Arnold & Company, 1937), 1.

The Social Impact of *BOMB DESTRUCTION*

The world-wide spread of radioactive fall-out material is sometimes suggested as a possible lethal agent for all persons on earth. While it is impossible to state how much damage it might do to human lives, even if the forms of attacks were given, it is nonetheless clear that the world-wide spread of the contaminant would be very uneven. Hence one can expect large population groups to remain free of serious irradiation, even if the amount of radioactive material produced were far in excess of the amount which could—if uniformly spread—cause lethal contamination in all populated areas. Fall-out has to be distributed by high-altitude winds in order to affect large areas.[39] Nearly all the likely targets in a possible all out war are located on the northern hemisphere. Thus, it follows that the populations which would be least affected are those on the southern hemisphere, most of which have a huge actual or potential rate of growth.

Those speculatively inclined, then, ought to picture the world after an all out nuclear war with extreme fall-out contamination not as a planet inhabited only by lower forms of plant life, immune to radioactivity, but as a world with expanding populations and perhaps thriving economies in South America, South Africa, Indonesia, Australia, and New Zealand. From this picture one might try to look still further ahead and perhaps reach the conclusion that the surviving generations would be further away from a peaceful millenium than ever because of the deep racial, religious, and ideological differences that divide the peoples of the southern hemisphere. Indeed—thus this speculation could continue—both Capitalism and Communism might survive, since both might be represented among the survivor nations. But the powerful states which fought for these issues would have disappeared from history —much as the Inca Empire and the realm of Carthage have ended forever.

[39] L. Machta, R. J. List, and L. F. Hubert, "World-wide Travel of Atomic Debris," *Science*, Vol. CXXIV, No. 3,220 (September 14, 1956), 474–77.

SELECTED BIBLIOGRAPHY

1. General

Brodie, Bernard. "Strategy Hits a Dead End," *Harper's Magazine* (October, 1955), 33–37.

———, ed. *The Absolute Weapon: Atomic Power and World Order*. New York, Harcourt, Brace, 1946.

Harris, Sir Arthur. *Bomber Offensive*. New York, The Macmillan Company, 1947. (The Royal Air Force campaign against Germany in World War II.)

Lapp, Ralph E. *Must We Hide?* Cambridge, Massachusetts, Addison-Wesley Press, Inc., 1949. (Evaluation of atomic bomb and possible measures against it. See also more recent articles by author in *The Bulletin of Atomic Scientists*.)

Possony, Stefan T. *Strategic Air Power*. Washington, Infantry Journal Press, 1949. (Strategic principles of bombing; transportation, industry, or morale as a target; importance of bottlenecks.)

Moore, Harry Estill. "Toward a Theory of Disaster," *American Sociological Review*, Vol. XXI (December, 1956), 733–37.

Titmuss, Richard M. *Problems of Social Policy. History of the Second World War*, United Kingdom Civil Series, ed. by W. K. Hancock. London, H. M. Stationery Office, 1950. (A very comprehensive evaluation of the British World War II experience in social administration, evacuation, relocation of homeless, and general welfare.)

The Social Impact of BOMB DESTRUCTION

U. S. Strategic Bombing Survey. 316 vols. Washington, Government Printing Office, 1946-47. (Reports of extensive field investigations of the effects of Allied air attacks against German and Japanese targets in World War II.)

2. Weapon Effects and Civil Defense

Cooper, Gershon, and Roland N. McKean. "Is Dispersal Good Defense," *Fortune* (November, 1954), 126ff.

The Effects of the Atomic Bombs at Hiroshima and Nagasaki—Report of British Mission to Japan. London, H. M. Stationery Office, 1946. (Good short report, effects on population, utilities etc.)

Great Britain, Medical Research Council. *The Hazards to Man of Nuclear and Allied Radiations.* Cmd. 9780. London, H. M. Stationery Office, 1956. (Mainly on peacetime radiation, good evaluation of genetic effects.)

Hawley, Amos H. "Urban Dispersal and Defense," *Bulletin of the Atomic Scientists,* Vol. VII (October, 1951), 307-12.

Muller, H. J. "The Genetic Damage Produced by Radiation," *Bulletin of the Atomic Scientists,* Vol. XI, No. 6 (June, 1955), 210ff.

National Academy of Sciences—National Research Council. *The Biological Effects of Atomic Radiation: Summary Reports.* Washington, 1956. (A judicious evaluation of the risks from radiation—primarily in peacetime.)

O'Brien, Terence H. *Civil Defense. History of the Second World War,* United Kingdom Civil Series, ed. by W. K. Hancock. London, H. M. Stationery Office, 1955. (Administrative aspects of civil defense.)

The Rand Corporation, R-322-RC, *Report on a Study of Non-military Defense,* Santa Monica, Calif., 1958.

U. S. Congress. Hearings before the Joint Committee on Atomic Energy. *The Nature of Radioactive Fallout and Its Effects on Man.* Summary Analysis of Hearings. Washington, Government Printing Office, 1957.

U. S. Department of Defense and U. S. Atomic Energy Commission.

Selected Bibliography

The Effects of Nuclear Weapons. Washington, Government Printing Office, 1957. (The authoritative and comprehensive treatise of weapon effects. Bibliography on biomedical effects.)

U. S. Strategic Bombing Survey. (Cited under 1.). European report No. 40, *Civilian Defense Division—Final Report;* and Pacific Report No. 11, *Final Report Covering Air Raid Protection and Allied Subjects in Japan.*

3. Evacuation

Bernert, Eleanor, and Fred C. Iklé. "Evacuation and the Cohesion of Urban Groups," *American Journal of Sociology,* Vol. LVIII, No. 2 (September, 1952).

Freud, Anna, and Dorothy Burlingham. *War and Children.* New York, International Universities Press, 1944. (Psychoanalytic study of the effects of evacuation on children.)

Great Britain, Ministry of Health. *Report on Conditions in Reception Areas.* London, H. M. Stationery Office, 1941. (Evacuation effects early in the war.)

Haverda, J. L. *"De Sociale Devolgen Van De Watersnood,"* Maandblad Voor de Geestelijke Volksgezondheid, Vol. VIII, No. 7/8 (July-August, 1953). (Evacuation from the floods in Holland in 1953).

Iklé, Fred C., and Harry V. Kincaid. *Social Aspects of Wartime Evacuation of American cities.* With Particular Emphasis on Long-Term Housing and Re-employment. Committee on Disaster Studies, National Academy of Sciences—National Research Council *Publication No. 393.* Washington, 1956.

Instituut voor Sociaal Onderzoek van het Nederlandse Volk. *Studies in Holland Flood Disaster, 1953.* 4 vols. Washington, National Academy of Sciences—National Research Council, Committee on Disaster Studies, 1955.

Padley, Richard, and Margaret Cole, eds. *Evacuation Survey: A Report to the Fabian Society.* London, George Roatledge & Sons, Ltd., 1940. (Psychological and sociological effects of evacuation of children.)

Titmuss Richard M. *Problems of Social Policy.* (Cited under 1.)

The Social Impact of BOMB DESTRUCTION

Vernon, Magdalen D. "A Study of Some Effects of Evacuation on Adolescent Girls," *The British Journal of Educational Psychology,* Vol. X (June, 1940), 114-34.

Wolf, Katherine M. "Evacuation of Children in Wartime," *The Psychoanalytic Study of the Child,* I, 389-404. New York, International Universities Press, 1945. (A survey of the literature.)

4. Human Behavior in Disasters and Administrative Controls

Demrath, Nicholas T., and Anthony F. C. Wallace, eds. "Human Adaption to Disaster," *Human Organization* (special issue), Annotated bibliography by J. Rayner, Vol. XVI, No. 2 (Summer, 1957).

Dinerstein, Herbert, and Leon Gouré. *Moscow in Crisis.* Glencoe, Illinois, The Free Press, 1955. (Political and social situation in Moscow during World War II when German forces threatened the city.)

Ferguson, Sheila, and Hilde Fitzgerald. *Studies in the Social Services. History of the Second World War,* United Kingdom Civil Series, ed. by W. K. Hancock. London, H. M. Stationery Office, 1954.

Form, William H. and Sigmund Nosow, *Community in Disaster.* New York, Harper and Brothers, 1958. (Study of individual behavior and organizational performance in a tornado disaster.)

Fritz, Charles E., and Eli S. Marks. "The NORC Studies of Human Behavior in Disaster," *The Journal of Social Issues,* Vol. X, No. 3 (1954), 26-41. (Description of studies by National Opinion Research Center, University of Chicago, on natural disaster in the United States.)

Fritz, Charles E., and J. H. Mathewson, *Convergence Behavior in Disasters: A Problem in Social Control.* Committee on Disaster Studies, National Academy of Sciences—National Research Council *Publication No. 476.* Washington, 1957. (An analysis of the movement of people, messages, and supplies toward disaster areas.)

Fritz, Charles E., and Harry B. Williams. "The Human Being in Disasters: A Research Perspective," *The Annals of the American*

Selected Bibliography

Academy of Political and Social Science, Vol. CCCIX (January, 1957), 42–51.
Gouré, Leon. *Soviet Administrative Controls During the Siege of Leningrad*. Santa Monica, California, The Rand Corporation, RM-2075, 1957.
Killian, Lewis M. "The Significance of Multiple-Group Membership in Disaster," *The American Journal of Sociology*, Vol. LVII (1952), 309–14.
Moore, Harry Estill. *Torandoes over Texas*. Austin, University of Texas Press, 1958. (Social organization and psychological reactions in two disaster communities.)
Perry, Stewart E., Earle Silber, and Donald A. Bloch. *The Child and His Family in Disaster: A Study of the 1953 Vicksburg Tornado*. Committee on Disaster Studies, National Academy of Sciences—National Research Council *Publication No. 394*. Washington, 1956.
U. S. Strategic Bombing Survey. (Cited under 1.). European report No. 646, *The Effects of Strategic Bombing on German Morale;* and Pacific report No. 14, *The Effects of Strategic Bombing on Japanese Morale*.
Wallace, Anthony F. C. *Human Behavior in Extreme Situations: A Survey of the Literature and Suggestions for Further Research*. Washington, National Academy of Sciences—National Research Council, Committee on Disaster Studies, 1956.

5. Psychological Effects, Panic

Cantril, Hadley. *The Invasion from Mars: A Study in the Psychology of Panic*. Princeton, Princeton University Press, 1947. (Study of the panic caused by a dramatic broadcast of Orson Wells' play.)
Daric, Jean. "L'Évolution de la Mortalité par Suicide en France et à l'Étranger," *Population*, Vol. XI (Paris, October, 1956), 673–700. (Decrease in suicides during wartime.)
Foreman, Paul B. "Panic Theory," *Sociology and Social Research*, Vol. XXXVII (1953), 295–304.
Glover, E. "Notes on the Psychological Effects of War Conditions on

the Civilian Population," *International Journal of Psychoanalysis*, Vol. XXIII (1942), 17-37. (Case studies from England.)

Grinker Roy R., and John P. Spiegel. *Men Under Stress*. Philadelphia, Blakiston, 1945. (Psychiatric study of pilots in combat during World War II.)

Janis, Irving L. *Air War and Emotional Stress*. New York, McGraw-Hill Book Company, Inc., 1951. (Thorough analysis of the psychological effects of bombing, particularly the atomic bombings in Japan.)

Panse, Friedrich. *Angst und Schreck*. In the series *Arbeit und Gesundheit*. Published by the Bundesministerium für Arbeit, N.F. No. 47, Stuttgart, Georg Thieme, 1952. (Interviews with persons who experienced actual dangers in the air raids in Germany.)

Quarantelli, E. L. "The Nature and Conditions of Panic," *The American Journal of Sociology*, Vol. LX (November, 1954), 267-75. (Excellent clarification of the problem of panic.)

Schmideberg, M. "Some Observations on Individual Reactions to Air Raids," *International Journal of Psychoanalysis*, Vol. XXIII (1942), 146-76. (Cases from a psychiatrist's practice in England.)

Scott, William A. *Public Reaction to a Surprise Civil Defense Alert in Oakland, California*. Survey Research Center, University of Michigan, 1955. (Reaction to a false alert, absence of panic.)

Svendsen, Bent Borup. "Psychiatric Morbidity Among Civilians in Wartime," *Acta Jutlandica*, Vol. XXIV, A. Kopenhagen, Aarhus University, 1952. (No definite changes in admissions to mental hospitals during wartime.)

Vernon, P. E. "Psychological Effects of Air-Raids," *Journal of Abnormal Psychology*, Vol. XXXVI (October, 1941), 457-76.

Wallace, Anthony F. C. *Tornado in Worcester: An Exploratory Study of Individual and Community Behavior in an Extreme Situation*. Committee on Disaster Studies, National Academy of Sciences—National Research Council *Publication No. 392*. Washington, 1956.

Wolfenstein, Martha. *Disaster: A Psychological Essay*. Glencoe, Illinois, The Free Press, 1957. (Psychiatric interpretation of studies on natural disasters.)

Selected Bibliography

6. Narratives of Bombing Experiences

FitzGibbon, Constantine. *The Winter of the Bombs: The Story of the Blitz of London*. New York, W. W. Norton, 1957.

Gräff, S. *Tod im Luftangriff*. Hamburg, H. H. Nölke, 1948.

Hachiya, Michihiko. *Hiroshima Diary*. Chapel Hill, University of North Carolina Press, 1955.

Hersey, John. *Hiroshima*. New York, Alfred A. Knopf, 1946.

Kiesel, O. E. *Die Unverzagte Stadt*. Volksbücherei Verlag Goslar, 1949. (About Hamburg.)

Nagai, Takashi. *We of Nagasaki*. New York, Duell, Sloan and Pearce, 1951.

Rumpf, Hans. *Der Hochrote Hahn*. Darmstadt, E. S. Mittler & Sohn, 1952. (About air raids on German cities.)

Seydewitz, Max. *Civil Life in Wartime Germany*. New York, Viking Press, 1945.

7. Man Power and Other Economic Factors

Great Britain, Food Ministry. *How Britain Was Fed in War Times: Food Control 1939–1945*. London, H. M. Stationery Office, 1946.

———, Ministry of Labour and National Service. *Report for the Years 1939–1946*. Cmd. 7225. London, H. M. Stationery Office, 1947.

———. *Statistics Relating to the War Effort of the United Kingdom*. Cmd. 6564. London, H. M. Stationery Office, 1944.

Hammond, R. J. *Food*, I. *History of the Second World War*, United Kingdom Civil Series, ed. by W. K. Hancock. London, H. M. Stationery Office, 1951.

Hargreaves, E. L., and M. M. Gowing. *Civil Industry and Trade. History of the Second World War*, United Kingdom Civil Series, ed. by W. K. Hancock. London, H. M. Stationery Office, 1952.

Kohan, C. M. *Works and Buildings. History of the Second World War*, United Kingdom Civil Series, ed. by W. K. Hancock. London, H. M. Stationery Office, 1952.

The Social Impact of BOMB DESTRUCTION

Long, Clarence D. *The Labor Force in War and Transition: Four Countries.* National Bureau of Economic Research *Occasional Paper 36.* New York, 1952. (Labor in United States, Canada, Germany, and Great Britain in World War II.)

Parker, H. M. D. *Manpower: A Study of War-time Policy and Administration. History of the Second World War,* United Kingdom Civil Series, ed. by W. K. Hancock. London, H. M. Stationery Office, 1957.

U. S. *Strategic Bombing Survey.* (Cited under 1.). European report No. 3, *The Effects of Strategic Bombing on the German War Economy;* Pacific report No. 53, *The Effects of Strategic Bombing on Japan's War Economy;* and Pacific report No. 55, *The Effects of Air Attack on Japanese Urban Economy.*

8. Casualties

Bodart, Gaston. *Losses of Life in Modern Wars (Austria-Hungary, France).* Oxford, Clarendon Press, 1916.

Dumas, Samuel, and K. O. Vedel-Petersen. *Losses of Life Caused by War.* Oxford, Clarendon Press, 1923. (Nineteenth-century war and World War I.)

Heinsohn. "Die Menschenverluste der Hansestadt Hamburg im 2. Weltkrieg," *Hamburg in Zahlen,* No. 26 (September, 1951). (Hamburg's air-raid casualties.)

Horstman, Kurt, et. al. "Deutsche Bevölkerungsbilanz des 2. Weltkrieges," *Wirtschaft und Statistik,* VIII, 493–500. (German population losses in World War II.)

Rumpf, Hans. "Die Verluste der westdeutschen Zivilbevölkerung im Luftkrieg," *Wehr-Wissenschaftliche Rundschau,* Vol. III (October, 1953), 493–97. (German civilian air-raid casualties in World War II.)

Sauvy, Alfred. "La Population de L'Union Soviétique," *Population* (Paris), vol. XI (July-September, 1956), 461–80. (Soviet World War II casualties, pp. 470ff.)

Simon, Peter, "Die Kölner Fliegeropferkartei," *Statistische Mitteilun-*

Selected Bibliography

gen der Stadt Köln, V (1950), 78–89. (Air-raid casualties in Cologne.)

Thompson, Warren S. *Plenty of People.* New York, Ronald Press, 1948. (Chap. V, "War and Population Growth.")

9. Postwar Reconstruction

Arndt, Martin, *Wiederaufbau und Bauwirtschaft.* Vol. V of *"Wiederaufbau Zerstörter Städte,"* series ed. by Kurt Blaum. Frankfurt, H. Cobert, 1947. (Data on degree of World War II destruction in Germany by size of city.)

Grebler, Leo. "Street Changes in the Rebuilding of European Cities," *The American City,* August, 1955.

―――. *Europe's Reborn Cities.* Urban Land Institute *Technical Bulletin No. 28.* Washington, 1956.

―――. "Continuity in the Rebuilding of Bombed Cities in Western Europe," *The American Journal of Sociology,* Vol. LXI (March, 1956), 463–69.

Hawley, Amos. "Land Value Patterns in Okayama, Japan, 1940–52," *The American Journal of Sociology,* Vol. LX, No. 5 (March, 1955), 487–92. (Effect of destruction on land values.)

Iklé, Fred C. "Reconstruction and Population Density in War-damaged Cities," *Journal of the American Institute of Planners,* Vol. XVI (Summer, 1950), 131–39.

―――. "The Effect of War Destruction upon the Ecology of Cities," *Social Forces,* Vol. XXIX, No. 4 (May, 1951), 383–91.

10. Social and Economic Postwar Effects

Baumert, Gerhard. *Jugend der Nachkriegszeit.* Darmstadt, Gemeindestudie des Instituts für Sozial-wissenschaftliche Forschung, E. Roether, 1952. (Youth in postwar Germany, effects of World War II.)

Cavers, David F. "Legal Measures to Mitigate the Economic Impact of Atomic Attack," *Bulletin of the Atomic Scientists,* Vol. IX, No. 7 (September, 1953), 269–72.

———. "The Economic Consequences of Atomic Attack," *Armed Forces Chemical Journal,* Vol. VIII (September-October, 1954), 13–17.

Hirshleifer, Jack. "Some Thoughts on the Social Structure after a Bombing Disaster," *World Politics,* Vol. VIII (January, 1956), 206–27.

La Farge, Henry, ed. *Lost Treasures of Europe.* New York, Pantheon Books, 1946. (A pictorial record of works of art destroyed in World War II.)

Schelsky, Helmut. *Wandlungen der deutschen Familie in der Gegenwart.* Dortmund, Ardey, 1953. (Effects of World War II on the German family.)

INDEX

Absenteeism of employees: 30, 124, 159, 160, 161–62, 167
Agriculture, employment in: 110
Air-raid alerts: 166
Area raids, in World War II: 75–76
Armed forces, mobilization for: 168–69
Atomic bomb: *see* tactical nuclear weapons
Australia: 2, 232

Behavior, determinants of: 12–13
Berlin, Germany: temporary housing, 68; evacuations from, 87; mobilization of labor, 173–74; delinquency rates, 221
Bikini Atoll: 21
Billeting: 63–65, 92–93, 112, 117, 182; *see also* evacuee-host relationship
Biological warfare: 36–39
Black Death: 208
Bomb destruction, total effect on war effort: 178ff.
Bombing experience: socioeconomic effects, 6–7; reactions to, 13–15; motivation for evacuation, 98ff.; psychiatric effects, 228–29
British Air Raids Precautions Department: 17
British Air Staff: 17
British restaurants: 149
Broken-backed warfare: 190–202
Burials: 158–59

Casualties: World War II rates, 16–19; from fall-out, 20–22; from chemical and biological warfare, 36–39
Casualties, impact of: morale, 27–34; organizational and legal, 34–36; housing density, 58–59; transportation, 124; man power, 157–58; long-term, 203–11
Chemical warfare: 36–39
Children and mothers, evacuation of: *see* evacuation, remedial
Churchill, Sir Winston, on nuclear warfare: 178
Cities: physical and social structures of, 5; readjustment of, after destruction, 8–9; redevelopment of, 211–24; evacuation from, *see* evacuation
Civil defense: inadequacy of, in U. S., *vi;* and communications, 132; absorption of man power by, 162–63; future importance of, 204; "Operation Alert," 206n.

The Social Impact of *BOMB DESTRUCTION*

Civilians, reactions of, to destruction: 12–15
Civilization, survival of: 224–32
Cologne, Germany, evacuations from: 85, 87
Communications: 131–37, 187
Community kitchens: 148, 149; *see also* mass feeding
Commuting: 121, 122, 125, 126, 127
Compensation for air-raid victims: 154–55
Construction workers: 163–65
Consumer density: 9–10
Consumer goods, durable: 141–43; availability of, 151–53; after destruction, 154–55
Consumer-resources ratio: 7–8, 9, 10, 121ff., 150
Conventional bombing: 39; casualty rates, 16–18
Coventry, England, food supply in: 146–47
Credit, monetary: 136
Culture: *see* civilization

Deaths: *see* fatalities
Decontamination: 23, 165
Delegation of authority: 187
Delinquency: 221
Destruction: readjustment of cities to, 8–9; resources prior to, 9–10; aftereffects, 11–12; social effects, 221–26
Disease: 23–27, 38; *see also* casualties and radiation sickness
Dresden, Germany, British bombing of: 201–202

Economy, after nuclear attack: 189; *see also* organization, economic
Elasticity of resources: 8–10, 11, 58, 121ff., 150–51, 183; housing, 41ff., 180, 196
Electrical systems: 137, 139–40, 185
Electricity, industrial consumption of: 138
Emergency housing and camps: 66–69
Emotional distress: 30
England: *see* Great Britain
Epidemics: see plague epidemics
Evacuation: 22–23, 59ff., 77ff., 98ff., 144, 159, 196, 205; *see also* evacuation, remedial; evacuation, strategic; evacuation, tactical

Index

Evacuation, remedial: definition of, 78–79; present British plans for, 88; possibility of, from New York City, 89; official conflicts, 96–97
Evacuation, strategic: definition of, 79; problems of, 106–108; employment, 109–11; billeting, 112–19; effect on man power, 161
Evacuation, tactical: definition of, 78; problems of, 82–83; proposed for U. S. cities, 84; effect on man power, 160–61
Evacuee-host relationship: 85, 89, 91–92, 93, 115–19
Evacuees: 182, 185, 194, 195, 196; return of, to cities, 89–91; assisted travel for, 94–96; reactions of, 98–99; employment of, 109–12; distribution of, 113
Excavation, forms of: 224–25

Fall-out: 20–23, 24–27, 53, 144n., 185, 186, 196, 204, 209, 210–11, 232
Family life, impact of bombing on: 228
Fatalities: 144, 171, 205, 209, 212; *see also* casualties
Field kitchens: *see* mass feeding
Fine arts: 227–28
Fire storms: 19–20
Flight, from cities: 100ff.
Flood, of 1953, in Holland: 4, 5, 93n., 113, 115–19, 155n.
Food: 5, 7, 9, 38, 141–42, 143, 144–52, 182, 186, 209; *see also* mass feeding
Frankfurt, Germany: casualties, 161; population density, 214; redevelopment of, 215, 223
Functionally homogeneous relationships (in urban society): 5ff.

Genes, effect of nuclear radiation on: 210–11
Germany: indiscriminate evacuation discouraged, 33; housing density, 47, 49; reaccommodation processes, 59–64; temporary housing, 68, 69; tactical evacuations, 83; evacuation problems, 94, 95; community kitchens, 148, 149; recruitment of labor, 172–73; railroad destruction, 188–89; morale, 198; male-female fatality ratio, 205
Great Britain: statistical information, 4–5; casualties, 17, 23, 24; nightly evacuations from cities, 82–83; evacuation in, 93, 94, 95, 97; wartime employment, 111; consumer goods available, 141–42; food supply, 143–44; attempted co-ordination of industry, 112n.; British

245

restaurants, 149; supply distribution, 152–53; loss of working hours, 160; civil defense, 163n.; rural-urban distribution, 212

Great Plague of 1665 (London): 32–33, 106

Hamburg, Germany: casualties, 16, 18, 24; medical problems, 25; morale, 30–31; population changes, 49–51; billeting, 64; housing density, 66; emergency homes, 67, 68; exodus from, in 1953, 83; post-raid flights, 103–105; vehicle destruction, 123; transit personnel, 124; travel statistics, 126–27; consumer-resources ratio, 128–29; destruction of telephone facilities, 134; water supply, 138; food supplies, 145; consumer goods supply, 153; man power, loss of, 161; bomb damage repair, 164; labor reallocation, 172; railroad yards destroyed, 188; redevelopment, 215; population loss, 213–14; population density (1880–1950), 217–20

Harris, Sir Arthur, comments of, on area raids: 75n.

Heat flash: 24

Hiroshima, Japan: atomic explosion, 3; casualties, 17, 20; radiation sickness, 21; medical facilities, 24; morale, 31; fatalities, 32; population loss, 41; temporary housing, 69; panic, 102; water and electrical supply, destruction of, 137; reaction of survivors, 179, 180; looting, 186n.; redevelopment, 212

Hirshleifer, Jack, comments of, on post-bombing economics: 229, 230

Holland, floods of 1953: 4, 5, 93n., 113, 115–19, 155n.

Hospitals: *see* medical facilities

Household goods: 153

Housing: 5, 6, 8, 9, 10, 182, 196; density of, 41ff., 114

Housing, destruction of: impact on population, 40ff.; disproportionality of population loss from, 71–76; effect on man power, 159

Huizinga, J., comments of, on Middle Ages: 231

Human relations, patterns of: 228

Hydrogen bomb: *see* tactical nuclear weapons

Indonesia: 232

Industry: communications essential to, 132; inefficiency after destruction, 166, 167–68; after nuclear bombing, 225

Industry, dispersal of: 77–78, 80–82, 109, 165–66

Injuries: *see* casualties

Index

Internal radiation: *see* radiation sickness

Janis, Irving L., comments of, on emotional stress: 28–29

Japan: statistical information, 4; indiscriminate evacuation discouraged, 33; housing density, 47–49; reaccommodation processes, 59, 62, 63; temporary dwelling units, 68–69; strategic evacuations, 79; morale, 179; disruption of railroads, 188–89; surrender of, 192; residual military capacity, 200, 201; atomic bombings, 202

Kobe, Japan: casualties, 16; temporary dwelling units, 69; telephone destruction, 133–34; food supply, 146

Kyoto, Japan, reallocation of labor in: 172

Labor force: *see* man power

Law and order, maintenance of: 186

Leningrad, Russia: population growth, 81n.; electrical supply, 140n.; rationing, 152n.

Leukemia: 210

Livestock: 37

London, England: casualties, 16–17; rocket bombings, 19; medical facilities, 25; "trekking," 82; exodus of evacuees from, 98; transportation, 130n.; repair of bomb damage, 164–65; Chelsea, borough of, population loss, 214; population recovery, 215; Stepney-Poplar Reconstruction Area, 223

Looting: 186

Mail services: 133

Man power: 156, 182, 189; factors reducing, 157–69; factors increasing, 169–77

Markets: 5

Marshall Islands: 3

Mass feeding: 144ff.

Mass shelters: 112

Medical facilities: 13, 23–27, 185

Middle Ages, plagues of: 4, 32, 208, 209, 231

Milan, Italy: 33

Military capabilities, residual: 200

Military forces: 184–85, 188

The Social Impact of *BOMB DESTRUCTION*

Mobile canteens: *see* mass feeding
Mobilization: 168–69
Morale: impact of casualties upon, 27–34; impact of bombing on civilian and military, 198–99
Moscow, Russia, population growth: 81n.
Munich, Germany, reconstruction in: 223
Mustard gas: 37; *see also* poison gas

Nagasaki, Japan: atomic explosion, 3; casualties, 17, 20; radiation sickness, 20, 21, 24; medical facilities, 25; morale, 31, 34; panic, 102; telephone losses, 133; food supply, 147; reaction of survivors, 179; redevelopment, 212; population density, 215–17
National-Socialist Welfare Agency (NSV): 145
Nevada: 3
New Mexico: 3
New York City, possibility of evacuation from: 93
New Zealand: 232
Nonessential production, conversion of, to defense: 171–77
North Korea: 30
Nuclear physicists: 11
Nuclear radiation (residual): *see* fall-out
Nuclear warfare: threat of, *v, vi;* Perception of Danger of, 12; hazards of, 16; casualty rates, 17; sudden effects of, 19; possible effects of, on housing, 52–53; possible reactions to, 108; effect of, on man power, 157–58, 173–74; possible aftermath of, 178–82; disruption resulting from, 183–84; continuity of government after, 185–88; transportation problems, 188–89; broken-backed warfare, 190–202; probable postwar results of, 203ff.

"Operation Alert": 206n.
Organization, economic: 11, 135–36, 209
Organization, governmental: 34–35, 185–88, 229, 230–31
Organizational services, vulnerability of: 136–37
Osaka, Japan: housing density, 61; recruitment of man power, 172

Pacific Ocean: 3
Panic: 13–15, 100ff., 186

Index

Paraguay, population loss (1865–70): 207
"Perception of Danger" principle: 19, 29, 33
Physicists: 3
Plague epidemics: 4, 32–33, 106, 208
Plants, effect of Strontium–90 on: 209
Plymouth, England, redevelopment of: 223
Poison gas: abstention from use of, in World War II, *v;* consequences of, 36–38; social effects from, 39
Population: impact of housing destruction upon, 40ff.; plight of, after nuclear attacks, 195; survivors, 204; loss of, 209; density of, 213, 215, 221
Postwar consequences, possible, of nuclear warfare: 203ff.

Radiation sickness: 21–22, 25–27, 194, 195–96, 203, 209–11, 231
Radioactivity: 39, 102
Radium, ingested: 210
Rationing: 8, 51n., 143, 147, 148n., 151
Reaccommodation: 52ff.
Reception areas: 98, 99, 100; employment in, 109–11; co-ordination of, 113; disproportionate crowding in some, 114–15; catering facilities, 145
Reconstruction: 222–24, 226
Remscheid, Germany, destruction of goods in: 152
Resources: *see* consumer-resources ratio; elasticity of resources
Restaurants: 10
Roman Empire, fall of: 231
Rotterdam, Holland, German bombing of: 201
Royal Air Force bomber command: 75n.
Rural-urban distribution of population: 212

School buildings: 10
Senate Armed Services Subcommittee on the Air Force, 1956: 206–207n.
Sewerage: 139
Siberia: 3
South America: 232
Spanish Civil War: 17

The Social Impact of *BOMB DESTRUCTION*

Stalingrad, Russia: 30
Stockpiles of food: 150–51
Strontium–90: 209–10
Students, employment of: 120
Surrender: after nuclear attacks, 191–93; factors determining, 197–98, 200, 201, 202
Survivors: 181, 204, 209

Tactical nuclear weapons: *v, vi, vii,* 3, 21, 39, 178, 180
Telephone facilities: 131, 132, 133, 134–35
Test nuclear explosions, data from: 3, 11
Tokyo, Japan: casualties, 17; evacuations from, 88; water supply, 138; Imperial Palace, 201
Transportation: 5, 6, 7, 9, 10; intra-urban, 121–31; components of, 122; destruction of vehicles, 122–23; augmentation of, by automobiles, 124–25; elasticity of resources, 128–30; nationwide, 188–89

Underground factories: 165–66
Union of Soviet Socialist Republics: urban growth in, 81n.; possible lethal effects of nuclear warfare against, 207n.
United States: civil defense in, *vi,* 36, 78; industrial dispersal encouraged in, 81n.; evacuation possibilities, 97; billeting possibilities, 113n.; stockpiles of food in, 182; urban concentration of technical personnel in, 137–40
United States Department of Agriculture, stock-piling of food by: 145n.
United States Employment Service: 111
Utilities, maintenance and housekeeping: 137–40

V–1 and V–2 rocket bombings of England: 19, 205–206

War effort, total effect of bomb destruction on: 178ff.
War production, conversion of, from nonessential: 171–77
Water supplies, disruption of: 137, 186
West Germany, population increase: 62n., 212; *see also* Germany
Women, employment of: 169
Workers: *see* man power
Working hours, loss of: 166–68
Work week, lengthening of: 170–71

www.ingramcontent.com/pod-product-compliance
Lightning Source LLC
Chambersburg PA
CBHW020747160426
43192CB00006B/267